C0-AQV-892

Crosswalk Coach PLUS for the Common Core State Standards, English Language Arts, Grade 8

Coach™

triumphlearning™

Crosswalk Coach PLUS for the Common Core State Standards, English Language Arts, Grade 8
T303NA
ISBN-13: 978-1-62362-654-9

Cover Image: © Thinkstock

Triumph Learning® 136 Madison Avenue, 7th Floor, New York, NY 10016

© 2014 Triumph Learning, LLC

All rights reserved. No part of this publication may be reproduced in whole or in part, stored
in a retrieval system, or transmitted in any form or by any means, electronic, mechanical,
photocopying, recording or otherwise, without written permission from the publisher.

Printed in the United States of America.

10 9 8 7 6 5 4 3 2 1

The National Governors Association Center for Best Practices and Council of Chief State School Officers
are the sole owners and developers of the Common Core State Standards, © Copyright 2010. All rights reserved.

Frequently Asked Questions about the Common Core State Standards

What are the Common Core State Standards?

The Common Core State Standards for mathematics and English language arts, grades K–12, are a set of shared goals and expectations for the knowledge and skills that will help students succeed. They allow students to understand what is expected of them and to become progressively more proficient in understanding and using mathematics and English language arts. Students are expected to meet each year's grade-specific standards as well as further develop the skills mastered in earlier grades.

Do the Common Core State Standards tell teachers how and what to teach?

No. Because the best understanding of what works in the classroom comes from teachers, these standards establish *what* students need to learn, but they do not dictate *how* teachers should teach. Instead, schools and teachers decide how best to help students reach the standards.

What do the Common Core State Standards mean for students?

The standards provide a clear, consistent understanding of what is expected of student learning across the country. Common standards do not prevent different levels of achievement among students, but they do ensure more consistent exposure to materials and learning experiences through curriculum, instruction, teacher preparation, and other supports for student learning. These standards give students the knowledge and skills they need to succeed in college and careers.

Do the Common Core State Standards focus on skills and content knowledge?

Yes. The Common Core Standards recognize that both content and skills are important. They require rigorous content and application of knowledge through higher-order thinking skills. The English language arts standards require certain critical content for all students, including classic myths and stories from around the world, America's founding documents, foundational American literature, and Shakespeare. The remaining crucial decisions about content are left to state and local determination. In addition to content coverage, the Common Core State Standards require that students systematically acquire knowledge of literature and other disciplines, such as social studies and science, through reading, writing, speaking, and listening.

In mathematics, the Common Core State Standards lay a solid foundation in whole numbers, addition, subtraction, multiplication, division, fractions, and decimals. Together, these elements support a student's ability to learn and apply more demanding math concepts and procedures.

The Common Core State Standards require that students develop a depth of understanding and ability to apply English language arts and mathematics to novel situations, as college students and employees regularly do.

Contents

Common Core Standards Correlation Chart

Standard	Grade 8	Coach Lesson(s)
Reading Standards for Literature		
Key Ideas and Details		
RL.8.1	Cite the textual evidence that most strongly supports an analysis of what the text says explicitly as well as inferences drawn from the text.	1–7
RL.8.2	Determine a theme or central idea of a text and analyze its development over the course of the text, including its relationship to the characters, setting, and plot; provide an objective summary of the text.	2–4
RL.8.3	Analyze how particular lines of dialogue or incidents in a story or drama propel the action, reveal aspects of a character, or provoke a decision.	2, 3
Craft and Structure		
RL.8.4	Determine the meaning of words and phrases as they are used in a text, including figurative and connotative meanings; analyze the impact of specific word choices on meaning and tone, including analogies or allusions to other texts.	6, 33
RL.8.5	Compare and contrast the structure of two or more texts and analyze how the differing structure of each text contributes to its meaning and style.	1, 5
RL.8.6	Analyze how differences in the points of view of the characters and the audience or reader (e.g., created through the use of dramatic irony) create such effects as suspense or humor.	3
Integration of Knowledge and Ideas		
RL.8.7	Analyze the extent to which a filmed or live production of a story or drama stays faithful to or departs from the text or script, evaluating the choices made by the director or actors.	
RL.8.8	(Not applicable to literature)	
RL.8.9	Analyze how a modern work of fiction draws on themes, patterns of events, or character types from myths, traditional stories, or religious works such as the Bible, including describing how the material is rendered new.	5
Range of Reading and Level of Text Complexity		
RL.8.10	By the end of the year, read and comprehend literature, including stories, dramas, and poems, at the high end of grades 6–8 text complexity band independently and proficiently.	1–7
Reading Standards for Informational Text		
Key Ideas and Details		
RI.8.1	Cite the textual evidence that most strongly supports an analysis of what the text says explicitly as well as inferences drawn from the text.	8–15
RI.8.2	Determine a central idea of a text and analyze its development over the course of the text, including its relationship to supporting ideas; provide an objective summary of the text.	8–11
RI.8.3	Analyze how a text makes connections among and distinctions between individuals, ideas, or events (e.g., through comparisons, analogies, or categories).	12
Craft and Structure		
RI.8.4	Determine the meaning of words and phrases as they are used in a text, including figurative, connotative, and technical meanings; analyze the impact of specific word choices on meaning and tone, including analogies or allusions to other texts.	16, 31

Standard	Grade 8	Coach Lesson(s)
Reading Standards for Informational Text *(continued)*		
Craft and Structure *(continued)*		
RI.8.5	Analyze in detail the structure of a specific paragraph in a text, including the role of particular sentences in developing and refining a key concept.	9, 11–13
RI.8.6	Determine an author's point of view or purpose in a text and analyze how the author acknowledges and responds to conflicting evidence or viewpoints.	11, 12
Integration of Knowledge and Ideas		
RI.8.7	Evaluate the advantages and disadvantages of using different mediums (e.g., print or digital text, video, multimedia) to present a particular topic or idea.	
RI.8.8	Delineate and evaluate the argument and specific claims in a text, assessing whether the reasoning is sound and the evidence is relevant and sufficient; recognize when irrelevant evidence is introduced.	11, 14
RI.8.9	Analyze a case in which two or more texts provide conflicting information on the same topic and identify where the texts disagree on matters of fact or interpretation.	11, 12
Range of Reading and Level of Text Complexity		
RI.8.10	By the end of the year, read and comprehend literary nonfiction at the high end of the grades 6–8 text complexity band independently and proficiently.	8, 9, 11–15
Writing Standards		
Text Types and Purposes		
W.8.1	Write arguments to support claims with clear reasons and relevant evidence.	
W.8.1.a	Introduce claim(s), acknowledge and distinguish the claim(s) from alternate or opposing claims, and organize the reasons and evidence logically.	17
W.8.1.b	Support claim(s) with logical reasoning and relevant evidence, using accurate, credible sources and demonstrating an understanding of the topic or text.	17
W.8.1.c	Use words, phrases, and clauses to create cohesion and clarify the relationships among claim(s), counterclaims, reasons, and evidence.	17
W.8.1.d	Establish and maintain a formal style.	17
W.8.1.e	Provide a concluding statement or section that follows from and supports the argument presented.	17
W.8.2	Write informative/explanatory texts to examine a topic and convey ideas, concepts, and information through the selection, organization, and analysis of relevant content.	
W.8.2.a	Introduce a topic clearly, previewing what is to follow; organize ideas, concepts, and information into broader categories; include formatting (e.g., headings), graphics (e.g., charts, tables), and multimedia when useful to aiding comprehension.	18
W.8.2.b	Develop the topic with relevant, well-chosen facts, definitions, concrete details, quotations, or other information and examples.	18
W.8.2.c	Use appropriate and varied transitions to create cohesion and clarify the relationships among ideas and concepts.	18
W.8.2.d	Use precise language and domain-specific vocabulary to inform about or explain the topic.	18
W.8.2.e	Establish and maintain a formal style.	18
W.8.2.f	Provide a concluding statement or section that follows from and supports the information or explanation presented.	18
W.8.3	Write narratives to develop real or imagined experiences or events using effective technique, relevant descriptive details, and well-structured event sequences.	

Standard	Grade 8	*Coach Lesson(s)*
	Writing Standards *(continued)*	
Text Types and Purposes *(continued)*		
W.8.3.a	Engage and orient the reader by establishing a context and point of view and introducing a narrator and/or characters; organize an event sequence that unfolds naturally and logically.	19
W.8.3.b	Use narrative techniques, such as dialogue, pacing, description, and reflection, to develop experiences, events, and/or characters.	19
W.8.3.c	Use a variety of transition words, phrases, and clauses to convey sequence, signal shifts from one time frame or setting to another, and show the relationships among experiences and events.	19
W.8.3.d	Use precise words and phrases, relevant descriptive details, and sensory language to capture the action and convey experiences and events.	19
W.8.3.e	Provide a conclusion that follows from and reflects on the narrated experiences or events.	19
Production and Distribution of Writing		
W.8.4	Produce clear and coherent writing in which the development, organization, and style are appropriate to task, purpose, and audience. (Grade-specific expectations for writing types are defined in standards 1–3 above.)	17–20, 23
W.8.5	With some guidance and support from peers and adults, develop and strengthen writing as needed by planning, revising, editing, rewriting, or trying a new approach, focusing on how well purpose and audience have been addressed. (Editing for conventions should demonstrate command of Language standards 1–3 up to and including grade 8.)	17–20, 23
W.8.6	Use technology, including the Internet, to produce and publish writing and present the relationships between information and ideas efficiently as well as to interact and collaborate with others.	23
Research to Build and Present Knowledge		
W.8.7	Conduct short research projects to answer a question (including a self-generated question), drawing on several sources and generating additional related, focused questions that allow for multiple avenues of exploration.	24
W.8.8	Gather relevant information from multiple print and digital sources, using search terms effectively; assess the credibility and accuracy of each source; and quote or paraphrase the data and conclusions of others while avoiding plagiarism and following a standard format for citation.	24
W.8.9	Draw evidence from literary or informational texts to support analysis, reflection, and research.	
W.8.9.a	Apply *grade 8 Reading standards* to literature (e.g., "Analyze how a modern work of fiction draws on themes, patterns of events, or character types from myths, traditional stories, or religious works such as the Bible, including describing how the material is rendered new").	21, 24
W.8.9.b	Apply *grade 8 Reading standards* to literary nonfiction (e.g., "Delineate and evaluate the argument and specific claims in a text, assessing whether the reasoning is sound and the evidence is relevant and sufficient; recognize when irrelevant evidence is introduced").	22, 24
Range of Writing		
W.8.10	Write routinely over extended time frames (time for research, reflection, and revision) and shorter time frames (a single sitting or a day or two) for a range of discipline-specific tasks, purposes, and audiences.	17–23

Standard	Grade 8	*Coach Lesson(s)*
Speaking and Listening Standards		
Comprehension and Collaboration		
SL.8.1	Engage effectively in a range of collaborative discussions (one-on-one, in groups, and teacher-led) with diverse partners on *grade 8 topics, texts, and issues,* building on others' ideas and expressing their own clearly.	
SL.8.1.a	Come to discussions prepared, having read or researched material under study; explicitly draw on that preparation by referring to evidence on the topic, text, or issue to probe and reflect on ideas under discussion.	25
SL.8.1.b	Follow rules for collegial discussions and decision-making, track progress toward specific goals and deadlines, and define individual roles as needed.	25
SL.8.1.c	Pose questions that connect the ideas of several speakers and respond to others' questions and comments with relevant evidence, observations, and ideas.	25
SL.8.1.d	Acknowledge new information expressed by others, and, when warranted, qualify or justify their own views in light of the evidence presented.	25
SL.8.2	Analyze the purpose of information presented in diverse media and formats (e.g., visually, quantitatively, orally) and evaluate the motives (e.g., social, commercial, political) behind its presentation.	26
SL.8.3	Delineate a speaker's argument and specific claims, evaluating the soundness of the reasoning and relevance and sufficiency of the evidence and identifying when irrelevant evidence is introduced.	26, 27
Presentation of Knowledge and Ideas		
SL.8.4	Present claims and findings, emphasizing salient points in a focused, coherent manner with relevant evidence, sound valid reasoning, and well-chosen details; use appropriate eye contact, adequate volume, and clear pronunciation.	27
SL.8.5	Integrate multimedia and visual displays into presentations to clarify information, strengthen claims and evidence, and add interest.	27
SL.8.6	Adapt speech to a variety of contexts and tasks, demonstrating command of formal English when indicated or appropriate. (See grade 8 Language standards 1 and 3 on page 52 for specific expectations.)	26, 27
Language Standards		
Conventions of Standard English		
L.8.1	Demonstrate command of the conventions of standard English grammar and usage when writing or speaking.	
L.8.1.a	Explain the function of verbals (gerunds, participles, infinitives) in general and their function in particular sentences.	28
L.8.1.b	Form and use verbs in the active and passive voice.	29
L.8.1.c	Form and use verbs in the indicative, imperative, interrogative, conditional, and subjunctive mood.	29
L.8.1.d	Recognize and correct inappropriate shifts in verb voice and mood.	29
L.8.2	Demonstrate command of the conventions of standard English capitalization, punctuation, and spelling when writing.	
L.8.2.a	Use punctuation (comma, ellipsis, dash) to indicate a pause or break.	30
L.8.2.b	Use an ellipsis to indicate an omission.	30
L.8.2.c	Spell correctly.	30
Knowledge of Language		
L.8.3	Use knowledge of language and its conventions when writing, speaking, reading, or listening.	
L.8.3.a	Use verbs in the active and passive voice and in the conditional and subjunctive mood to achieve particular effects (e.g., emphasizing the actor or the action; expressing uncertainty or describing a state contrary to fact).	29

Standard	Grade 8	*Coach Lesson(s)*
Language Standards *(continued)*		
Vocabulary Acquisition and Use		
L.8.4	Determine or clarify the meaning of unknown and multiple-meaning words or phrases based on *grade 8 reading and content*, choosing flexibly from a range of strategies.	
L.8.4.a	Use context (e.g., the overall meaning of a sentence or paragraph; a word's position or function in a sentence) as a clue to the meaning of a word or phrase.	31
L.8.4.b	Use common, grade-appropriate Greek or Latin affixes and roots as clues to the meaning of a word (e.g., *precede, recede, secede*).	32
L.8.4.c	Consult general and specialized reference materials (e.g., dictionaries, glossaries, thesauruses), both print and digital, to find the pronunciation of a word or determine or clarify its precise meaning or its part of speech.	31
L.8.4.d	Verify the preliminary determination of the meaning of a word or phrase (e.g., by checking the inferred meaning in context or in a dictionary).	31
L.8.5	Demonstrate understanding of figurative language, word relationships, and nuances in word meanings.	
L.8.5.a	Interpret figures of speech (e.g. verbal irony, puns) in context.	6
L.8.5.b	Use the relationship between particular words to better understand each of the words.	32–33
L.8.5.c	Distinguish among the connotations (associations) of words with similar denotations (definitions) (e.g., *bullheaded, willful, firm, persistent, resolute*).	33
L.8.6	Acquire and use accurately grade-appropriate general academic and domain-specific words and phrases; gather vocabulary knowledge when considering a word or phrase important to comprehension or expression.	16, 31–33
Reading Standards for Literacy in History/Social Studies		
Key Ideas and Details		
RH.8.1	Cite specific textual evidence to support analysis of primary and secondary sources.	8, 12, 17, 24
RH.8.2	Determine the central ideas or information of a primary or secondary source; provide an accurate summary of the source distinct from prior knowledge or opinions.	8, 12, 17
RH.8.3	Identify key steps in a text's description of a process related to history/social studies (e.g., how a bill becomes law, how interest rates are raised or lowered).	13
Craft and Structure		
RH.8.4	Determine the meaning of words and phrases as they are used in a text, including vocabulary specific to domains related to history/social studies.	16, 31
RH.8.5	Describe how a text presents information (e.g., sequentially, comparatively, causally).	12, 13
RH.8.6	Identify aspects of a text that reveal an author's point of view or purpose (e.g., loaded language, inclusion or avoidance of particular facts).	11
Integration of Knowledge and Ideas		
RH.8.7	Integrate visual information (e.g., in charts, graphs, photographs, videos, or maps) with other information in print and digital texts.	14
RH.8.8	Distinguish among fact, opinion, and reasoned judgment in a text.	15
RH.8.9	Analyze the relationship between a primary and secondary source on the same topic.	12
Range of Reading and Level of Text Complexity		
RH.8.10	By the end of grade 8, read and comprehend history/social studies texts in the grades 6–8 text complexity band independently and proficiently.	8, 9, 11–15

Standard	Grade 8	Coach Lesson(s)
Reading Standards for Literacy in Science and Technical Subjects		
Key Ideas and Details		
RST.8.1	Cite specific textual evidence to support analysis of science and technical texts.	8, 9
RST.8.2	Determine the central ideas or conclusions of a text; provide an accurate summary of the text distinct from prior knowledge or opinions.	8–10
RST.8.3	Follow precisely a multistep procedure when carrying out experiments, taking measurements, or performing technical tasks.	13
Craft and Structure		
RST.8.4	Determine the meaning of symbols, key terms, and other domain-specific words and phrases as they are used in a specific scientific or technical context relevant to *grades 6–8 texts and topics*.	16, 31
RST.8.5	Analyze the structure an author uses to organize a text, including how the major sections contribute to the whole and to an understanding of the topic.	9, 11
RST.8.6	Analyze the author's purpose in providing an explanation, describing a procedure, or discussing an experiment in a text.	13
Integration of Knowledge and Ideas		
RST.8.7	Integrate quantitative or technical information expressed in words in a text with a version of that information expressed visually (e.g., in a flowchart, diagram, model, graph, or table).	14
RST.8.8	Distinguish among facts, reasoned judgment based on research findings, and speculation in a text.	15
RST.8.9	Compare and contrast the information gained from experiments, simulations, video, or multimedia sources with that gained from reading a text on the same topic.	12, 24
Range of Reading and Level of Text Complexity		
RST.8.10	By the end of grade 8, read and comprehend science/technical texts in the grades 6–8 text complexity band independently and proficiently.	8, 9, 11–15
Writing Standards for Literacy in History/Social Studies, Science, and Technical Subjects		
Text Types and Purposes		
WHST.8.1	Write arguments focused on *discipline-specific content*.	
WHST.8.1.a	Introduce claim(s) about a topic or issue, acknowledge and distinguish the claim(s) from alternate or opposing claims, and organize the reasons and evidence logically.	17
WHST.8.1.b	Support claim(s) with logical reasoning and relevant, accurate data and evidence that demonstrate an understanding of the topic or text, using credible sources.	17
WHST.8.1.c	Use words, phrases, and clauses to create cohesion and clarify the relationships among claim(s), counterclaims, reasons, and evidence.	17
WHST.8.1.d	Establish and maintain a formal style.	17
WHST.8.1.e	Provide a concluding statement or section that follows from and supports the argument presented.	17
WHST.8.2	Write informative/explanatory texts, including the narration of historical events, scientific procedures/experiments, or technical processes.	
WHST.8.2.a	Introduce a topic clearly, previewing what is to follow; organize ideas, concepts, and information into broader categories as appropriate to achieving purpose; include formatting (e.g., headings), graphics (e.g., charts, tables), and multimedia when useful to aiding comprehension.	18
WHST.8.2.b	Develop the topic with relevant, well-chosen facts, definitions, concrete details, quotations, or other information and examples.	18

Standard	Grade 8	Coach Lesson(s)
	Writing Standards for Literacy in History/Social Studies, Science, and Technical Subjects *(continued)*	
Text Types and Purposes *(continued)*		
WHST.8.2.c	Use appropriate and varied transitions to create cohesion and clarify the relationships among ideas and concepts.	18
WHST.8.2.d	Use precise language and domain-specific vocabulary to inform about or explain the topic.	18
WHST.8.2.e	Establish and maintain a formal style and objective tone.	18
WHST.8.2.f	Provide a concluding statement or section that follows from and supports the information or explanation presented.	18
Production and Distribution of Writing		
WHST.8.4	Produce clear and coherent writing in which the development, organization, and style are appropriate to task, purpose, and audience.	17–20, 22
WHST.8.5	With some guidance and support from peers and adults, develop and strengthen writing as needed by planning, revising, editing, rewriting, or trying a new approach, focusing on how well purpose and audience have been addressed.	17, 18, 20, 22, 23
WHST.8.6	Use technology, including the Internet, to produce and publish writing and present the relationships between information and ideas clearly and efficiently.	23
Research to Build and Present Knowledge		
WHST.8.7	Conduct short research projects to answer a question (including a self-generated question), drawing on several sources and generating additional related, focused questions that allow for multiple avenues of exploration.	24
WHST.8.8	Gather relevant information from multiple print and digital sources, using search terms effectively; assess the credibility and accuracy of each source; and quote or paraphrase the data and conclusions of others while avoiding plagiarism and following a standard format for citation.	24
WHST.8.9	Draw evidence from informational texts to support analysis, reflection, and research.	22
Range of Writing		
WHST.8.10	Write routinely over extended time frames (time for reflection and revision) and shorter time frames (a single sitting or a day or two) for a range of discipline-specific tasks, purposes, and audiences.	17–20, 22–24

CHAPTER

1 Reading Literature

Chapter 1: Diagnostic Assessment

Lesson 1: Literary Structure
RL.8.1, RL.8.5, RL.8.10

Lesson 2: Plot and Setting
RL.8.1, RL.8.2, RL.8.3, RL.8.10

Lesson 3: Character
RL.8.1, RL.8.2, RL.8.3, RL.8.6, RL.8.10

Lesson 4: Theme and Summary
RL.8.1, RL.8.2, RL.8.10

Lesson 5: Patterns in Literature
RL.8.1, RL.8.5, RL.8.9, RL.8.10

Lesson 6: Figurative Language
RL.8.1, RL.8.4, RL.8.10, L.8.5.a

Lesson 7: Supporting Inferences
RL.8.1, RL.8.10

Chapter 1: Cumulative Assessment

1 Diagnostic Assessment

Read the passage and answer the questions that follow.

The Railway Train
by Emily Dickinson

I like to see it lap the miles,
And lick the valleys up,
And stop to feed itself at tanks;
And then, prodigious, step

5   Around a pile of mountains,
And, supercilious, peer
In shanties by the sides of roads;
And then a quarry pare

To fit its sides, and crawl between,
10 Complaining all the while
In horrid, hooting stanza;
Then chase itself down hill

And neigh like Boanerges;
Then, punctual as a star,
15 Stop—docile and omnipotent—
At its own stable door.

prodigious: enormous
supercilious: haughty
shanties: huts
pare: split
Boanerges: a loud preacher or orator
docile: yielding
omnipotent: all-powerful

1. What part of this passage's structure makes it a poem?

   A. It contains figurative language.

   B. It is broken into lines.

   C. It includes difficult words.

   D. It is not very long.

2. The train is compared to a star to show that the train

   A. is dependable.

   B. has bright lights.

   C. runs only at night.

   D. is very far away.

3. The setting of the poem is BEST described as

   A. the countryside.

   B. a train yard.

   C. a beach.

   D. the city.

4. What analogy is being made in this poem?

   A. A train is to a countryside as a river is to a valley.

   B. A train's whistle sounds like the voice of a loud speechmaker.

   C. A train is like a hungry cat.

   D. The train moving along the track is like a horse galloping through the countryside.

5. In a famous Greek legend, the god Prometheus is chained to a rock because he gives humankind the power to make fires. Prometheus has come to be a symbol of energy restrained. How is the train like Prometheus in this poem?

   _____

   _____

   _____

   _____

Duplicating any part of this book is prohibited by law.

Read the passage and answer the questions that follow.

adapted from

The Last Leaf
by O. Henry

Joanna and Susan moved to New York in the spring. They were close friends, determined to support each other as artists. They shared a studio apartment on the third story of an old brick apartment building where many other artistic people lived. They loved the lively talent spilling out of the vibrant city.

In the winter, a nasty new visitor came in and around the streets of their neighborhood. He had long fingers that stretched in and around corners. Although he didn't shake everyone's hand, he was full of surprises and caught even some of the strongest souls in his grasp. He spared Susan but set his sights on Joanna. A girl fresh from the California sunshine was no match for such an experienced visitor. His name was Pneumonia and he held Joanna tightly in his grip.

Joanna wandered slowly through her illness—breathing heavily, sleeping and sighing often. The constant struggle of her new life in the city had already sapped her will to live. Nothing was pleasing or exciting anymore. Joanna resigned herself to her fate. She began to write good-bye notes.

Heartbroken and helpless, Susan watched her friend begin to fade away. One day, she took a deep breath and asked the doctor if Joanna was ever going to get better. The doctor hesitated and finally broke the news to Susan. Joanna's only chance was to *want* to get better. Without a change of heart, Joanna would linger and then pass away. Susan cried into her handkerchief and then went to sit at her friend's side once again.

Susan sat by Joanna's bed, trying to interest her in new drawings. She heard Joanna quietly whispering. "Eleven, ten, nine," and then a little bit later, "eight, seven, six." Susan wondered what she could possibly be counting. All she could see out the window was an old wall with ivy leaves growing on it. There had been so much wind in the last few days that the leaves were just about gone.

"What are you counting, Joanna?" Susan asked.

"The leaves. When they are gone, I will go, too. It's getting so much closer now. I don't need anything to eat or drink. My head hurt from counting them before, but now it's very close to my time."

"What are you talking about? Leaves have nothing to do with getting better! I am shutting the curtains for the night now, and we are not talking about this again," Susan exclaimed.

Susan quickly shut the curtains and told Joanna that she had to run downstairs. There was an old painter who lived there. Despite his occasional grumpiness, the old man was a friend. He listened carefully as Susan, full of despair, spilled her plan to him. He would not listen at first. He did not understand how leaves could be so important to Joanna. But soon he would oblige her.

That night, Susan worked on her drawings while listening to the wind blow, the rain fall, and small pieces of hail hit the tin roof. The next morning, Susan was exhausted. She stared at the curtains, knowing that all of the ivy leaves would surely have fallen from the wall in the rainstorm. When Joanna awoke, she demanded that the curtains be opened. Holding her breath, Susan drew back the curtains. Her heart leaped with joy. One leaf remained.

"It's the last leaf. I was sure it would be gone," Joanna sighed. All through the day the lone leaf hung, clinging to the wall. Darkness fell, and the curtains were once again closed. Susan was exhausted with fear for her friend, but lay awake as the rain fell through the night once again.

In the morning, Joanna cried for the curtains to be opened. Once again the leaf clung delicately to the wall. For an hour she watched as the leaf refused to leave the safety of the vine and join its brothers on the ground. She called to Susan.

"Susan, it was sinful to wish my life away. I know we will go to Italy one day and draw its beautiful landscapes."

Susan was nearly overcome with relief and happiness. She immediately sent a telegram to the doctor to ask his opinion. The doctor came at once and reassured her that if Joanna continued to progress, she would make a full recovery and be ready for anything by spring.

Later that week, Joanna was indeed greatly improved. Susan sat on Joanna's bed, looking at some sketches she had been working on. She looked up at Joanna, her eyes suddenly sad. "Joanna, I need to tell you something. Our neighbor from downstairs passed away from pneumonia a few days ago. He was clutching a palette and a paintbrush when he died. His clothes were soaking wet. He had finished painting a masterpiece."

"What masterpiece?" Joanna asked.

Susan paused, and then she said, "The leaf he painted on the wall the night the last leaf fell."

Duplicating any part of this book is prohibited by law.

6. Which detail BEST supports the following statement about Susan?

   It can safely be said that Susan has a supportive personality.

   A. Susan asked the doctor if Joanna would ever get better.

   B. Susan moved to New York with Joanna.

   C. Susan asked the painter to make Joanna a painting.

   D. Susan was happy when Joanna said she wanted to live.

7. How is this passage divided?

   A. into stanzas

   B. into paragraphs

   C. into acts and scenes

   D. into chapters

8. What causes the conflict in the passage?

   A. Joanna and Susan move to New York.

   B. The neighbor paints an oak leaf.

   C. Susan talks to the doctor.

   D. Joanna catches pneumonia.

9. What is the theme of the passage?

   A. peace

   B. honesty

   C. ambition

   D. friendship

10. Explain what the painter's actions reveal about him.

_____

_____

_____

_____

1 Literary Structure

RL.8.1, RL.8.5, RL.8.10

Getting the Idea

Fiction, poetry, and drama are three different genres, or types, of literature. Certain literary structures, or ways works are organized, help define each genre. Fiction, poetry, and drama all have specific features that make up their structures.

Fiction

Fiction has a certain structure. A work of fiction may have characters and dialogue, like drama. However, in fiction, text is broken up into paragraphs. Also, you may learn far more about a character's thoughts in fiction than in drama. Large sections of paragraphs together, organized around a common idea or plot event, make up chapters. A **chapter** is a section of a book. In some books, the chapters have numbers or names. When you open a book, look at the first few pages to find its **table of contents**. This is the list of chapters and the page numbers where each chapter begins.

Poetry

The structure of poetry can be very different from poem to poem. However, every poem has lines. Many poems are broken up into **stanzas,** or groups of lines, set apart by spaces. Usually, each stanza in a poem builds upon the last. Poets may use more than one stanza to help develop their ideas in a poem. There are two stanzas in the poem below.

Plowboy
by Carl Sandburg

After the last red sunset glimmer,
Black on the line of a low hill rise,
Formed into moving shadows, I saw
A plowboy and two horses lined against the gray,
5   Plowing in the dusk the last furrow.
The turf had a gleam of brown,
And smell of soil was in the air,
And, cool and moist, a haze of April.

I shall remember you long,
10   Plowboy and horses against the sky in shadow.
I shall remember you and the picture
You made for me,
Turning the turf in the dusk
And haze of an April gloaming.

Meter is the pattern of stressed and unstressed syllables in a line of poetry. Read the following lines from Edgar Allan Poe's poem "The Raven" aloud. Notice that the syllables in bold are stressed.

> **While** I **nod**ded, **near**ly **nap**ping,
> **Sud**denly there **came** a **tap**ping,
> **As** of **some**one **gent**ly **rap**ping,
> **Rap**ping **at** my **cham**ber **door**.

Notice how the stressed syllables occur at regular intervals. We also call this *rhythm*.

Drama

Drama also has specific elements that make up its structure. Unlike poetry, drama does not have to be broken up into separate lines. It also does not have to rhyme. Most dramas are divided into acts and scenes. A **scene** takes place in one location. A collection of scenes is called an **act**. Here are some scenes from one act of a drama:

Act I

Scene 1

Heidi and Nathan are sitting at the dinner table.

HEIDI: We've come here for dinner way too often. Four times in one month?

NATHAN: I know, but the pasta dishes are delicious.

Scene 2

Heidi and Nathan are walking home after their meal. It is snowing.

NATHAN: (*groaning*) Why did we go there again?

HEIDI: I can't believe you're asking me that question.

In a drama, the characters' names are often all in capital letters and followed by a colon. The words after the colon show the **dialogue**, or what the characters are saying. The words in italics are the **stage directions**. Sometimes, stage directions show what characters are doing or thinking. They can also show how a character's line should be spoken.

Duplicating any part of this book is prohibited by law.

Thinking It Through

Read the following passage, and then answer the questions that follow.

from

Sad to Go
Chapter 2

At the airport, Diana watched silently as her little brother, Adam, climbed onto the red suitcase at her feet and made himself comfortable. On any other occasion, she would have scolded him and made him get off. Today, all she wanted to do was give him a big hug. She wouldn't have thought it was possible, but she was really going to miss him.

"You're going to have a great time—don't worry," her dad said. He was sitting in the blue plastic seat next to her.

Diana sighed. At first, she had been excited about spending a month at her aunt's farm during the summer. However, as the date of her departure had neared, she had realized how much she loved being with her parents and her brother. She was also going to miss her friends, her bedroom, the creaky swing in the backyard, even her goldfish. Diana stared at the large airplane sitting on the runway. Maybe it wasn't too late to change her mind.

What kind of literature is this passage? What is its structure?

_____

_____

_____

_____

_____

HINT Poems have verses and stanzas, dramas have acts and scenes, and fiction has paragraphs and chapters.

Coached Example

Read the passages and answer the questions.

from

The Westwood Stables
Act II, Scene 1

Walter and Bharati are standing by the old stables.

WALTER: What do you think?

BHARATI: (*sighing loudly*) I don't know, Walter. This horse
sure has taken a bad fall.

WALTER: But she'll be okay, right?

BHARATI: I think she'll be okay. Her leg is beginning to heal
already, see? But she's not as young and strong as she once was.

WALTER: She's definitely getting older. You know, I can still remember the first
time I rode Starlight. The sun was so bright, I had to squint and hold my head
sideways just to see her.

BHARATI: And was she friendly?

WALTER: (*smiling*) She seemed to be calling my name as I walked up to her.

BHARATI: I think she'll be okay.

from

The Westwood Stables
Chapter 2

Walter and Bharati stood by the old family stables. It was around sundown,
and a slight chill was in the air. Bharati knew Walter would ask how Starlight was
doing, and when he asked, Bharati let out a long sigh.

"I don't know," said Bharati. "This horse sure has taken a bad fall." He had a
hunch the injuries weren't so bad, but he didn't want to give Walter false hope.
"I think she'll be okay. You can see where she's started to heal. But Walter, she's
not as young and strong as she once was. You know that."

Walter said wistfully, "I know. I still remember the first time I rode her. The
sun was so bright, I had to squint to see her."

"Was she friendly then?" Bharati asked. "She's not always so obliging." He
could tell that Walter had a deep bond with the horse. That alone might be
enough to keep Starlight going.

Walter grinned. "I could have sworn she was calling my name when I went up to her."
Chances were good, Bharati thought, that Starlight would be okay.

1. In the first passage, the words <u>sighing loudly</u> are italicized because they are

    A. meters.

    B. dialogue.

    C. stage directions.

    D. table of contents.

HINT What do the italicized words seem to be telling the reader?

2. Which of the following would come before the second passage?

    A. Act I

    B. Chapter 1

    C. Stanza 1

    D. Line 1

HINT Look under the title of this passage to help answer this question.

3. What information does the second passage tell you that the first passage doesn't?

_____

_____

_____

_____

_____

_____

Lesson Practice

Use the Reading Guides to help you understand the passages.

Reading Guide

What do you notice about the way the lines of this passage are grouped?

What is the subject of this passage?

How does the writer feel about this subject?

Song of a Second April
by Edna St. Vincent Millay

April this year, not otherwise
    Than April of a year ago,
Is full of whispers, full of sighs,
Of dazzling mud and dingy snow;
5   Hepaticas that pleased you so
Are here again, and butterflies.

There rings a hammering all day,
    And shingles lie about the doors;
    In orchards near and far away
10   The grey wood-pecker taps and bores;
    The men are merry at their chores,
    And children earnest at their play.

The larger streams run still and deep,
Noisy and swift the small brooks run
15   Among the mullein stalks the sheep
    Go up the hillside in the sun,
    Pensively,—only you are gone,
You that alone I cared to keep.

hepaticas: an herb with delicate flowers
mullein: an herb with distinctive yellow flowers

Duplicating any part of this book is prohibited by law.

What details about spring do you notice in this passage?

In what way is the structure of this passage different from the structure of the first passage?

excerpted and adapted from

The Wind in the Willows
by Kenneth Grahame

The Mole had been working very hard all the morning, spring cleaning his little home. First with brooms, then with dusters; then on ladders and steps and chairs, with a brush and a pail of whitewash; till he had dust in his throat and eyes, and splashes of whitewash all over his black fur, and an aching back and weary arms. Spring was moving in the air above and in the earth below and around him, penetrating even his dark little house with its spirit of discontent and longing. It was small wonder, then, that he suddenly flung down his brush on the floor, said "Bother!" and ran out of the house without even waiting to put on his coat. Something up above was calling him imperiously, and he made for the steep little tunnel which answered in his case to the gravelly carriage-drive owned by animals whose residences are nearer to the sun and air. So he scraped and scratched and scrabbled and then he scrabbled and scratched and scraped, working busily with his little paws and muttering to himself, "Up we go! Up we go," till at last, *pop*! his snout came out into the sunlight, and he found himself rolling in the warm grass of a great meadow.

"This is fine!" he said to himself. "This is better than whitewashing!" The sunshine struck hot on his fur, soft breezes caressed his heated brow, and after the seclusion of the cellarage he had lived in so long, the carol of happy birds fell on his dulled hearing almost like a shout. Jumping off all his four legs at once, in the joy of living and the delight of spring without its cleaning, he pursued his way across the meadow till he reached the hedge on the further side.

Duplicating any part of this book is prohibited by law.

Answer the following questions.

1. What kind of literature is the first passage?

   A. poem

   B. drama

   C. fiction

   D. act

2. Read this line from the first passage.

   **The larger streams run still
   and deep**

   Which of the following correctly shows the stressed syllables of this line?

   A. **The** larg**er** streams **run** still
   and deep

   B. The **larg**er **streams** run **still**
   and **deep**

   C. **The** larg**er streams** run **still**
   and **deep**

   D. The larg**er** streams **run** still
   and deep

3. What is the structure of the second passage?

   A. two acts of a play

   B. two chapters of a novel

   C. two scenes from a play

   D. two paragraphs from a longer work

4. What change would make the second passage look more like the first?

   A. More dialogue would have to be added.

   B. The character names would have to appear in capital letters.

   C. The lines would have to be broken.

   D. More paragraphs would have to be added.

5. How does the structure of the second passage help teach you about its characters? Use examples from the passage in your response.

   _____

   _____

   _____

   _____

   _____

   _____

   _____

Use the Reading Guides to help you understand the passages.

Reading Guide

"The Ant and the Grasshopper" is a fable, a type of fiction in which characters—often animals—learn a lesson. As you read, look for clues that reveal the story's lesson.

What details in the story tell you more about the ant? What details tell you more about the grasshopper?

How are the ant and the grasshopper different?

The Ant and the Grasshopper

Long ago in a meadow of grass lived an ant and a grasshopper. Every day the tiny ant arose at dawn and hurried to the distant farmer's field. She had work to do and little time to rest. In the field she picked up a grain of wheat; holding it tightly, she scurried back to her home and stored it in her larder. All day she repeated this journey, collecting grain after grain of wheat.

Nearby, the grasshopper watched and smiled to himself. As the busy ant rushed by, the grasshopper spoke to her. "Dear ant, it is a beautiful summer's day. Why do you waste it laboring so hard? I will sing for you, and we can dance across the meadow—come, put down that heavy grain of wheat, and let us enjoy the day!" But the ant paid no attention to the laughing grasshopper; she continued on, making one trip after another to the farmer's field.

When the seasons changed, the sun faded, and the frozen land became mantled in snow, the grasshopper had no warm place to go, and no food to eat, so he paid a visit to his friend, the ant.

Hearing a knock at her door, the ant answered it and found the shivering grasshopper standing there. "My friend ant!" the grasshopper said, "I have come to sing for you! Invite me in to sit by your fire, and feed me some of your delectable grains of wheat."

The ant smiled and said, "I worked all summer to store food to feed myself over these winter days, while you played and sang in the meadow, laughing at me. I have no warmth or food to share with you. I fear that you will have to fend for yourself. Goodbye!" The grasshopper jumped back as the ant's door slammed.

It was then that the grasshopper realized just why the ant worked so hard all summer, and why he would now be called to pay for his frolicking days of the past.

Journey
by Edna St. Vincent Millay

Reading Guide

As you read, follow the changing ideas in each stanza.

What overall idea does the poet express?

How are the structures of the poem and the fable on the previous page similar? How are they different?

Ah, could I lay me down in this long grass
And close my eyes, and let the quiet wind
Blow over me,—I am so tired, so tired
Of passing pleasant places! All my life,
5   Following Care along the dusty road,
Have I looked back at loveliness and sighed;
Yet at my hand an unrelenting hand
Tugged ever, as I passed. All my life long
Over my shoulder have I looked at peace;
10 And now I would fain lie in this long grass
And close my eyes.

      Yet onward!

       Cat-birds call
Through the long afternoon, and creeks at dusk
15 Are guttural. Whip-poor-wills wake and cry,
Drawing the twilight close about their throats.
Only my heart makes answer. Eager vines
Go up the rocks and wait; flushed apple-trees
Pause in their dance and break the ring for me;
20 Dim, shady wood-roads, redolent of fern
And bayberry, that through sweet bevies thread
Of round-faced roses, pink and petulant,
Look back and beckon ere they disappear.
Only my heart, only my heart responds.

25 Yet, ah, my path is sweet on either side
All through the dragging day,—sharp underfoot
And hot, and like dead mist the dry dust hangs—
But far, oh, far as passionate eye can reach,
And long, ah, long as rapturous eye can cling,
30 The world is mine: blue hill, still silver lake,
Broad field, bright flower, and the long white road;
A gateless garden, and an open path;
My feet to follow, and my heart to hold.

Answer the following questions.

6. Read each characteristic in the box below. Decide whether it describes the first passage, the second passage, or both passages. Write the characteristic in the correct column.

Sentences grouped into paragraphs	Lines grouped into stanzas	Dialogue expresses characters' words
Includes details	Speaker expresses thoughts	Contains a message

First Passage	Second Passage	Both Passages
_____	_____	_____
_____	_____	_____
_____	_____	_____

7. **Use your answer to Part A to answer Part B.**

Part A

What does the structure of the first passage BEST help you understand about its two characters?

A. They have similar opinions about eating wheat.

B. They have similar opinions about singing and dancing.

C. They have different opinions about hard work.

D. They have different opinions about keeping warm.

Part B

Circle the paragraphs in the first passage in which you discover the opinions you identified in Part A.

8. **Use your answer to Part A to answer Part B.**

    Part A

    Reread lines 1 to 15 of "Journey." Circle the line that indicates the speaker has made an important decision.

    Part B

    How does the structure of this line indicate that it is significant? There is more than one correct choice listed below.

    A. It rhymes with the previous line.

    B. It does not describe a detail the speaker sees.

    C. It describes the speaker's journey.

    D. It is not a part of a stanza.

    E. It is an exclamation.

    F. It is indented.

    G. It is shorter than other lines.

    H. It indicates the speaker is lazy.

---

9. **Use your answer to Part A to answer Part B.**

    Read the following sets of lines from "Journey."

Ah, could I lay me down in this long grass / And close my eyes, and let the quiet wind / Blow over me
I am so tired, so tired / Of passing pleasant places!
All my life, / Following Care along the dusty road, / Have I looked back at loveliness and sighed

    Part A

    Circle the set of lines that would BEST describe the actions of Grasshopper in the first passage.

    Part B

    Underline one detail from the first passage that describes those same actions.

Duplicating any part of this book is prohibited by law.

2 Plot and Setting

RL.8.1, RL.8.2, RL.8.3, RL.8.10

Getting the Idea

Plot is the sequence of events in fiction or drama. For example, the basic plot of most detective stories can be summed up as follows: 1) a crime occurs; 2) a detective talks to suspects and investigates the crime; 3) the criminal is revealed and brought to justice. A plot has certain elements, as explained in the chart below.

Elements of Plot	
conflict	a struggle or problem that a character must resolve
rising action	the bulk of the story, during which the character works to resolve the problem
climax	the turning point in a story, usually the most exciting part
resolution	the ending of the story, when the conflict is resolved

In Enid Bagnold's novel *National Velvet*, a fourteen-year-old girl named Velvet sees a magnificent stallion running in a field. She has always loved horses, and so she decides that she wants to own the untamed horse, train it, and enter it in the Grand National steeplechase, an important and difficult horse race. Velvet is also determined to ride the horse herself, even though she is a young girl. Training a horse can be challenging, even for experienced riders. The novel's conflict is Velvet's struggle to train the horse, find a way to enter the race, and win it. The rising action describes how Velvet acquires the horse and trains it. The climax, of course, is the big race, the exciting moment when all of Velvet's work is put to the test, as she competes against many very skilled riders. The resolution is the result of the race, when Velvet and her horse win.

Setting is the location and time in which a story takes place. Physical location is often part of the plot development. In *The Wonderful Wizard of Oz*, for example, Dorothy's misery is a direct result of her life on a Kansas farm and the gray dreariness of her surroundings. The land of Oz is vibrant and colorful—a sharp contrast in setting. However, Dorothy rejects Oz for Kansas, as she learns to appreciate her home and family.

The time period is another important element in a story. In the novel *A Connecticut Yankee in King Arthur's Court*, by Mark Twain, the central character is transported back in time, from nineteenth-century Connecticut to early medieval England. Hank Morgan's knowledge of the science and technology of his time helps him succeed in a superstitious society that believes in magic.

If the setting is not directly stated, look for clues, such as the available technology and a society's customs, to figure out the setting.

Thinking It Through

Read the following paragraph, and then answer the question that follows.

Sun Yi stared dejectedly at the grade on her English paper. This was her second C this semester. How could this be? Her teacher, Mr. O'Neill, suggested she sign up for after-school tutoring. Although she didn't want to, Sun Yi went to tutoring three times a week. She also spent extra time writing her next English paper. She put a tremendous amount of effort and imagination into it. When Mr. O'Neill handed back the papers, Sun Yi grinned with delight. She had earned a B+! Sun Yi's hard work had been rewarded.

Which part of the story is the climax?

_____

_____

 The climax usually occurs near the end of the story.

 How is the setting of this story important to the plot?

Coached Example

Read the passage and answer the questions.

Eli forced himself to take another step forward. Before him, the burning sand glittered like a golden carpet. He had been walking for hours, the sun's rays harsh on his skin.

Eli stopped and raised the plastic water bottle to his lips. Not a single drop of water trickled into his mouth. He tossed the empty bottle aside and stumbled forward. He fell onto the sand.

An image of Jessica's face filled his mind. They had argued that morning. Eli had taken a job in another city without consulting Jessica. Jessica had been angry. Eli had stormed out of the apartment without his cell phone and jumped into his car. After driving for miles, his car broke down. Eli realized he was in the middle of nowhere, and he began a long march for help. Soon, he was lost.

Now he was in need of a miracle. Suddenly, he heard a helicopter. Eli rose and waved his T-shirt frantically.

---

1. What is the setting of the passage?

   A. a desert

   B. a beach

   C. a forest

   D. a park

   HINT The passage includes details that provide clues to the setting.

2. What is the main conflict in the passage?

   A. Eli needs to buy a new car.

   B. Eli is struggling to stay alive.

   C. Eli is torn about taking a new job.

   D. Eli had an argument with Jessica.

   HINT The main conflict is the biggest problem that Eli is facing in the passage.

Lesson Practice

Use the Reading Guide to help you understand the passage.

Reading Guide

Look for clues to the setting as you read the passage. These may include descriptions of the weather, references to technology, or references to historical figures.

What is the main conflict in the passage?

The Peasant Astrologer
adapted from an Italian folktale

There was once a king who had a valuable ring. It was solid gold with a giant ruby and sparkling diamonds. One morning, when he reached into his jewelry chest for the ring, he came up empty-handed. The ring was gone. The desperate king searched everywhere. Could someone have stolen it? The king issued a proclamation. Any astrologer in the land who could tell him where to find his ring would be richly rewarded.

Astrologers from all over flocked to the royal castle. The king spoke to each one of them. Though each astrologer boldly announced that *he* was the only one who could find the king's ring, each one failed to produce it.

Now, a poor peasant named Nicolo had also heard the proclamation. He could not read or write. However, he was sharp. He was always able to figure out solutions to tricky problems. Having nothing to lose, he decided to join the search for the ring. He lived far from the castle and owned neither horse nor carriage. So, he walked for three miles along dusty roads, with only a crusty piece of bread and a block of cheese to eat.

Eventually, he arrived at the castle, where he presented himself to the king with the confidence of a real astrologer. By stroking his chin thoughtfully, he made himself seem very impressive. "Your Majesty," he said with a bow, "though I am poorly dressed, I am the astrologer who will solve the mystery of your missing ring. If you will lead me to my room, I shall begin my studies."

"Very well," the king replied.

So, Nicolo was taken to a room, furnished only with a bed and a table, upon which was a large book, a bottle of ink, and a quill pen. Nicolo sat at the table and turned the pages and scribbled on the paper, pretending to read and write.

The servants, who came in and out of the room bringing him food for the next few weeks, thought he was a great astrologer. They grew nervous, for they were the ones who had stolen the ring. It seemed to them that Nicolo cast severe glances at them, as if he accused them with his eyes. They wondered how long it would be before they were found out.

What are the key events in the plot?

Which part of the story is the resolution?

In fact, Nicolo had suspected them from the beginning, and their nervousness confirmed his suspicions. But how could he prove it? One day, his wife came to visit, and Nicolo had an idea.

"Hide under the bed," he told her, "and when a servant enters, say, 'That's the first one.' When the next one enters, say, 'That's another one,' and so on. Trust me, this should work."

Soon, the first servant entered with Nicolo's dinner. Immediately, the wife said, "That's the first one." Then, the second servant entered, and the wife said, "That's another one." The servants were frightened. They did not know where the voice was coming from but were certain that their guilt had been uncovered.

The servants decided to confess and beg the astrologer not to betray them to the king. They entered the room again and bowed before Nicolo.

"Great astrologer, you have uncovered our crime. We are poor people. Please take the ring back and do not denounce us to the king."

Nicolo had a better idea. "If you wish to keep your lives, take the ring and make the turkey in the courtyard swallow it. And never speak of this again."

The servants did as they were told. Then, Nicolo went to the king and said, "After toiling for nearly a month, I have discovered the location of the ring. A turkey swallowed it."

The king was ecstatic to have his ring back. He presented Nicolo with a large purse of money and appointed him court astrologer. Nicolo was a peasant no more.

astrologer: someone who makes predictions based on the constellations

Answer the following questions.

1. What is the conflict at the beginning of the passage?

   A. The king owns a ruby and diamond ring.

   B. The king needs a new astrologer.

   C. The king issues a proclamation.

   D. The king loses his valuable ring.

2. What is the setting of the passage?

   A. a modern-day capital city

   B. a small-town village

   C. Nicolo's farmhouse

   D. a kingdom long ago

3. Which event in the passage is part of the rising action?

   A. The king reaches into his jewelry chest.

   B. The king makes Nicolo court astrologer.

   C. Nicolo pretends to read and write.

   D. The king gets his ring back.

4. Which event is the climax in the passage?

   A. Nicolo tells the king where to find the ring.

   B. Nicolo is appointed court astrologer.

   C. Nicolo's wife hides under the bed.

   D. Nicolo arrives at the king's court.

5. How is Nicolo able to solve the problem, even though he is only a peasant? Use examples from the passage in your response.

   _____

   _____

   _____

   _____

Use the Reading Guide to help you understand the passage.

Reading Guide

The setting and the plot work together to reveal the themes or central ideas of a literary text. As you read the passage, think about how the narrator feels and acts in response to a surprising incident.

What conflict arises in this part of the passage?

Often an element of the setting will propel the action of the plot. What does the narrator do after discovering the footprint on the beach?

excerpted and adapted from

Robinson Crusoe

by Daniel Dafoe

In this place also I had my grapes growing, which I principally depended on for my winter store of raisins, and which I never failed to preserve very carefully, as the best and most agreeable dainty of my whole diet; and indeed they were not only agreeable, but medicinal, wholesome, nourishing, and refreshing to the last degree.

As this was also about half-way between my other habitation and the place where I had laid up my boat, I generally stayed and lay here in my way thither; for I used frequently to visit my boat, and I kept all things about or belonging to her in very good order. Sometimes I went out in her to divert myself, but no more hazardous voyages would I go, scarcely ever above a stone's cast or two from the shore. I was so apprehensive of being hurried out of my knowledge again by the currents or winds, or any other accident. But now I come to a new scene of my life. It happened one day, about noon, going towards my boat. I was exceedingly surprised with the print of a man's naked foot on the shore, which was very plain to be seen on the sand. I stood like one thunderstruck, or as if I had seen an apparition. I listened, I looked round me, but I could hear nothing, nor see anything; I went up to a rising ground to look farther; I went up the shore and down the shore, but it was all one; I could see no other impression but that one. I went to it again to see if there were any more, and to observe if it might not be my fancy; but there was no room for that, for there was exactly the print of a foot—toes, heel, and every part of a foot. How it came thither I knew not, nor could I in the least imagine; but after innumerable fluttering thoughts, like a man perfectly confused and out of myself, I came home to my fortification, not feeling, as we say, the ground I went on, but terrified to the last degree, looking behind me at every two or three steps, mistaking every bush and tree, and fancying every stump at a distance to be a man. Nor is it possible to describe how many various shapes my affrighted imagination represented things to me in; how many wild ideas were found every moment in my fancy; and what strange, unaccountable whimsies came into my thoughts by the way.

How does the footprint affect the narrator when he is nearby? How does the footprint affect him when he moves away from it?

Often, characters use setting details to draw conclusions that move the plot forward. Whom does the narrator conclude made the footprint?

When I came to my castle (for so I think I called it ever after this), I fled into it like one pursued. Whether I went over by the ladder, as first contrived, or went in at the hole in the rock, which I had called a door, I cannot remember; no, nor could I remember the next morning, for never frightened hare fled to cover, or fox to earth, with more terror of mind than I to this retreat.

I slept none that night; the farther I was from the occasion of my fright, the greater my apprehensions were. This is something contrary to the nature of such things, and especially to the usual practice of all creatures in fear; but I was so embarrassed with my own frightful ideas of the thing, that I formed nothing but dismal imaginations to myself, even though I was now a great way off. Sometimes I fancied it must be the devil, and reason joined in with me in this supposition; for how should any other thing in human shape come into the place? Where was the vessel that brought them? What marks were there of any other footstep? And how was it possible a man should come there?

Answer the following questions.

6. Decide whether each text detail on the left BEST supports the location, time, or conflict within the passage. Draw a line between the detail and the correct box on the right.

A. ". . . this was also about half-way between my other habitation and the place where I had laid up my boat."

1. time

2. location

B. "I went to it again to see if there were any more, and to observe if it might not be my fancy; but there was no room for that, for there was exactly the print of a foot."

3. conflict

C. "But now I come to a new scene of my life. It happened one day, about noon."

7. Read this excerpt from paragraph 2 of the passage.

> . . . there was exactly the print of a foot—toes, heel, and every part of a foot. How it came thither I knew not, nor could I in the least imagine; but after innumerable fluttering thoughts, like a man perfectly confused and out of myself, I came home to my fortification, not feeling, as we say, the ground I went on, but terrified to the last degree, looking behind me at every two or three steps, mistaking every bush and tree, and fancying every stump at a distance to be a man.

Underline the details in the paragraph that propel the narrator to return home in fear.

8. **Use your answer to Part A to answer Part B.**

Part A

What is the relationship between the setting and the narrator's inability to sleep?

A. The narrator spends the night searching for a vessel.

B. Closeness to the footprint causes the narrator to feel apprehensive.

C. The narrator spends the night searching the shore for more footprints.

D. Distance from the footprint causes the narrator's imagination to run wild.

Part B

Which text detail BEST supports your answer in Part A?

A. "... I went up to a rising ground to look farther; I went up the shore and down the shore, but it was all one."

B. "... the farther I was from the occasion of my fright ... I formed nothing but dismal imaginations to myself."

C. "This is something contrary to the nature of such things."

D. "... I was so embarrassed with my own frightful ideas of the thing."

E. "Sometimes I fancied it must be the devil, and reason joined in with me in this supposition."

9. Read each setting detail in the box below. Choose three details that BEST support the central idea that unexplained incidents cause people to feel fear. Write them in the chart.

"mistaking every bush and tree"	"fancying every stump at a distance to be a man"	"scarcely ever above a stone's cast or two from the shore"
"in this place also I had my grapes growing"	"not feeling, as we say, the ground I went on, but terrified"	

Setting Detail 1	Setting Detail 2	Setting Detail 3

3 Character

RL.8.1, RL.8.2, RL.8.3, RL.8.6, RL.8.10

Getting the Idea

A **character** is a person or animal in a story, play, or poem. In fact, a character can be any creature that comes from the author's imagination. Characters are essential parts of a literary work, and understanding them can enhance a reader's understanding of the text.

Characters have **traits**, or qualities that define them. For example, think about the character traits of some well-known characters. Tom Sawyer is mischievous, Goldilocks is curious, and Paul Bunyan is strong. Read the chart below to find out more about how characters are shaped.

| Elements That Reveal Character Traits ||
Element	Example
actions	*Lisa snuck into her brother's room and took five dollars from his wallet.* Lisa's trait is dishonesty.
dialogue	*"Will you hurry up? I don't have all day!" Ed yelled.* Ed's trait is impatience.
thoughts and emotions	*Taariq wondered if he would ever dare say hello to Aisha.* Taariq's trait is shyness.
interaction with other characters	*Casey rushed to open the door as Ty approached on crutches. He helped Ty into a seat and brought him a drink.* Casey's trait is thoughtfulness.
the author's direct statements	*Brenda had always been ambitious. She worked twelve-hour days, hoping for a promotion.* Brenda's trait is persistence.

Most characters have more than one trait, and they often change during a story. For instance, a greedy boy may learn to share with others. In the story of King Midas, a greedy man is granted the power to turn everything he touches to gold. He learns his lesson when he loses many things and people he loves this way. Read carefully, though: in some stories, a good character may become evil.

Characters have **motivations**, or reasons why they act the way they do. In a famous novel by Alexandre Dumas called *The Count of Monte Cristo*, the main character, Edmond Dantès, is betrayed by his friend and unjustly imprisoned. His suffering is so immense that when he escapes from prison, he sets an elaborate plan into action to destroy his enemies. His motivation is revenge, and it guides the plot throughout the novel. This is a true suspense story: as Dantès faces each obstacle, we truly never know what the outcome is going to be.

Sometimes, we feel suspense *because* we know and anticipate a certain outcome. An author might choose to give the reader information that a character in the story does not know. When we know something more than a character does, we might anticipate a conflict to take place and think, *Don't do it!* This literary device is called **dramatic irony**. An author uses **point of view**—the perspective from which a story is told—to reveal as much or as little to the reader as the author chooses. For instance, in William Shakespeare's *Othello*, the audience knows that Iago is evil and is deceiving Othello because Shakespeare reveals Iago's private conversations. However, Othello constantly refers to Iago as a good and honest friend. This creates suspense as the audience waits for the moment that Othello learns the truth.

The setting can have a direct effect on characters. The novel *Brave New World*, by Aldous Huxley, takes place mostly in London in the twenty-sixth century. In this futuristic society, people are free from war, poverty, and disease. However, the government controls every aspect of their lives, eliminating their freedom and individuality. The setting causes things to happen to the characters that would not happen otherwise.

Thinking It Through

Read the following paragraph, and then answer the question that follows.

Rick leaned back in the recliner and watched the credits roll on the TV screen. His show was over, but he'd left the remote control by the cable box. He'd have to get up from the recliner to change the channel. Rick thought about that as he watched a shampoo commercial. He almost got up during the car commercial. He was still contemplating his situation during a sneakers commercial. Finally, he realized that someone was bound to come into the living room sooner or later. All he had to do was wait.

Which word BEST describes Rick, and why?

_____

_____

HINT   Pay attention to Rick's actions and thoughts.

Coached Example

Read the passage and answer the questions.

The curtain opens on a thirteen-year-old boy named Ben. He giggles to himself as he climbs a stepladder and carefully positions a large water balloon on the top of a partly opened door. He climbs down the ladder and pushes it out of the way. Still giggling, he hurries over to the living room couch and sits.

BEN: *(calling)* Hey, Jake, come here a minute!

JAKE: *(off-stage)* What is it?

BEN: *(stifling a chuckle)* Just come here! You gotta see this!

JAKE: *(off-stage)* All right. Be right there.

(Ben sits up eagerly in anticipation. A moment later, Jake enters through the door. The water balloon falls on his head, soaking him. He wipes water off his face and glares at Ben.)

JAKE: *(furiously)* Another trick? When are you going to grow up?

(Ben points at Jake and breaks out into loud laughter.)

JAKE: I'm telling Mom. Let's see how funny you think it is then.

Jake turns and exits. Ben jumps to his feet, a worried look on his face.

BEN: *(running)* Jake, wait!

(Ben exits.)

---

1. Ben's actions suggest that he is

   A. a grouch.

   B. a prankster.

   C. careless.

   D. trustworthy.

HINT Choose the trait that best suits Ben's actions in the play.

2. The interaction between Ben and Jake shows that they

   A. have a lot of fun together.

   B. are both very sneaky.

   C. depend on each other.

   D. do not always get along.

HINT Reread the dialogue. The characters' words are revealing.

Lesson Practice

Use the Reading Guide to help you understand the passage.

Reading Guide

Think about the ways that these characters' words reveal their character traits.

How does the girls' interaction help you understand their characters?

What Do You Want to Be?

"So, what did you write your essay on?" Keisha asked Ruby.

The girls had written an essay in English class in which they explained what they wanted to be when they grew up.

"A kindergarten teacher," Ruby said.

"You're kidding!" Keisha exclaimed, opening up the milk carton on her lunch tray.

"Hey, girls, what's going on?"

Keisha and Ruby greeted Nandi and Mia as they joined them at the cafeteria table.

"Well," Keisha began, answering Mia's question, "you know the essay we just wrote in Mr. Martin's class? Ruby said she wants to be a kindergarten teacher."

"What's wrong with that?" Nandi asked, unwrapping a chicken burrito.

"Nothing," Keisha answered, "if you like babysitting noisy brats for six hours a day. "

Ruby frowned. Keisha was always such a know-it-all. She thought she had a better idea about almost everything. "I won't be a babysitter, Keisha. Teaching is one of the most important jobs in the world."

Keisha shrugged. "Whatever. While you're in a classroom pulling your hair out, I'll be in outer space exploring the galaxy. I'm going to be an astronaut."

"Hey!" Mia exclaimed. "I want to open a skydiving school when I grow up. I see neither of us is afraid of heights." She smiled at Keisha.

"Well, I'm going to be just a *little bit* higher up than you, Mia," said Keisha.

"You're so sarcastic, Keisha. First you made fun of Ruby and now you're making fun of Mia."

Keisha shrugged again. "So what do you want to be, Nandi?"

Nandi's frown dissolved into a smile. "A painter. I want to be the next Picasso or Joan Miró."

"Joan Miró, huh?" Keisha said. "Never heard of her." She took a bite of her grilled cheese sandwich.

How does the setting contribute to the events in the passage?

Nandi laughed. "That shows how much you know. Joan Miró was a man. He was from Spain, and he changed modern art."

Keisha swallowed and made a face. "Whatever. This cheese sandwich is as cold as an iceberg. I'm bringing it back to the lunch lady. Be right back."

"I'm not surprised you want to be a painter, Nandi," Mia said. "You're really good in art class."

"Thanks. One day my paintings will hang in art galleries and museums for the whole world to see. Everyone's going to know my name."

"You really want to open a skydiving school, Mia?" asked Ruby.

Mia grinned. "Yes! I've always wanted to skydive, but my parents won't let me. As soon as I'm old enough, I'm hitting the skies! I can't wait. The thrill of jumping out of a plane and rushing toward the ground, feeling the air in my face, and knowing that I have to pull the cord at the right time or—"

Ruby held up her hand and cut in. "Okay, stop. How is that fun? I know teaching kindergarten may not be exciting, but at least it's safe!"

"And boring!" Keisha added, sliding back into her seat. She placed a fresh sandwich on her tray. "I'm with you, Mia. When I think of sitting in a space shuttle and shooting off into space a thousand miles an hour, I get chills. One day I'm going to be in a space station, looking down on Earth. It's gonna be amazing! Oh—oops! I have to get a napkin."

Ruby scowled at Keisha's back as she walked away. Then, she grabbed a salt shaker and poured it into Keisha's milk carton. She stirred it quickly with a straw as Mia and Nandi looked on.

"Ruby! That's not nice," Mia said, but she couldn't help smiling. Nandi was smiling, too.

"Hope she takes a big, long gulp," Nandi said.

Answer the following questions.

1. Which girls have the MOST in common?

   A. Nandi and Ruby

   B. Mia and Nandi

   C. Keisha and Mia

   D. Keisha and Ruby

2. Which of the following is MOST LIKELY true of Ruby?

   A. She likes children.

   B. She wants to be rich.

   C. She likes to take risks.

   D. She does not like school.

3. Nandi's words suggest that her motivation for being a painter is

   A. money.

   B. fame.

   C. freedom.

   D. curiosity.

4. Which word BEST describes Mia?

   A. imaginative

   B. intelligent

   C. unfriendly

   D. adventurous

5. Why does Ruby pour salt into Keisha's milk? Use examples from the passage in your response.

   _____

   _____

   _____

   _____

Use the Reading Guide to help you understand the passage.

Reading Guide

Where and when is the story set? As you read, keep in mind the effect that the setting has on the characters.

How do Liam's actions reveal aspects of his character?

Think about the importance of the word *soil* in the story and how it shapes the characters.

Foreign Soil

Liam Gallagher kicked the wilting leaves of the sugar beet plants that dotted the field of his family's farm. Usually, after such an act of rebellion, he would gaze around to ensure that his father hadn't seen him. In such cases, Liam would become the object of a lecture about respecting nature and his family's livelihood. Today, however, Liam didn't care whether his father saw him or not. He was furious and looking for an argument.

He had known for weeks, months even, that the farm was failing. In fact, all the local farms were in danger of failing. It was as if the Irish soil, so loved by the generations of families who worked the land, was betraying its people. Industrial jobs in the cities lured the poor and starving farmers away from their meager potatoes and sugar beets. He couldn't blame them, really; after all, every family's survival depended on monetary income. Yet, somehow, he had believed that his family's sugar beets would thrive and that his father would find a wealthy buyer. Liam's father's words, uttered around the family dinner table the previous evening, echoed in Liam's ears: "America. We're going to America to join my brother and his family in New York."

Liam often accompanied his father to the store to buy farm supplies. Here, the local men gathered and exchanged gossip. Liam had overheard discussions about America. For strong men, America offered respectable construction jobs building canals, railroads, streets, and sewers. For women, there were jobs in factories and mills. Liam's uncle, Patrick, had immigrated to New York two years ago. He had forwarded letters describing his life in America. He and his family lived in a neighborhood with other Irish Catholics, and both he and his wife had found work. They were making a decent living. Most of the letters to Liam's father ended with the same invitation: "Please think about joining us, Aidan." Liam missed his comical and affectionate uncle, but he had always assumed that Uncle Patrick would return to Ireland one day. He never dreamed that their reunion might take place on foreign soil.

Dramatic irony occurs when one character is unaware of information that another character or the reader may have. As you read, consider how dramatic irony might affect the conflicts that the characters face.

What aspects of the characters are revealed in their thoughts, words, and actions?

When Aidan Gallagher proclaimed his plan to immigrate to America with his wife and children, it was accompanied by a sense of urgency that went unperceived by the rest of the family, given the frenzied reaction to his decree. Recently, the American legislature had set in place quotas on immigration, restricting the number of immigrants from any particular country. Aidan alone realized the implications of this Immigration Act of 1924: If they didn't act quickly, it was possible that the family would be denied permission to relocate to America at all.

Still, he had to try. He couldn't remain inactive and watch his family drift further into poverty. Aidan regretted his hesitation two years earlier when Patrick had pleaded with him to come to America. "Come with me, brother; Ireland cares nothing for your rumbling belly." Aidan had been a fool to think that the sugar beets would yield sweetness instead of heartache.

Aidan printed each family member's name meticulously on the immigration forms. Looking up from his battered desk near the window, he glimpsed his son Liam kicking sugar beets in the field. He appreciated that Liam was distraught about the prospect of leaving Ireland. Liam loved farming, and he had friends and a girlfriend, Siobhan, in the village. Saying goodbye wouldn't be easy, but Aidan trusted that his son would come to terms with the arrangement in time. Aidan wasn't as convinced that the American government would let his family in. He knew that many Irish families had already departed for America. He didn't know how many openings remained. Would there be enough room left for his family? He prayed so.

Looking back at the house, Liam could see his father sitting at his desk. *That's it*, Liam thought, *I'm going to march in there and tell him that I'm not going. I'm old enough to strike out on my own, and I'm going to do it in Ireland.* Dust fluttered around Liam's feet as he started walking, moving rapidly across the field. Halfway to the house, though, Liam's pace slowed. *How can I choose this sad piece of soil over family and loyalty?* he thought to himself, his anger and resolve fading.

Aidan saw his son coming slowly toward the house, the boy's face a study in melancholy. Aidan sighed noisily. It was time to tell his son the truth about the urgency that the family faced. Maybe knowledge would have the power to heal their rift.

Answer the following questions.

6. Read each line of dialogue on the left. Then match the dialogue to the character trait on the right that it BEST reveals.

A. "Yet, somehow, he had believed that his family's sugar beets would thrive and that his father would find a wealthy buyer."

1. cautious

2. lazy

B. "Liam missed his comical and affectionate uncle, but he had always assumed that Uncle Patrick would return to Ireland one day."

3. dishonest

4. optimistic

C. "Aidan regretted his hesitation two years earlier when Patrick had pleaded with him to come to America."

5. family-oriented

6. rebellious

D. "*That's it*, Liam thought, *I'm going to march in there and tell him that I'm not going.*"

7. Which of the following motivates Aidan to move his family to America? There is more than one correct choice listed below.

A. friends in the village

B. quota on number of immigrants

C. gossip at the farm store

D. Liam's anger

E. Liam's girlfriend

F. conversation at the family dinner table

G. the poor sugar beet crop

8. **Use your answer to Part A to answer Part B.**

    Part A

    What information do Aidan and the reader have that Liam does not have?

    A. details from gossip at the general store

    B. knowledge about the failure of the crop

    C. knowledge of legislation regarding American immigration

    D. information from Uncle Patrick's letters home

    Part B

    In what way does this information affect the story?

    A. It makes Liam's behavior at the beginning of the story more humorous.

    B. It adds a bittersweet tone to Liam's relationship with Siobhan.

    C. It reveals Uncle Patrick's motivations for wanting the family to move to America.

    D. It creates suspense because Liam is unaware that the family might not be permitted to stay in America.

    E. It makes Liam seem cruel for not wanting to accompany his family to America.

9. **Use your answer to Part A to answer Part B.**

    Part A

    Read paragraph 7 of the passage. Underline a thought or an action that supports the theme that family members must sometimes sacrifice individual desires for the good of the family.

    Part B

    How does this thought or action BEST indicate that Liam has changed?

    A. He realizes he can make new friends in America.

    B. He becomes excited at the prospect of finding work in America.

    C. He understands that his family will never be successful in Ireland.

    D. He discovers his own independent nature.

    E. He determines that he is not good at farming.

4 Theme and Summary

RL.8.1, RL.8.2, RL.8.10

Getting the Idea

The **theme** of a literary work is its central message or lesson. Many stories, plays, and poems have themes, although they are usually not stated directly in the text. One exception is the fable, in which the author often states the moral at the end of the story. Themes are general statements about life and people. The specific characters and events in the texts are just a means of expressing these statements.

Think about the tale of the shepherd boy who cried wolf. He cries "Wolf! Wolf!" repeatedly, bringing the villagers running to help; time after time they discover he was lying. Finally, when a wolf actually appears, they ignore the boy's cries, and the wolf devours his sheep. The story teaches the importance of telling the truth. Its theme could be stated as "Honesty is the best policy." Common themes in literature include the following:

- If at first you don't succeed, try again.
- People get what they deserve.
- Sacrifices often bring rewards.
- Be happy with what you have.
- Appearances can be deceiving.
- Good triumphs over evil.
- Love conquers all.

A text may have more than one theme. William Shakespeare's plays often teach multiple lessons on love, friendship, greed, pride, and trusting the wrong person.

Authors sometimes develop a theme through the use of recurring images in a setting, or similar events in a plot. In other words, they use repetition to draw attention to an important idea. In *Death of a Salesman*, playwright Arthur Miller refers to planting many times. At the beginning of the play, the central character, Willy Loman, complains, "The grass don't grow anymore, you can't raise a carrot in the backyard." Toward the end of the play, he looks for a seed store because he wants to plant peas and carrots. Later, he goes out to plant seeds in the middle of the night.

The idea of planting seeds is central to the play's themes. Near the end of his life, Loman realizes that he has failed as a salesman, a husband, and a father. His attempt to plant seeds shows that he wants to leave something behind after he is gone. This could be security for his family, a legacy, or something to show he led a meaningful life. Loman never gets to plant his garden, supporting the themes of failure and unfulfilled dreams.

While a theme captures an essential message of a story, a **summary** is a short retelling of the story in the reader's own words. It should give the basic elements: the main idea or theme and the most important details of the story. It should not include minor details, information from outside the story, or the reader's opinion or judgments about the story.

A summary of Washington Irving's "The Legend of Sleepy Hollow," for example, would include only the major plot points. It might look like this: *Schoolmaster Ichabod Crane is an outsider competing against local hero Brom Bones for Katrina Van Tassel's hand in marriage in the supposedly haunted town of Sleepy Hollow. One night Crane attends a party at Van Tassel's home, where he plans to propose to her. Instead, Crane leaves the party rejected and spooked from the ghost stories Bones and others tell. On his ride home, Crane runs into the legendary Headless Horseman, who throws his head at him. Crane is never heard from again, and his mysterious disappearance becomes another ghost story.* This summary gives you a good sense of what the story is about without getting into too many details.

Thinking It Through

Read the following paragraph, and then answer the question that follows.

> Meg looked at the spinach on her plate and scrunched up her nose. It looked awful. But her mother was staring at her from across the table. Meg raised a forkful of spinach to her mouth and took a bite. She was happily surprised.

What is the theme of the passage?

_____

_____

 What lesson does Meg learn?

DISCUSS How would you summarize this passage? How is the summary different from the theme?

Coached Example

Read the passage and answer the questions.

The Birds, the Beasts, and the Bat
adapted from a fable by Aesop

Long ago, the birds were at war with the beasts. Through the years, the power shifted. Sometimes the birds won the battle, and sometimes the beasts won. The bat, never knowing how a battle might end, always fought on the side he felt was the strongest. Finally, peace was made, and the birds and the beasts became friends. The bat's dishonest conduct became apparent to both sides. The birds and the beasts decided to punish the disloyal bat and drove him away. From that day, the bat has hidden himself in dark places and is friends with neither birds nor beasts.

1. What is the theme of the passage?

   A. One who plays for both sides will end up friendless.

   B. It is better to try and fail than not to try at all.

   C. Birds and beasts should live separately.

   D. Nothing good comes of war.

   HINT Think about what happens to the bat and choose the best answer.

2. Which word from the passage gives the BEST clue about the theme?

   A. strongest

   B. disloyal

   C. beasts

   D. war

   HINT The correct answer is the word most directly related to the theme.

Lesson Practice

Use the Reading Guide to help you understand the passage.

Reading Guide

Think about the central message or lesson the writer wants to communicate.

Look for recurring images or events as you read the passage.

Jian Writes a Book Report

Jian yelled, "Go long!" and tossed the football to his brother, Li. The ball sailed through the air. Jian watched as Li made a spectacular catch. In an instant, Li whipped the ball back to Jian.

"Not bad!" Jian called out, running to catch Li's return.

"Not bad?" Li scoffed. "That doesn't mean much, coming from you. You catch like a girl."

"Thank you," their sister, Bai, said from the back porch. "I'll take that as a compliment."

Jian grinned as he hurled the ball into the air. "I'm so sure that's what Li meant."

Bai got up to go indoors. "Okay, guys, I have to do my homework. Jian, don't you have a book report due next week?"

Jian shrugged and dove for the ball. "I've got plenty of time. Next week's a long way off."

"That's what you always say," Bai replied before going into the house.

Later that afternoon, Jian sat down at his computer to write his book report. It had been a long time since he had even looked at the book. He scanned the first few pages, and then he stared at the computer screen. It stared back, uncooperative. Li came into their room and asked him if he wanted to play a board game. Jian enthusiastically agreed and turned off his computer. Then they settled into a long game of Risk, his favorite.

As they were playing, their mom came home from work. She called Jian into the kitchen and opened the refrigerator door. "It's your turn to clean out the refrigerator. I reminded you this morning."

"Sorry, Mom. I meant to, but I've been working on this book report."

Bai heard Jian's words from the living room and cleared her throat loudly. Jian pretended not to notice. "I'll do it right now, Mom."

"It's too late now. It's dinnertime. Please do it tomorrow."

Why does Bai tell Jian about the fable?

How does the ending of the passage support the theme?

Jian promised and returned to the living room, glaring at Bai as he walked by. As their mother prepared dinner, Bai watched her brothers play. Finally, she said, "You know who you remind me of, Jian? Those beavers in that fable who wanted to play with their friends instead of building a dam. Next thing they knew, they had no homes. They were also being chased by wolves."

Jian glanced up from the board game. "Luckily, we don't live near wolves."

Bai shrugged. "We'll see who laughs last."

The next day, Jian got himself a snack from the refrigerator. He paused as he looked inside, remembering he was supposed to clean it. But Jian figured he still had three hours before his mom came home. He sat down to watch his favorite show on TV.

His friend Chris called him halfway through the show. "Hi, Jian. Did you speak to your Little League coach about my trying out for the team? You'd said you would."

"Oh, um . . . well . . ."

"Oh, come on, Jian! You've been saying you're going to ask him for two weeks now. What are you waiting for?"

Jian thought that was a really good question. Unfortunately, he didn't have a really good answer. He promised to ask Coach Rivers the next day.

Later that night, Jian heard his mother yell for him from the kitchen. After their conversation, he super-promised her he would clean the refrigerator the next day. She super-promised to ground him for a week if he didn't keep his super-promise.

Two nights later, Jian stayed up all night writing his book report. His sister walked past his room, singing, "Someone's in trouble." She was right. Jian received a D on his report, and the teacher called his mother in for a consultation. Jian realized he was going to be grounded after all.

Answer the following questions.

1. Which character in the passage learns a lesson?

   A. Bai

   B. Jian

   C. Li

   D. Chris

2. What is the theme of the passage?

   A. Think of others before you think of yourself.

   B. Don't put off till tomorrow what you should do today.

   C. If at first you don't succeed, try again.

   D. You can't always get what you want.

3. How does the author demonstrate the theme?

   A. by stating it directly in the passage

   B. by showing how well Jian and Li get along

   C. through a description of Bai's secret thoughts

   D. through repeated examples of Jian's lack of action

4. Which element in the passage MOST helps develop the theme?

   A. the dirty refrigerator

   B. the football game

   C. the mother's job

   D. the back porch

5. What is the connection between the fable Bai mentions and Jian? Use examples from the passage in your response.

   _____

   _____

   _____

   _____

Reading Guide

As you read, reflect on the main plot points that help you understand what happens to the narrator.

What causes Jim and his mother to travel to the neighboring hamlet?

Remember that repeated ideas often point to a theme. What idea is repeated in paragraph 1?

excerpted and adapted from

Treasure Island

by Robert Louis Stevenson

The narrator, Jim, lives with his mother at his family's inn, the Admiral Benbow. An old sailor, Billy, has been staying at the inn. In ill health, Billy is cared for by Doctor Livesey and has received visits from a former shipmate, Black Dog, and from a mysterious blind man. As the passage begins, Billy has just had a fatal stroke.

I lost no time, of course, in telling my mother all that I knew, and perhaps should have told her long before, and we saw ourselves at once in a difficult and dangerous position. Some of the man's money—if he had any—was certainly due to us, but it was not likely that our captain's shipmates, above all the two specimens seen by me—Black Dog and the blind beggar—would be inclined to give up their booty in payment of the dead man's debts. The captain's order to mount at once and ride for Doctor Livesey would have left my mother alone and unprotected, which was not to be thought of. Indeed, it seemed impossible for either of us to remain much longer in the house; the fall of coals in the kitchen grate, the very ticking of the clock, filled us with alarm. The neighborhood, to our ears, seemed haunted by approaching footsteps; and what between the dead body of the captain on the parlor floor and the thought of that detestable blind beggar hovering near at hand and ready to return, there were moments when, as the saying goes, I jumped in my skin for terror. Something must speedily be resolved upon, and it occurred to us at last to go forth together and seek help in the neighboring hamlet. No sooner said than done. Bareheaded as we were, we ran out at once in the gathering evening and the frosty fog. . . .

As you read a detail or description, think about whether or not it belongs in a summary of the text.

What realization do Jim and his mother come to in paragraph 3?

Remember that a summary is objective. It includes the main idea or theme and the most important details, not your own thoughts about the story.

It was already candle-light when we reached the hamlet, and I shall never forget how much I was cheered to see the yellow shine in doors and windows; but that, as it proved, was the best of the help we were likely to get in that quarter. For—you would have thought men would have been ashamed of themselves—no soul would consent to return with us to the Admiral Benbow. The more we told of our troubles, the more—man, woman, and child—they clung to the shelter of their houses. The name of Captain Flint, though it was strange to me, was well enough known to some there, and carried a great weight of terror. Some of the men who had been to field-work on the far side of the Admiral Benbow remembered, besides, to have seen several strangers on the road, and, taking them to be smugglers, to have bolted away; and one at least had seen a little lugger in what we called Kitt's Hole. For that matter, anyone who was a comrade of the captain's was enough to frighten them to death. And the short and the long of the matter was, that while we could get several who were willing enough to ride to Doctor Livesey's, which lay in another direction, not one would help us to defend the inn.

They say cowardice is infectious; but then argument is, on the other hand, a great emboldener; and so when each had said his say, my mother made them a speech. She would not, she declared, lose money that belonged to her fatherless boy. "If none of the rest of you dare," she said, "Jim and I dare. Back we will go, the way we came, and small thanks to you big, hulking, chicken-hearted men! We'll have that chest open, if we die for it. And I'll thank you for that bag, Mrs. Crossley, to bring back our lawful money in."

Answer the following questions.

6. Read the final paragraph of the passage. Circle a theme that the paragraph supports. Underline a detail you might include in a summary of the passage.

_____

7. **Use your answer to Part A to answer Part B.**

Part A

Which theme is BEST supported by paragraph 2 of the passage?

A. Strangers make people fearful.

B. Bravery is not common among those in a small town.

C. Fear can overcome the desire to help others.

D. People are motivated by fear to argue with others.

Part B

Which two details from the paragraph BEST support the answer to Part A?

A. "The more we told of our troubles, the more—man, woman, and child—they clung to the shelter of their houses."

B. "I shall never forget how much I was cheered to see the yellow shine in doors and windows; but that, as it proved, was the best of the help we were likely to get in that quarter."

C. "The name of Captain Flint, though it was strange to me, was well enough known to some there, and carried a great weight of terror."

D. "For—you would have thought men would have been ashamed of themselves—no soul would consent to return with us to the Admiral Benbow."

E. "It was already candle-light when we reached the hamlet."

8. **Use your answer to Part A to answer Part B.**

Part A

Which BEST describes how the author uses repetition to develop a theme in paragraph 1?

A. He relates the conversations between Jim and his mother to develop a theme relating to the dangers of running an inn.

B. He discusses the sailor's money to develop a theme relating to the ways in which money can be dangerous.

C. He details noises the characters hear to develop a theme relating to how people are frightened by sound.

D. He describes ways the characters are frightened to develop a theme relating to how one reacts to fear.

Part B

Underline three details in the paragraph that support your answer to Part A.

9. **Use your answer to Part A to answer Part B.**

Below are three events described in the passage.

Events	Jim and his mother ask residents of the hamlet for help.
	Men working near the inn describe strangers near the road.
	Jim's mother says they will return to defend the inn.

Part A

Circle the two events that would be BEST to include in a summary of the passage.

Part B

On the lines below, write a three-sentence summary of the passage. Include information from the two sentences you chose in Part A in your summary.

_____

_____

_____

5 Patterns in Literature

RL.8.1, RL.8.5, RL.8.9, RL.8.10

Getting the Idea

Contemporary, or modern, fiction often uses the same themes, patterns of events, or character types as stories from long ago. Often, these are stories that have been popular throughout the ages because they speak to some general themes that all people experience, such as love, revenge, and hope.

Here are some examples of patterns that have been repeated in old and new fiction.

Rags to Riches: The main character begins the story living in poverty. By the end of the story, this character becomes rich. Some fairy tales follow this pattern, such as the story of Cinderella. While becoming rich, the character often learns things about the world.

Coming of Age: A character moves from childhood to adulthood, and the challenges that many adolescents face are often carefully detailed. *A Tree Grows in Brooklyn* by Betty Smith is an example of this kind of story.

The Great Quest: The characters must go on a long journey, physically or emotionally, often to find or to accomplish something, such as a way to destroy an evil ring as in J.R.R. Tolkien's *The Lord of the Rings*. On the way, they often face challenges or meet new friends. Some fantasy, crime, and adventure books follow this story line.

Two Rivals: Two characters are pitted against each other in a competition for the same thing, such as winning a contest. Sometimes, one character represents good, while the other represents evil. The books in J.K. Rowling's *Harry Potter* series include two rivals fighting against each other.

Forbidden Love: Two people fall in love but, for some reason, cannot be together. Some stories end in tragedy, and the couple remains apart forever. This is the case in William Shakespeare's *Romeo and Juliet*. In other stories, the two people find a way to be together, in spite of the obstacles that surround them.

Growth and Learning: As characters learn more about life or about themselves, they grow. Some stories focus on this process, following a character's change from innocence and ignorance to experience and understanding. Harper Lee's *To Kill a Mockingbird* includes characters that grow and change by the end of the story.

Certain character types repeat from story to story as well. These types include the damsel in distress, the naïve youngest brother, the trickster, the selfish hermit, the wise village elder, the tyrannical master, the kind ruler, the dangerous criminal, and others.

Even when the same themes, patterns of events, and character types are repeated in two stories, other elements may change. For instance, some stories take place in the past and others in the future, so settings and characters can change a lot. If a story that was once a novel becomes a drama, different changes occur. In a novel, the characters' thoughts and feelings may be clearly stated. However, in a drama, the actors must *show* the characters' thoughts and feelings rather than say them out loud.

Thinking It Through

Read the following paragraph, and then answer the question that follows.

Leon stared at Hannah through the window of the car. Today was the day he had been dreading for weeks: the day he would leave Hannah. Leon's parents thought they'd been spending way too much time together lately. But he could hardly believe that they were sending him away to summer camp *just* to make sure he didn't get a chance to see Hannah for a couple of months. Hannah was standing on the front porch, her face tear-stained and somber. Knowing she would not be able to see Leon for such a long time, she had cried herself to sleep the night before. Leon took a deep breath. This was going to be a long summer.

What common story line described in the lesson do you see in this passage? Explain your answer.

_____

_____

_____

 HINT There are two characters in this passage who want to be together.

DISCUSS Can you think of any other stories with a similar story line?

Coached Example

Read the passages and answer the questions.

The Tale of Arachne
adapted from a Greek myth

There once lived a girl named Arachne who was a talented weaver and spinner. People would come from miles around to see her beautifully spun cloths. Arachne was vain and smugly proud of her work. One day, the goddess Athena challenged Arachne to a weaving contest. They set up their looms and went to work, spinning and weaving all night. In the morning, Athena had spun a cloth showing the gods and goddesses doing nice things for others. However, Arachne's cloth showed the gods and goddesses falling down and getting in trouble. Athena was so angry, she cursed Arachne forever by turning her into a spider.

Vote for Me!
excerpted from a short story

Jen walked down the main hall at school, putting up posters as she went. "Jen Davies for Senior Class President," the signs proudly proclaimed. She had spent hours working on this campaign. The posters and speeches had taken her weeks. Suddenly, Jen spotted Robin strolling down the hall, laughing and talking with her friends. Robin seemed as if she didn't have a care in the world. Yet Robin was also running for class president! Jen and Robin stared at each other across the hall. Today was the day of the school election. Each girl was thinking: may the best candidate win.

---

1. What common story line do you see in both of these passages?

    A. Rags to Riches

    B. Two Rivals

    C. The Great Quest

    D. Growth and Learning

    HINT Think about what the characters want in both stories.

2. How does the story line change from the myth to the story?

    A. The myth has elements of magic in the plot, while the story does not.

    B. The myth has characters who are enemies, while the story does not.

    C. The story has animals in the plot, while the myth does not.

    D. The story has characters who are friends, while the myth does not.

    HINT Think about the basic characteristics of myths and stories.

Lesson Practice

Use the Reading Guides to help you understand the passages.

Genteel means polite and having manners.

How does Eliza change from the beginning to the end of this passage?

excerpted and adapted from

Pygmalion

by George Bernard Shaw

Eliza Doolittle is a young woman selling flowers on the street in the early 1900s in London, England. Like many other people who work in the streets selling their goods, Eliza does not speak clearly or well and she is not at all refined. One day, Eliza meets a professor, Henry Higgins, who wants to teach her how to speak properly.

ELIZA: I want to be a lady in a flower shop instead of selling at the street corner. But they won't take me unless I can talk more genteel. You said you could teach me. Well, here I am ready to pay you.

HIGGINS: Sit down. Eliza, you are to live here for the next six months, learning how to speak beautifully, like a lady in a florist's shop.

(*After a few months, Eliza attends a party at the home of Professor Higgins's mother, Mrs. Higgins. At the party, Mrs. Eynsford Hill and her two grown children, Clara and Freddy, meet Eliza.*)

ELIZA: (*speaking with complete correctness of pronunciation and great beauty of tone*) How do you do, Mrs. Higgins? (*She gasps slightly in making sure of the H in* Higgins, *but is quite successful.*) Mr. Higgins told me I might come.

MRS. HIGGINS: Quite right: I'm very glad indeed to see you.

MRS. EYNSFORD HILL: I feel sure we have met before, Miss Doolittle. I remember your eyes.

ELIZA: How do you do? (*She sits down on the ottoman gracefully in the place just left vacant by Higgins.*)

MRS. EYNSFORD HILL: Please meet my daughter, Clara.

ELIZA: How do you do?

CLARA: How do you do? (*She sits down on the ottoman beside Eliza.*)

FREDDY: (*coming to their side of the ottoman*) The pleasure is mine.

MRS. EYNSFORD HILL: That is my son, Freddy.

ELIZA: How do you do?

(*Freddy bows and sits down in the Elizabethan chair. The others later remark what a lovely young woman Ms. Eliza Doolittle is.*)

Skateboard Success

Rob and Javier live in modern-day Venice, California. They have gone to school together for years, but they are not really friends. Rob is an amazing skateboarder, and kids often come to the park just to watch him practice. Javier is one of those kids. Today, Javier and his friend Greg are at the park to watch Rob skateboard.

JAVIER: (*sighing*) I can't believe how good he is! It's like he's an expert or something. Man, I wish I could skateboard like that.

GREG: Yeah, I heard he's been in competitions all over the state.

(*Rob walks over to them.*)

ROB: Hey, you're Javier, right?

JAVIER: Um, yeah. Why?

ROB: Well, I heard you were doing really well in Mrs. Ying's class.

JAVIER: I guess. So what?

ROB: Well, see, I haven't been doing so great. And my dad says if I don't bring my grades up, I can't skateboard anymore.

JAVIER: Wow, that's tough. But why are you telling me all this?

ROB: I've seen you come watch me here in the park a few times. I was wondering if maybe we could trade. You tutor me in math, and I'll teach you to skateboard.

JAVIER: (*surprised*) Wow! Really? That… that would be cool.

(*For the next few weeks, Rob teaches Javier to skateboard. Javier falls a lot at first and then seems to get better and better. One day, Greg comes by the park to watch Javier skateboard.*)

GREG: Hey, Javier. How's it going?

JAVIER: Eh, I wouldn't say I'm an expert just yet. (*laughing*)

GREG: Yeah, that would be amazing. But let's see what you got.

JAVIER: Okay, yeah. Check this out.

(*Javier skateboards from one ramp to the next. He even does a few tricks, jumping off his skateboard and landing back on safely.*)

GREG: Whoa! That was awesome. I can't believe how good you got this fast!

JAVIER: Yeah, Rob's a pretty good teacher. And, guess what? He got a B on Mrs. Ying's last test, too.

Answer the following questions.

1. What theme appears in both passages?

    A. competition

    B. forgiveness

    C. forbidden love

    D. growth and learning

2. The MAIN difference between the passages lies in the

    A. conflict.

    B. setting.

    C. plot events.

    D. characters' traits.

3. How are Eliza and Javier alike?

    A. They both change by the end of the passage.

    B. They both remain the same at the end of the passage.

    C. They both argue with other characters.

    D. They both have trouble making new friends.

4. Read this sentence from passage 1.

    I want to be a lady in a flower shop instead of selling at the street corner.

    Which of the following sentences from passage 2 is most similar to this one?

    A. "Well, see, I haven't been doing so great."

    B. "But why are you telling me all this?"

    C. "Man, I wish I could skateboard like that."

    D. "Eh, I wouldn't say I'm an expert just yet."

5. How are the story lines in passage 1 and passage 2 different? Use examples from the passages in your response.

    _____

    _____

    _____

    _____

    _____

Use the Reading Guides to help you understand the passages.

Reading Guide

"The Minotaur" is an adaption of the Greek myth of Theseus and the Minotaur. It was written by Hawthorne in 1853 as part of a collection of myths adapted for children. As you read, think about why an author might be interested in adapting a myth for a different audience.

Theseus engages in a long physical journey. What is he trying to accomplish?

What are Theseus's character traits? How does he resemble other characters with whom you're familiar?

What is the outcome of the conflict? Why is Theseus successful?

excerpted and adapted from

The Minotaur

by Nathaniel Hawthorne

The Minotaur is a half-man, half-bull monster. He is kept in a labyrinth, or maze, by King Minos of Crete. As a penalty for losing a war with Crete, the king of Athens, Theseus's father, must send fourteen people each year to be sacrificed to the Minotaur. Theseus volunteers to face the Minotaur, and Minos's daughter Ariadne agrees to help Theseus.

As he passed onward, the clouds gathered over the moon, and the labyrinth grew so dusky that Theseus could no longer discern the bewilderment through which he was passing. He would have left quite lost and utterly hopeless of ever again walking in a straight path if, every little while, he had not been conscious of a gentle twitch at the silken cord. Then he knew that the tender-hearted Ariadne was still holding the other end . . . And at last, in an open space, at the very center of the labyrinth, he did discern the hideous creature. . . .

Without more words on either side, there ensued the most awful fight between Theseus and the Minotaur . . . [T]he monster, in his first headlong rush against Theseus, . . . missed him by a hair's breadth and [broke] one of his horns short off against the stone wall. On this mishap, he bellowed so intolerably that a part of the labyrinth tumbled down . . . Smarting with the pain, he galloped around the open space . . . After this, the two antagonists stood valiantly up to one another and fought, sword to horn, for a long while. At last, the Minotaur made a run at Theseus, grazed Theseus's left side with his horn, and flung him down. Thinking that he had stabbed Theseus to the heart, the Minotaur cut a great caper in the air, opened his bull mouth from ear to ear, and prepared to snap Theseus's head off. But by this time, Theseus had leaped up and caught the monster off his guard. Fetching a sword stroke at the Minotaur with all his force, Theseus hit him fair upon the neck . . .

"Thou hast slain the monster," cried Ariadne, clasping her hands.

"Thanks to thee, dear Ariadne," answered Theseus, "I return victorious."

The Running Back

Reading Guide

As you read this passage, think about how the story line resembles that of "The Minotaur."

In what ways is Tucker similar to Theseus? In what ways is he different?

Notice that the story takes place in a more contemporary setting. How does that affect the actions of the main character? How might Theseus react in a similar setting?

Tucker was poised to explode into a run as soon as the center snapped the ball. Seconds earlier, the quarterback had called a running play. Tucker was about to receive a handoff. His nerves tingled with electricity, but he wasn't afraid. He possessed powerful weapons against the opposing team's defense—large hands, strength, and speed. His team was down by three points, and the clock showed limited precious minutes of play, but Tucker was no ordinary football player. He was a hero, and he would save his teammates from destruction.

The center snapped the ball, and Tucker's body moved ahead of his brain. He felt the speckled skin of the oblong football in his hands and locked eyes briefly with his quarterback, whose nod was almost imperceptible. Before Tucker could acknowledge the support, he realized that he had begun to move. The end zone wasn't visible, and the field was littered with defensive traps. Tucker dodged one player with a quick move to the left, but he was immediately attacked by another player who dove too early. Tucker leaped over his fallen opponent. More dangers remained, however. Tucker felt as if he were moving through a maze as he shifted left and then right to avoid defensive tackles. The end zone still wasn't visible, but Tucker raced toward safety and victory by instinct.

Finally, Tucker broke free of the bodies into open space. The end zone lay gleaming before him. He was conscious of his breath and the pounding of his heart as he pumped his legs and pulled the football tighter to his torso. Then, from the right, Tucker caught site of a defender in pursuit. This man was large, bigger than Tucker, who noted the deadly curvature of the player's arm muscles. Tucker was stunned at how fast a man this large could move. It was as if he wasn't human. Tucker was tired, but he knew that he would have to run faster to beat the oncoming hit. This was the moment when an athlete becomes a champion, the moment when mental composure exceeds physical ability. Tucker stayed his course and ran toward the goal line, crossing it just as he felt the defender grab his waist.

Answer the following questions.

6. **Use your answer to Part A to answer Part B.**

   Below are four patterns of events that are common to many fictional plots.

Patterns of Events	
	Rags to Riches
	Coming of Age
	The Great Quest
	Forbidden Love

   Part A

   Circle the pattern of events that is BEST reflected in both "The Minotaur" and "The Running Back."

   Part B

   Underline text evidence from each passage that supports your answer to Part A.

   _____

7. Read each name in the Characters box below. Decide whether the character is BEST described as a hero, a villain, or a sidekick. Write the name of the character on a line under the appropriate type.

Characters		
Theseus	Ariadne	Quarterback
The Minotaur	Tucker	Defender

Hero	Villain	Sidekick
_____	_____	_____
_____	_____	_____

8. Which choices below BEST describe ways in which "The Running Back" draws on elements within "The Minotaur"? There is more than one correct choice listed below.

A. Tucker is competing against an opponent.

B. Tucker receives encouragement.

C. Tucker does not destroy his opponent.

D. Tucker acknowledges that his opponent is worthy.

E. Tucker must protect the football.

F. Tucker battles as part of a team.

9. **Use your answer to Part A to answer Part B.**

Part A

Choose the theme that is BEST reflected in both passages.

A. It is never easy to accomplish something alone.

B. Monsters can be found almost anywhere.

C. Life's greatest challenges can bring out the best in people.

D. A difficult journey does not always result in victory.

Part B

Which detail from "The Running Back" BEST supports your answer to Part A?

A. "Tucker was tired, but he knew that he would have to run faster to beat the oncoming hit."

B. "Tucker leaped over his fallen opponent."

C. "He possessed powerful weapons against the opposing team's defense—large hands, strength, and speed."

D. "Tucker was stunned at how fast a man this large could move. It was as if he wasn't human."

E. "Tucker was poised to explode into a run as soon as the center snapped the ball."

6 Figurative Language

RL.8.1, RL.8.4, RL.8.10, L.8.5.a

Getting the Idea

The job of a writer is, among other things, to communicate something—an idea, a story, a feeling—with words. Many writers use figurative language to help them. **Figurative language** is language that does not mean exactly what it says. It is language that is used beyond its literal meaning for effect or to create an image in the reader's mind. Figurative language is typically colorful and creative. One type of figurative language is the analogy. An **analogy** illustrates the relationship between two unfamiliar things by comparing it with another relationship readers may know. Read this analogy, for example:

> The outfielder is to baseball what the fullback is to soccer.

In this analogy, the writer makes a comparison between two similar positions in two different sports. If you know much about baseball, you know that the outfielder is important to the game, but not at the center of the action. The same is true of the fullback in soccer—the team couldn't win without a fullback, but he's probably not the hardest-working player on the field.

An **allusion** is an indirect reference to a well-known person, place, event, or object in history or in a literary work. In other words, an allusion refers to an idea familiar to many readers. Read this sentence:

> A modern-day Scrooge, Will conveniently forgot his friends' birthdays.

The author does not directly state that Will is stingy, but the allusion to Scrooge allows the reader to draw that conclusion. Scrooge is the notorious penny-pincher in Dickens's *A Christmas Carol*.

Irony is a kind of figurative language that usually means the exact opposite of what it says, rather than suggesting an image or impression. As discussed in Lesson 3, **dramatic irony** occurs when the reader or audience knows something that a character does not. **Verbal irony** is slightly different. It is the use of words to express something different from their literal meaning, sometimes for humorous effect. It often sounds like sarcasm. For example, Trudy says, "I love it when Mrs. Montoya gives us surprise quizzes!" She doesn't mean that she loves surprise quizzes, of course. Very few people probably are happy to have surprise quizzes. Trudy is being ironic; what she means is that she hates surprise quizzes.

A **pun** is a play on words in which one word is used that either sounds like or is identical to another; the sentence and the word can usually be interpreted in more than one way. Puns are often used for humorous effect, although not always. For example, when Mercutio is dying in Shakespeare's *Romeo and Juliet*, he says: "Ask me tomorrow, and you shall find me a grave man." In this case, he is making a play on the word *grave*. It means "serious" here, but it also suggests that Mercutio will be dead, or in his grave. Although Mercutio's use of the word is clever, it contributes to the severe tone of the tragic play. Shakespeare's **tone**, or attitude toward the subject, in this section is intense and violent.

Thinking It Through

Read the following paragraph, and then answer the question that follows.

> Brandon was a walking history book. He earned an A on every social studies exam. "What's your secret?" his friend Keith asked him once. Brandon smiled, and then he leaned forward and whispered, "I read a lot and I study."

What is the irony in this paragraph?

_____

_____

HINT   Dramatic irony occurs when the reader knows something not known to a character or characters.

Read the passage and answer the questions.

excerpted from

A Night-Piece

by William Wordsworth

Bent earthwards; he looks up—the clouds are split
Asunder,—and above his head he sees
The clear Moon, and the glory of the heavens.
There, in a black-blue vault she sails along,
5   Followed by multitudes of stars, that, small
And sharp, and bright, along the dark abyss
Drive as she drives: how fast they wheel away,
Yet vanish not!—the wind is in the tree,
But they are silent;—still they roll along
10   Immeasurably distant; and the vault,
Built round by those white clouds, enormous clouds,
Still deepens its unfathomable depth.
At length the Vision closes; and the mind,
Not undisturbed by the delight it feels,
15   Which slowly settles into peaceful calm,
Is left to muse upon the solemn scene.

1. The poet uses the word *still* in line 9 to make a pun about the stars. How can the word be interpreted?

   A. The stars are quiet and not moving.

   B. The stars are quiet even as they continue across the sky.

   C. The stars are immovable and unchanging.

   D. The stars are quiet and eventually disappear.

   HINT Note the poet's description of how the stars appear to move and the comparison made to the wind.

2. The poet uses figurative language to describe what the traveler actually sees in the sky, along with the vision that occurs in his mind. This language suggests that

   A. the view of what the traveler sees in the sky is not real.

   B. the traveler's mind is closed to the beauty of the stars and the moon.

   C. the traveler is remembering a dream.

   D. the traveler not only sees what is in the sky, but experiences an emotional change.

   HINT Reread the last four lines of the poem.

Lesson Practice

Use the Reading Guide to help you understand the passage.

Reading Guide

An analogy is a comparison between dissimilar things. What is the analogy in paragraph 1?

Alex the Terror

There were many words people used to describe Alex, Cathy's new puppy. *Sweet, quiet,* and *calm* were not on the list. If the house was a beach, Alex was a tsunami. It was amazing how much damage he could do. And that's when he was in a good mood. When Alex was mad, he'd get this look in his eye, and his face would twist in this terrifying way that could make a grown person run. Then he got to work. He broke dishes, glasses, vases, and everything else breakable.

People sometimes wondered why Alex acted the way he did. Everyone had a different explanation. One theory was that he had been raised by angry Doberman pinschers. Another was that Alex was not a dog but a space alien, sent to destroy Earth. Aunt Nancy always blamed it on Cathy's parents.

"Stop giving him everything he wants! Just because he asks for a snack doesn't mean he should have it. You're spoiling him too much. You're creating a monster."

Cathy agreed with Aunt Nancy. Her parents should have been good with animals, but they had no luck with Alex. Cathy finally learned that if she wanted to keep Alex from chewing on her CDs or dropping dog bones in her shoes, she was going to have to keep her door locked at all times.

One day, Cathy's parents decided that they needed some time by themselves, away from the dog. They arranged for Cathy to stay with her grandfather, but there was no room at the place where they usually left Alex. And Alex couldn't go with Cathy. He might cause too much commotion for Grandpa Louie. Grandpa might end up in the hospital! So, they offered Aunt Nancy the use of their summer cottage for a week. Their secret plan was to bring Aunt Nancy some delicious food once she'd settled in, and then bring Alex along.

They invited Aunt Nancy over for dinner. "So what do you think?" Alex's mom asked. "The cottage is five minutes from the beach. It's fully stocked. The weather's going to be great. You'll have a wonderful time."

In paragraph 9, why does the author compare Alex to a fish?

What is the dramatic irony in this passage?

Aunt Nancy was thrilled. "You'd do that for me? You're too kind! My boss, Max, is driving me crazy. I could really use a break."

Just then there was a loud crash. Alex had just knocked a glass off the coffee table.

"OK, well, sounds great. I'll take the keys," Aunt Nancy said, shaking her head. "Silly dog! I didn't mean that kind of break."

Aunt Nancy tried to pick him up and sit him on her lap. But Alex was like a fish on a hook. He squirmed so violently that Aunt Nancy finally let him drop.

Cathy had sat quietly through dinner, listening to the conversation. Now, she didn't want to jump to conclusions, but she had overheard her parents buying two plane tickets to Hawaii. You wouldn't have to be Einstein to figure out what was going on. Cathy loved Aunt Nancy and hated to see this happen. And she was tired of her parents' inability to control Alex.

She took a deep breath and spoke. "Aunt Nancy, Mom and Dad are planning on saddling you with Alex while they go to Hawaii."

Cathy's parents gasped. Her father shot her a look that had "Benedict Arnold" and "traitor" written all over it. But their guilt silenced them.

Aunt Nancy looked like she had just bitten into the rotten part of a red, shiny apple.

Cathy noticed that her aunt was ready to burst. Then, Cathy spoke up again. "Take that week in the cottage, Aunt Nancy. Mom and Dad can take Alex with them on vacation. They'll have fun together!"

As if he heard what the humans were saying, Alex started to bounce around and yelp happily.

Cathy's mom sighed deeply. "Of course."

Answer the following questions.

1. Which sentence from the passage is an analogy?

   A. "If the house was a beach, Alex was a tsunami."

   B. "She took a deep breath and spoke."

   C. "People sometimes wondered why Alex acted the way he did."

   D. "But Alex was like a fish on a hook."

2. The author makes an allusion to Einstein in paragraph 11 to make a point about Cathy's

   A. trustworthiness.

   B. frustration.

   C. curiosity.

   D. intelligence.

3. What is the pun in the passage?

   A. a play on the word *terror*

   B. a play on the words *great* and *grate*

   C. a play on the two meanings of *monster*

   D. a play on the two meanings of *break*

4. Which is an example of dramatic irony in the passage?

   A. Cathy's parents buy two tickets to Hawaii but leave her behind with Grandpa Louie.

   B. Aunt Nancy is unaware that Cathy's parents are planning to leave Alex with her.

   C. Alex breaks a glass.

   D. Cathy reveals her parents' plans to Aunt Nancy.

5. What is the significance of the allusion to Benedict Arnold? Use examples from the passage in your response.

   _____

   _____

   _____

   _____

Finding A Way

Reading Guide

Think about the description in the first paragraph. To what is the tree compared?

As you read paragraph 3, think about the irony reflected in the description of Jonathan's ride.

Jonathan Potter slumped against the tree and slid to the ground in complete exhaustion, fully aware that he could go no farther. If this was to be his final resting place, then the tree would make a good and sturdy marker. At least it was peaceful.

It seemed hours since Jonathan had panicked at the sight of British soldiers intercepting those he had been following. If Paul Revere, Billy Dawes, and Dr. Samuel Prescott had been arrested, was not all lost? Had they warned enough people in the area to be on the lookout for the British militia, who reportedly were on the move from Boston to Concord?

Jonathan was thankful that his horse had been so much slower than those ridden by the other three. Otherwise he too would have been arrested. Jonathan had guided his horse into the woods and had quickly abandoned the animal when he realized that crashing through the bushes was likely to draw the attention of the soldiers. Without much concentration on where he was going, Jonathan had dashed deep into the forest, leaping and running as any deer would from a dreaded hunter. Now here he was in the dark with no horse and no idea where he was.

More gloomy thoughts seeped into Jonathan's imagination. Was he a coward for running as he had? Should he just return to Boston, confess to the other patriots, and ask them to toss him into the harbor with the British tea that been thrown there two years before? Jonathan shook his head to clear his mind. His mother was right; he had a tendency to extreme thoughts that did him no service in an emergency. He was sixteen, too old to act like a fearful child.

Think about the language the author uses to describe Jonathan's surroundings. How does it help you visualize the setting in your mind?

Remember that figurative language does not mean exactly what it says. What figurative language do you encounter as you read the passage?

After several deep breaths, he tried to get a sense of where he was, but only his ears could pick up any clues. Listening carefully in the dark, Jonathan heard frogs croaking, which meant that water was nearby. Jonathan thought hard about the ponds he knew in this area in relation to where he had last been on the road to Lexington and Concord, but there were so many small ponds that he knew such speculation was useless. "Some fine messenger I am," he muttered to himself. "I'm a credit to the entire patriotic movement."

It was then that he became aware that his surroundings were less dark. The moon had risen, but the clouds were so thick that the light was extremely dim. However, Jonathan felt a spark of hope. Maybe the moon could shed some light on his situation. He squinted into the distance and began to walk, arms outstretched to prevent a headlong crash into a tree. He followed the frog sounds and eventually found the pond.

"Where do I go from here?" Jonathan muttered. Suddenly, as though in answer to his plea, the clouds parted and the pond was bathed in bright moonlight. Jonathan gasped at the beautiful sight.

Then he spied another light in the distance. Could that be a house? Jonathan carefully walked in that direction. As he got closer, he was excited to see that it was a house he recognized.

He knocked on the door and called out softly but firmly, "It is Jonathan Potter." The door opened a crack, revealing William Howell's surprised face. Howell immediately pulled him into the house. Jonathan told his story, leaving nothing out. He knew he could trust Howell, who supported the patriots' cause.

"If Revere, Dawes, and Prescott are not able to complete their ride, you must continue to warn people," Howell said. "I will loan you a horse." Jonathan promised that he would return the horse in the morning if he was not arrested.

"Be clever and quiet enough not to let that happen," Howell cautioned.

Jonathan was thankful that the moon had once again retreated behind the clouds, so the light that had led him out of the woods was now dim enough to cloak his passage. He was still scared, but resolute. At the next farm, he knocked on the door. When it was open, he announced, "The British are on the march and heading toward Concord."

Answer the following questions.

6. **Use your answer to Part A to answer Part B.**

   Part A

   Which of the following sentences from the passage is an analogy?

   A. "He squinted into the distance and began to walk, arms outstretched to prevent a headlong crash into a tree."

   B. "After several deep breaths, he tried to get a sense of where he was, but only his ears could pick up any clues."

   C. "Without much concentration on where he was going, Jonathan had dashed deep into the forest, leaping and running as any deer would from a dreaded hunter."

   D. "Suddenly, as though in answer to his plea, the clouds parted and the pond was bathed in bright moonlight."

   Part B

   What is the author trying to illustrate through the analogy?

   A. the desperate, senseless fear that the main character feels

   B. the sudden change in the main character's plight

   C. the extreme challenges faced by the main character

   D. the attempts by the main character to improve his situation

---

7. **Use your answer to Part A to answer Part B.**

   Part A

   Circle an example of verbal irony in paragraph 5 of the passage.

   Part B

   Why is the example you chose ironic?

   A. Jonathan is not really lost.

   B. Jonathan actually feels that he has failed.

   C. Frogs do not really make croaking noises.

   D. Jonathan had never actually traveled to Lexington and Concord.

   E. There actually are not many ponds in the area.

8. **Use your answer to Part A to answer Part B.**

   Part A

   Read paragraph 4 from the passage. Which of the following examples of figurative language does the paragraph contain?

   A. allusion

   B. analogy

   C. dramatic irony

   D. pun

   Part B

   What does this figurative language indicate?

   A. Jonathan doesn't realize that his patriot friends participated in the Boston Tea Party.

   B. Jonathan thinks his patriot friends consider him a coward.

   C. Jonathan's patriot friends had participated in the Boston Tea Party.

   D. Jonathan's patriot friends had participated in the Boston Massacre.

   E. Jonathan doesn't think the Boston patriots should drink British tea.

   ---

9. **Use your answer to Part A to answer Part B.**

   Part A

   Read paragraph 6 from the passage. Underline the pun in the paragraph.

   Part B

   Choose the two BEST interpretations of the pun.

   A. make him feel more hopeful

   B. point him toward the north

   C. identify the frogs he heard

   D. help him figure out his location

   E. lessen his fear of the British

   F. allow him to see in the dark

7 Supporting Inferences

RL.8.1, RL.8.10

Getting the Idea

When you read a passage, you may not understand what the author is trying to tell you immediately. Sometimes, the passage may not include every last bit of information you need to grasp it. However, as you read, you may need to make a brief statement about a passage. The statement might be for a paper, or it might be for your own understanding. This kind of statement is called a **generalization**. If all the information is not supplied, you'll need to make an inference or two. An **inference** is an educated guess that should always be based on information and evidence in a passage. Your prior knowledge, or the knowledge you have before you read a passage, will also help you to make an inference. Read the sentences below.

> Jan was a brilliant up-and-coming composer and arranger in Los Angeles. Her success wasn't a fluke, though—she was the hardest working musician in town.

In this example, the author directly tells the reader that Jan is brilliant and hardworking. The reader does not have to infer it. Now read these sentences.

> She never took a day off, and would often pull all-nighters trying to come up with the right melody. In just five years working in Los Angeles, she had scored three movies, adapted music for two plays, and written seven award-winning songs.

If you had to describe Jan, what would you say, based on the sentences above? This author does not directly describe Jan as brilliant and hardworking, but the reader can infer these qualities based on the **text evidence** presented. The author writes that Jan has written music for numerous movies and plays and would regularly stay up all night making music. This shows a hardworking spirit. Many of her songs had received awards: this should tell you that she had a certain level of brilliance.

So, as you read the following sentence, think about whether it is supported by the text: *Jan was a successful composer and even more caring person.* The sentence is supported partially: her accomplishments show that she is successful. However, the text doesn't comment on her caring nature.

Prior knowledge is a valuable tool in making inferences. For example, suppose you read a passage about a girl who puts on a bathing suit and packs a basket with sandwiches and water and a knapsack with suntan lotion and a towel. Think about times when you might do these things. Your previous experiences help you make a reasonable inference: the girl is going to the beach or a pool.

If you make a broad statement about a text as part of a book report or informational report, it must be supported by evidence in the text. Imagine a story about a boy who quickly hides a small piece of paper when the teacher approaches his desk during an exam. What do you think is on the piece of paper? The facts are that the boy is taking a test and that he hides the paper from his teacher. It's safe to guess that the paper has answers on it and that the boy is cheating.

Thinking It Through

Read the following paragraph, and then answer the question that follows.

> Raoul watched helplessly as his Wild Tiger boomerang flew into a tree and stayed there. As he walked closer, he spotted several branches low enough for him to climb on. Two days later, the kids in his class lined up to sign the cast on his arm.

What happened to Raoul, and how do you know?

_____

_____

_____

HINT Your inference should be based on the clues you see in the paragraph.

Coached Example

Read the passage and answer the questions.

When I Heard the Learn'd Astronomer
by Walt Whitman

When I heard the learn'd astronomer,
When the proofs, the figures, were ranged in
    columns before me,
When I was shown the charts and diagrams, to
    add, divide, and measure them,
When I sitting heard the astronomer where he
    lectured with much applause in the lecture-
    room,
5 How soon unaccountable I became tired
    and sick,
Till rising and gliding out I wander'd off
    by myself,
In the mystical moist night-air, and from time
    to time,
Look'd up in perfect silence at the stars.

1. Why does the astronomer's lecture make the speaker feel tired and sick?

   A. The speaker is jealous of the applause the astronomer receives for his lecture.

   B. The speaker notes errors in the astronomer's proofs, figures, charts, and diagrams.

   C. The speaker does not appreciate the astronomer's scientific explanation.

   D. The speaker is unable to understand the astronomer's addition, division, and measurement.

   HINT Compare and contrast the images at the beginning of the poem with the images at the end of the poem.

2. What event described in the poem BEST supports the inference in question 1?

   A. He feels the moist air of the night.

   B. He appreciates the simple, quiet nature of the night sky.

   C. He examines the astronomer's charts and diagrams.

   D. He hears the applause in the lecture room.

   HINT Consider the meanings of the words *mystical* and *perfect*.

Lesson Practice

Use the Reading Guide to help you understand the passage.

Reading Guide

Based on paragraph 1, make an inference about where Tyrell is landing.

What can you infer from the dad's reaction to the rocket car?

A Trip to Remember

Tyrell looked out of the square window as the shuttle approached for a landing. The end of the trip was approaching! He was a long way from Earth. His eyes lit up at the sight of the craters. He had only seen them in pictures and videos on Earth. In real life, they looked as if you could disappear in their depths forever.

"Quite a sight, huh?" Tyrell's dad asked. He was seated next to Tyrell. He could only imagine the thoughts going through Tyrell's mind.

Tyrell nodded his head eagerly. A two-seat rocket car flew by the window. Tyrell's dad followed it longingly with his eyes. "Wow, that's the latest model. They've gotten faster since I was a kid."

Tyrell smiled. "I hear those go for a hundred thousand Earth units, Dad," he said. "Do you think we'll ever be able to afford one?"

Tyrell's father sighed. "Maybe one day."

A shuttle attendant began to walk down the aisle, handing out oxygen masks attached to small metal canisters.

"Ladies and gentlemen, we'll be arriving on the moon in five minutes. Please be sure to keep your gravity boots on at all times. Please put on your masks before disembarking. The concentrated oxygen will last for up to three hours. The warning light will flash when it's running low. You can refill it at various oxygen stations on the surface. Should you have an oxygen emergency, press the alarm on the side of the canister, and an oxygen engineer will be with you in a matter of seconds."

Tyrell grinned in anticipation. Finally! The flight from Earth had taken less than two hours, but he could barely sit still through it. "I can't believe Mom is missing this," he said.

Tyrell's Mom had gone with them to the shuttle terminal in New America. She had planned to come on the trip. But as she had watched the shuttles depart and imagined herself traveling at such incredible speed, her knees had gone weak. She had decided to stay on solid ground.

Why doesn't anyone wear glasses anymore in this passage?

Use your prior knowledge to figure out what the Underground Comet is.

Tyrell and his dad put on their masks and slipped on their gravity boots. They followed the other passengers toward the exit and entered Luna Terminal. The terminal was brightly lit with huge generator-powered lights. They bathed the terminal in a golden light. The passengers could hear the gentle whirring of fans that kept the terminal at a steady temperature.

Tyrell's head spun left and right, his eyes eagerly taking in every detail of his surroundings. The terminal was crowded today. Two men in metallic suits strode past them. Tyrell noticed that they wore glasses with very dark lenses.

Tyrell pressed the "talk" button on his oxygen mask. "Dad, why are those men wearing lenses? I thought no one wore glasses anymore."

"They're part of the underground renovation project. They spend six to eight hours a day below the surface. Those glasses protect their eyes."

"Oh, there's an Underground Comet station. Can we go on the Underground Comet before we leave, Dad? I told my friends back home I was going."

"Sure, son. But let's explore first. There's a lot to see once we get out of the terminal."

"I hope there's a lot to eat! I'm hungry."

"Didn't you take your energy pill this morning?"

"I forgot. I was too excited!"

"I guess that's okay just this once... I've heard the Rima Restaurant is good. It's a controlled environment. We won't need our masks."

A woman in a floating zip-cart whizzed by Tyrell. He watched her maneuver through the crowd, two feet above the ground.

"Dad! Can we rent one of those?" Tyrell asked, tugging on the sleeve of his father's space suit.

"One thing at a time, son."

Tyrell and his father walked out of the terminal.

Answer the following questions.

1. Why is it MOST LIKELY that Tyrell's dad will not buy the rocket car?

   A. He thinks it goes too fast.

   B. Saving money is important to him.

   C. He does not like the way it looks.

   D. He read negative reviews about it.

2. Using clues from the passage, you can infer that the mom decides not to take the trip because

   A. she gets sick at the last minute.

   B. she is angry at the dad.

   C. she is afraid of flying.

   D. she wants some time alone.

3. Why do the men Tyrell sees in the terminal MOST LIKELY wear glasses with dark lenses?

   A. They like how the glasses look with the suits.

   B. The glasses help them work underground.

   C. They do not want to be recognized.

   D. The bright lights hurt their eyes.

4. Read the following statement.

   The trip to the moon is a new and exciting experience for Tyrell.

   Which of the following sentences from the story BEST supports the above statement?

   A. "Tyrell noticed that they wore glasses with very dark lenses."

   B. "Tyrell looked out of the square window as the shuttle approached for a landing."

   C. "Tyrell pressed the 'talk' button on his oxygen mask."

   D. "The flight from Earth had taken less than two hours, but he could barely sit still through it."

5. Does this passage take place in the past, the present, or the future? Explain how you know. Use examples from the passage in your response.

   _____

   _____

   _____

   _____

A Balcony Seat at the Movies

Reading Guide

An author may not state the setting of a story directly. Readers must use prior knowledge and textual evidence to infer where and when a story takes place.

Sometimes characters make inferences, as the narrator does when she assumes her mother will lose a job. On what historical and textual evidence does the narrator make this determination?

My first meeting with Liza Ann didn't go well.

After exiting the empty movie theater, I squirted the lemony homemade ammonia mixture onto the glass candy counter and wiped away the smudges and fingerprints left by children begging their parents for cinnamon jelly candies or suckers. Liza Ann's family owned the theater, and my mom worked there as a cleaning lady. Often, my mom dragged me along to help with the work.

As I finished wiping down the candy counter and moved on to the front windows, I noticed a slight motion behind me. I looked around, but I didn't see anything. I sprayed the window and started to use my thumbnail to scrape at the tape residue left behind when Liza Ann's father had removed the sign that read, "Colored Entrance Upstairs." Although Liza Ann's father had followed the law by removing the sign, some things hadn't changed much in our tiny Alabama town. The colored entrance to the theater was still upstairs, and the sun-yellowed tape residue wouldn't yield to my scraping.

"What are you doin'?" Liza Ann questioned.

Startled, I spun around, and forgetting that she was the white girl whose family employed my mother, I answered in the same way I would have if I'd caught my little brother spying on me, "None of your business. Now, leave me alone." She sucked in her breath sharply, blinked twice, and walked away.

Dread filled my heart over the following days. I waited to hear that my mother had been fired, but the news never came. A few weeks later, I was wiping down the candy counter again, and I saw the edge of a green dress peeking through the doorway to the theater.

"You might as well come on out. No need for spying," I said.

A few seconds later, Liza Ann stepped through the doorway, and we became friends over a shared box of salt-water taffy. She confessed that she was more intrigued than put off by my bold words. I confessed that I admired how she handled her own affairs without tattling.

In paragraph 11, the narrator's mother refers to the Justices of the Supreme Court. In 1954, the Justices ruled against segregation in public places in a famous case known as *Brown v. Board of Education*.

The narrator and Liza Ann have looked forward to the premiere for weeks. Yet, they sit apart. Why? Review paragraph 3.

From this point, I didn't mind when my mother took me to work with her. Sure, I wiped down that candy counter more times than I care to recollect, but afterward, my time was my own. Liza Ann and I spent hours reading magazines about fashion and movie stars. We cut out flips, bouffants, afros, and beehives and pasted them on pictures of ourselves as we imagined more glamorous lives. We followed the love life of Elizabeth Taylor with avid interest.

However, Liza Ann's favorite actress was Julie Andrews. She had loved Andrews in *Mary Poppins*, and after hearing that Andrews would star in *The Sound of Music*, Liza Ann started counting the days to the movie's premiere. She made me read Maria von Trapp's autobiography so that we could discuss the characters. We memorized the words to "Sixteen Going on Seventeen" and held two-person concerts in the movie theater. When we hung the poster for the movie in the window of the theater, Liza Ann rubbed her hand lovingly across the shiny paper to smooth out any wrinkles. "Perfect," she whispered.

My mom didn't allow me to attend the movie theater during business hours. We didn't have much extra money to spare, and she said she'd need a Supreme Court Justice to escort her if she decided to attend a movie there. I wasn't sure why she'd want to go to the movie with a Justice, but, after weeks of begging, she relented and said that I could go to the premiere of *The Sound of Music* if I used my own money to buy the ticket.

On the night of the premiere, I took a seat near the front of the balcony so that I could get a good view of the audience below. I craned my neck, trying to get a glimpse of Liza Ann before the lights dimmed. Finally, I spotted her. She was smiling and talking to some girls from school who were sitting next to her. We locked eyes briefly just before the theater went dark and the images on the screen flickered to life.

Answer the following questions.

6. **Use your answer to Part A to answer Part B.**

   Part A

   What is the setting of the story?

   A. northern United States in the late 1950s–early 1960s

   B. southern United States in the late 1950s–early 1960s

   C. northern United States in the late 1990s–early 2000s

   D. southern United States in the late 1990s–early 2000s

   Part B

   Circle two pieces of evidence in paragraph 3 of the passage that BEST support the inference in Part A.

   ---

7. **Use your answer to Part A to answer Part B.**

   Below are three possible reasons that the narrator fears her mother might be fired from her job at the movie theater.

The African American narrator befriends the white daughter of the mother's employers.
The African American narrator insults the white daughter of the mother's employers.
The African American narrator attends a movie premiere with the white daughter of the mother's employers.

   Part A

   Circle the reason that is BEST supported by textual evidence in the passage.

   Part B

   Underline two pieces of evidence in the passage that support the reason you chose in Part A.

8. Read each piece of textual evidence in the box below. Choose the evidence that BEST supports the inference. Write the evidence below the inference.

said that I could go to the premiere	didn't have much extra money to spare
used my own money to buy the ticket	need a Supreme Court Justice to escort her

---

Inference: If the narrator's mother attended a movie, she would likely refuse to sit in the colored balcony.

Textual Evidence:

---

9. **Use your answer to Part A to answer Part B.**

Part A

Why are the narrator and Liza Ann not sitting together at the movie premiere?

A. Liza Ann attends with other friends.

B. The girls' parents do not allow it.

C. The girls sit in segregated sections.

D. The narrator does not have a ticket.

Part B

Which evidence from the passage BEST supports your answer to Part A?

A. "I took a seat near the front of the balcony so that I could get a good view of the audience below."

B. "My mom didn't allow me to attend the movie theater during business hours."

C. "Liza Ann's family owned the theater, and my mom worked there as a cleaning lady."

D. "The colored entrance to the theater was still upstairs."

Cumulative Assessment

Read the passage and answer the questions that follow.

Early Rising

When I wake up
the sun is still asleep
(Mom and Dad are asleep too)
I tell myself
5   I have schoolwork:
a project   a report   some math problems…
I tell myself I have to keep myself ahead
But really
I'm up this early
10   because I like to see the sun wake up
Early times like this
are when the sun shows off its colors
its red and yellow and even pink

Sun, you are the flag
15   of the universe
I salute you by raising my blinds
I salute you a second time
by opening my window
Even though
20   you can't salute me back
it is enough
that you shine over me
and everyone else
all day long
25   I could go back to sleep
But why?
You'll keep me company
won't you?

1. Which of the following BEST states the theme of this poem?

   A. Morning is the best time for hard work.

   B. It is sensible to wake up early.

   C. It is best not to oversleep.

   D. Waking up is a meaningful experience.

2. Which of the following is the analogy in this poem?

   A. The speaker's attitude toward the sun is equivalent to a citizen's attitude toward the flag.

   B. The sun, when it is asleep, is like a sleeping child.

   C. The speaker's relationship with the sun is like the relationship of two very close friends.

   D. The speaker is to the sun as a soldier is to a general.

3. When does this poem take place?

   A. early afternoon

   B. late morning

   C. at dawn

   D. at dusk

4. Read the following statement about the passage.

   The speaker feels best in the morning.

   Which of the following lines from the poem BEST supports this statement?

   A. I salute you a second time

   B. I'm up this early/because I like to see the sun wake up

   C. You'll keep me company

   D. I tell myself/I have schoolwork:

5. What is the difference between stanza 1 and stanza 2 of this poem? Use examples from the poem in your answer.

   _____

   _____

   _____

   _____

Read the passage and answer the questions that follow.

excerpted and adapted from

One Day More

by Joseph Conrad

Act I
Scene 1

Curtain rises disclosing Carvil and Bessie moving away from the sea-wall. Bessie, about twenty-five, wears a black dress and a black straw hat. Her face is pale and she is very quiet. Carvil is blind with reddish whiskers and a big, immovable face.

CARVIL: (*hanging heavily on Bessie's arm*) Careful! Go slow! Want your poor blind father to break his neck? In a hurry to get home and start that everlasting yarn with your chum the lunatic?

BESSIE: I am not in a hurry to get home, father.

CARVIL: Well, then, go steady with a poor blind man. Blind! Helpless! (*strikes ground with stick*) Never mind! I've had enough time to make enough money to have ham and eggs for breakfast every morning. You haven't known a single day of hardship in all your days of your idle life. Unless you think that a blind, helpless father—

BESSIE: What is there for me to be in a hurry for?

CARVIL: You want to waste your time with that lunatic. Anything to get away from your duty.

BESSIE: Captain Hagberd's talk never hurt you or anybody else.

CARVIL: Go on. Stick up for your only friend.

BESSIE: Is it my fault that I haven't another soul to speak to?

CARVIL: (*snarls*) It's mine perhaps. Can I help being blind? You're upset because you want to be out having fun—with a helpless man left all alone at home. Your own father, too.

BESSIE: I haven't been away from you half a day since mother died.

CARVIL: He's a lunatic, that Captain Hagberd! That's what he is. Has been for years— long before those doctors destroyed my sight. (*growls angrily*)

BESSIE: Perhaps Captain Hagberd is not so mad as the town takes him for.

CARVIL: (*grimly*) Don't everybody know how he came here from the North to wait till his missing son turns up—here of all places in the world. His boy that ran away to sea sixteen years ago and never did give a sign of life since! Don't I remember seeing people dodge around corners out of his way when he came along High Street. Seeing him, I tell you. (*groans*) He bothered everybody so with his silly talk of his son being sure to come back home—next year—next spring—next month. What is it by this time, hey?

BESSIE: Why talk about it? He bothers no one now.

CARVIL: Cause they've learned how to shut him up. All you have to do is make a remark about his sail-cloth. All the town knows it. But he's got you to listen to his crazy talk whenever he chooses. Don't I hear you two at it, jabber, jabber, mumble, mumble—

BESSIE: What is there so mad in keeping up hope?

CARVIL: (*with scathing scorn*) Not mad! Starving himself to save up money—for that son. Filling his house with furniture he won't let anyone see—for that son. Advertising in the papers every week, these sixteen years—for that son. Not mad! Boy, he calls him. Boy Harry. His boy Harry. His lost boy Harry. Yah! Let him lose his sight to know what real trouble means. And the boy—the man, I should say—must have been put away safe in Davy Jones's locker for many a year—drowned—food for fishes—dead ... Stands to reason, or he would have been here before, smelling around the old fool's money.

BESSIE: Poor man. Perhaps he never had a son.

CARVIL: What are you up to? Are you after his money?

BESSIE: Father! How can you? It never entered my head.

CARVIL: Then you are a bigger fool than he is. Take me home. I want to rest.

6. Which word BEST describes Bessie?

    A. nervous

    B. light-hearted

    C. angry

    D. compassionate

7. What is the conflict in the passage?

    A. Carvil wants Bessie to pay attention to him, but she is distracted.

    B. Carvil wants his health to improve, but it gets worse every day.

    C. Bessie wants to help Carvil but can't find a way to do it.

    D. Bessie wants to spend time with Hagberd, and her father doesn't like him.

8. Which scene of the play is this?

    A. Act 3, Scene 1

    B. Act 2, Scene 2

    C. Act 1, Scene 1

    D. Act 1, Scene 2

9. How does Bessie MOST LIKELY feel about her home life?

    A. She is unhappy about it because she feels she has no freedom.

    B. She is satisfied with it and plans to stay where she is for many years.

    C. She wishes she had someone to help with Carvil, but she is otherwise satisfied.

    D. She wants to get married and bring her husband home with her.

10. What pattern from literature is at work in this passage? Use examples from the passage in your response.

_____

_____

_____

_____

Chapter 2: Diagnostic Assessment

Chapter 2: Cumulative Assessment

Diagnostic Assessment

Read the passage and answer the questions that follow.

Bookmaking

Did you ever pick up a book and wonder how it was made? It might take you only a few days or weeks to read a book, but it took a long process to make it. There are many people involved in making a book. From the writer to the publisher to the printer, a book goes through many stages before it ends up on a bookstore or library shelf.

Making books has changed in major ways since humans first began to put their words on paper. In fact, early books were not written on paper. They were written on parchment or vellum, which was made from treated animal hides. They were also not typed or printed because this technology did not exist. Books were entirely handwritten or copied by hand using a feather pen and ink pot. Any copies of a book were produced the same way. This work was done by copyists called scribes. Can you imagine how long it took to produce a book this way? Today's bookmaking process relies heavily on technology.

A book begins with a manuscript written by the author. Most authors today use word processing software to write their manuscripts, but there are those rare holdouts who still use a typewriter. Creating a manuscript on a typewriter is not a good idea. Not only does it have obvious limitations, but most publishers today require that a manuscript be submitted in digital form. So, an author who refuses to embrace modern technology may have trouble publishing his or her manuscript.

When the manuscript arrives at the publisher, it is revised by an editor. Depending on the nature of the manuscript and the procedures of the publisher, it may take weeks or months before the manuscript is ready to go to the printer. The manuscript must be edited and then "set" onto a page so that it is in the precise order and form that the final book will be in. In many publishing firms, this is the job of the graphic designer.

A graphic designer also creates graphics, or images, using specialized software. The drawings, pictures, charts, and countless other images that you see in books are not randomly placed on the page. They are precisely positioned for best effect and fit. The position is decided by the editor and the designer. In this digital age, adding graphics to a book is a fairly simple process. It was much different when manuscripts were illustrated by hand. Today, a graphic designer places a digital image of a famous painting on a book page. Thousands of copies of the book are printed, along with that image. It can't get much easier than that. But in medieval times, each image was created individually by hand. So, an illustrator—or illuminator, as one was called back then—drew and colored in every painting for every page for every copy of the manuscript. Modern graphic design, while still requiring work and the skills of a trained digital artist, is an easier and faster way to create a book.

After the manuscript has been edited, designed, and shaped into its final form, it is sent to the printer. Different methods of printing have been used in modern times. Today, most books are printed using photolithography, also known as offset printing. Offset printing is the most cost-effective way to produce large quantities of books. In offset printing, the inked image is offset, or transferred, from a plate to a rubber blanket to the printing surface. Books are printed in signatures, or units of pages. Believe it or not, the pages are not printed in the order they will appear in the book. The pages are positioned on the printing plate so that they will be in the right order when the pages are folded.

The next step is binding the pages. First, the pages are gathered and assembled in the right order, a process done by a gathering machine. They are sorted into groups called signatures. Then, the signatures are fastened, typically on a flexible sewing machine. Flexible sewing allows the pages to turn easily and lay flat. Next, the endpapers that help hold the book in the cover are attached to each end of the fastened signatures. Then, glue is applied to the spine to hold the signatures together. Finally, the cover is attached to the book at the casing-in machine.

Thanks to modern technology, thousands of books can be printed in a relatively short time. Despite its reliance on technology, the publishing industry would not exist without the combined creative talents of authors, editors, and graphic designers.

Parts of a Typical Case-Bound Book

1. If you could add another label to the diagram, what would it be?

   A. spine

   B. table of contents

   C. title

   D. illustration

2. Which sentence from the passage is an opinion?

   A. "Books are printed in signatures, or units of pages."

   B. "It can't get much easier than that."

   C. "When the manuscript arrives at the publisher, it is revised by an editor."

   D. "Books were entirely handwritten or copied by hand using a feather pen and ink pot."

3. Briefly summarize the main ideas of the passage.

    _____

    _____

    _____

    _____

4. The diagram in the passage helps the reader understand that the shoulder is attached to the

    A. cover.

    B. liner.

    C. signatures.

    D. endpaper.

Read the passage and answer the questions that follow.

The Medieval Manuscript

In today's world, computers, printing presses, and copy machines make it relatively easy to produce great quantities of books and other writings in a short time. However, hundreds of years ago—before Johannes Gutenberg invented a printing press that used movable type in the fifteenth century—creating just one book could take weeks, months, or even years.

Early Scribes

For most of the European Middle Ages (the time period from approximately 500 to 1500 CE) books were produced and copied by hand. In fact, the word *manuscript*, which means a handwritten or typed composition, comes from the Latin word *manus* (hand) and *scriptus* (to write). Early copyists, or scribes, were usually monks who lived in monasteries. Within the walls of these religious communities, the monks could spend long hours each day in the scriptorium. This was the room set aside for copying books as well as composing letters and documents. The scriptorium was usually cold, and the monks worked by natural light, since candles were a fire risk. Books were produced for a monastery's own use or on commission for someone else.

Writing the Text

Medieval manuscripts were not composed on paper as we know it today. Paper was made from treated animal hides, typically from sheep, goats, or calves. Scribes used untanned skins, called parchment, or tanned skins, called vellum. Vellum was considered a higher grade of writing material. When the scribe sat down to copy a book, the first thing he did was to lightly draw or score lines across the page as a guide. Then, in silence and with painstaking effort, he would begin to create the manuscript. Dipping a quill feather or reed pen into the ink pot, the scribe artfully drew each letter onto the page. The text of many medieval manuscripts looks very similar because scribes used standard forms of script. Script, or book handwriting, varied and developed through the ages. For example, in early Rome, scribes typically used all uppercase letters. Centuries later, a script called the Caroline minuscule, which used lowercase letters, became very popular. One of the chief differences between medieval script and modern script is the time and care that medieval scribes put into writing every letter. People today just wouldn't have the patience for that.

Illuminating the Manuscript

Most of the medieval manuscripts that survive today are found in museums, libraries, or universities. Many of them are exquisite works of art. This is because, like today, books were often illustrated. However, medieval illustrations were not the black-and-white or color reproductions one finds in modern books. Each illustration was an original miniature painting created with brilliant colors and remarkable detail. It took real artistic talent to create such elaborate designs in spaces that were often only inches wide. Manuscripts were also adorned with decorated initials and borders. The term *illuminated* technically refers to any manuscript that was decorated with gold and silver, because these colors added brightness and light to the manuscript. However, it is commonly used today to describe illustrated manuscripts in general.

After a scribe created the written text, he passed the manuscript on to an illuminator. Often, it took multiple illuminators with different artistic abilities to illustrate a text. Some illuminators painted on the borders and added other decorative details. Others created the miniature paintings. For color, illuminators used a binding agent, such as gum arabic, and mixed it with a variety of pigments. For example, they used ultramarine for blue, verdigris for green, and arsenic sulfide for yellow. For the red ink typically used in book titles and headings, illuminators used a red earth pigment called *rubrica*. (This is why titles and headings are sometimes called *rubrics*.) Monks experimented with pigments to get just the right color.

Types of Texts

So what were the most common topics of medieval manuscripts? The most frequently copied books in medieval Europe were bibles and other religious writings. Topics like medicine, law, astronomy, and mathematics were also popular. The writings of Greek and Latin authors like Virgil and Aristotle were also reproduced. But one specific type of medieval manuscript may have been the most popular of all. It was called the "book of hours." Books of hours were devotional books containing a calendar, psalms, meditations, and prayers for specific hours of the day. Often, these books were commissioned by wealthy nobles, who spared no expense in acquiring the most lavishly illuminated manuscripts.

The Legacy

In a world of mass-produced books, the artistry of bookmaking has long been forgotten. Today's readers want books in larger quantities, and in more varieties, than people of medieval times could imagine. As a result, books' quality has gone downhill. The books are printed on cheaper paper and so the pages don't look as nice. Also, the covers are designed to draw in readers, and so they use lots of flashy colors. Nonetheless, medieval illuminated manuscripts are an enduring reminder that talent, meticulous care, and pride in one's work can produce extraordinary results.

5. The author could BEST support his argument that the older ways of making books are superior by

    A. reproducing some text from a medieval book.

    B. offering a diagram of a book constructed in medieval times.

    C. providing a chart comparing book quantities in medieval times with quantities now.

    D. providing an illustration of a page from an older book.

6. Which step was done before a scribe began to create a manuscript?

    A. He would pass it on to an illustrator.

    B. The book was placed in a scriptorium.

    C. The illustrator would create images for the book interior.

    D. He would draw light lines on the page.

7. Which sentence from the passage is a fact?

    A. "For example, in early Rome, scribes typically used all uppercase letters."

    B. "So what were the most common topics of medieval manuscripts?"

    C. "People today just wouldn't have the patience for that."

    D. "Many of them are exquisite works of art."

8. Which types of manuscripts were the most commonly produced?

    A. histories

    B. romances

    C. science books

    D. religious writings

9. According to BOTH passages, what has been a major effect of modern technology on bookmaking?

    A. People do not read as much as they used to.

    B. Books can be mass produced relatively quickly.

    C. Books are not as beautifully decorated as in the past.

    D. Books are of higher quality than books of the past.

10. How are the two authors' approaches to the topic of books different? Use examples from the passages in your response.

_____

_____

_____

_____

Duplicating any part of this book is prohibited by law.

8 Cite Textual Evidence

RI.8.1, RI.8.2, RI.8.10, RH.8.1, RH.8.2, RH.8.10, RST.8.1, RST.8.2, RST.8.10

Getting the Idea

When you analyze a text, you interpret what you have read and state your opinions and conclusions about the content. To support your analysis, it's important to cite **textual evidence** that indicates why your interpretation is reasonable and accurate. Textual evidence consists of facts, details, and examples that you cite or quote directly from the text to support your opinions and conclusions. Read the paragraph below.

> The driving force behind transportation has always been the desire to make life easier and more profitable. Throughout history, inventive minds have wrestled with the challenge of moving people and goods faster and more comfortably in order to boost a society's trading and selling power. Meeting this challenge has led to the development of larger and faster ships that were first powered by wind pushing sails, then by steam, and finally by oil. On land, wagons led to trains that were first powered by coal and steam and then by diesel fuel. At last, in search of speed, people invented airplanes, which now have technology that has made every part of the planet reachable within hours.

When you analyze this paragraph, you might infer that new technology in transportation is developed to allow people to go farther and faster. To support this claim, you could refer to details in the second sentence. You could also cite the detail about development in ship power and, in the last sentence, the statement that airplane travel has made it possible to travel long distances in hours.

When citing textual evidence, be sure to select details that strongly support your analysis or inference. You may want to quote the text exactly by stating "According to the text" or "The author says" and then citing the text in quotation marks. Then explain how the textual evidence supports your analysis. For example:

Technological advances in transportation have resulted from the need to go farther and faster. The author claims that this need for speed is nothing new. According to the text, the desire for faster travel spurred the development of ships "that were first powered by wind pushing sails, then by steam, and finally by oil." Airplanes greatly sped up travel and, as a result, "made every part of the planet reachable within hours."

The reader supported the response stated in the first sentence of the above paragraph with textual evidence from the quoted paragraph near the top of this page. This evidence illustrates the purpose behind technological advances in transportation.

Thinking It Through

Read the following paragraph, and then answer the question that follows.

In the twentieth century, the airplane made it possible for people and goods to be transported worldwide in a short period of time. While air travel remains the fastest way to travel long distances, airports and airplanes are now overcrowded and less comfortable. A new version of an old vehicle may provide an alternative: high-speed trains called maglevs. Germany and Japan are developing maglevs that use electromagnets to propel the train along a guideway instead of on steel tracks. The trains themselves have no engines and so are quiet as they speed along. The magnetic field raises the train as it travels so that it floats on air above the guideway. The trains can travel up to 310 miles per hour, which is twice as fast as a conventional train and compares to a passenger jet that can fly at about 565 miles per hour. A maglev train could go from Paris, France, to Rome, Italy, in a little more than two hours. Maglevs may be the future of transportation for those who no longer find air travel convenient.

Circle the sentence that BEST supports the argument that maglevs could be an alternative to air travel. Which details support the claim that maglevs improve upon older technology?

_____

_____

HINT Which facts illustrate how maglevs are different from conventional trains?

 DISCUSS Write an objective summary of the paragraph in your own words and share it with a partner.

Duplicating any part of this book is prohibited by law.

Coached Example

Read the passage and answer the questions.

The First Working Submarine

The first practical idea for an underwater craft was proposed in 1578. British mathematician William Bourne wrote about a craft covered with waterproof leather and propelled with oars. But it was Cornelius Drebbel who actually built the world's first known working submarine in the 1620s. The vessel was probably based on a rowboat with tall sides and decking installed over the top to join the sides. Drebbel's craft was similar to Bourne's proposal. It was covered completely with greased leather for waterproofing and was powered by four oars protruding through leather-sealed holes in the sides. There was also a waterproof hatch near the center. Tubes held above the surface of the water by flotation devices supplied air to the occupants. Under the oarsmen's seats, Drebbel installed large pigskin bladders connected to pipes that extended outside the vessel. Ropes tied the bladders closed until the occupants were ready to submerge. When the ropes were untied, the bladders filled to submerge the vessel ten to fifteen feet. To surface, the crew compressed the bladders to force the water out.

1. Which sentence BEST summarizes the text?

   A. Both William Bourne and Cornelius Drebbel were important inventors.

   B. Bladders helped to submerge and surface the first working submarine.

   C. Cornelius Drebbel built the first working submarine.

   D. A rowboat was used as the basis for building the first submarine.

   HINT A summary focuses on the central idea rather than on a single detail.

2. Which detail from the passage supports the claim that Drebbel's submarine included ideas proposed by Bourne?

   A. "The vessel was probably based on a rowboat with tall sides and decking installed over the top . . ."

   B. "It was covered completely with greased leather for waterproofing . . ."

   C. "There was also a waterproof hatch near the center."

   D. "Under the oarsmen's seats, Drebbel installed large pigskin bladders . . ."

   HINT Look for the detail that relates back to the sentence that describes what Bourne proposed.

Lesson Practice

Use the Reading Guide to help you understand the passage.

Reading Guide

As you read, think about what inferences you can draw from the text. Cite textual evidence to support your inferences.

After citing textual evidence, be sure to explain how this evidence supports your claims about the text.

What claim does the author make about the smartphone as a miniature computer in paragraph 3?

Smartphones and Their Capabilities

The first smartphones developed when electronics companies began to combine and improve upon the capabilities of two already existing devices, the cell phone and the personal digital assistant (PDA). The IBM Simon is recognized as the first smartphone. It was designed in 1992 and was released to the public two years later. This mobile phone had many features of a PDA, including a calendar, an address book, a calculator, e-mail, simple games, and the ability to send and receive facsimiles. Over the next decade or so, other companies released similar devices. As technology developed, electronics companies included additional features such as a digital camera, text messaging, and video games on their devices in an effort to gain market share.

Early smartphones required the user to interact with the device by using a stylus, keypad, or small keyboard. That changed when the original Apple iPhone was released in 2007. The iPhone was the first widely used smartphone to employ touchscreen technology. Touchscreen technology allowed a larger screen area because a keypad was no longer necessary. This type of user interface soon appeared for nearly all of the most popular smartphones. Although Apple dominated the early smartphone market, competitors such as Samsung released touchscreen devices that greatly reduced Apple's market share.

Since 2007, technology related to the physical components of smartphones as well as to their operating systems and the networks on which they function has developed greatly. Today's smartphones combine the communication capabilities of the cell phone and the PDA, including voice calling, texting, and e-mail. They also serve many other functions. They usually include a digital camera that takes photos and records videos, and they can store these media along with digital music. Smartphones also allow users to download video games. These additional functions for personal entertainment are important to many people. The smartphone has become so advanced that many see it as a miniature computer.

What evidence does the author use in paragraph 4 to support the claim that smartphones are comparable to miniature computers?

When you analyze a text, think about what the author has said about the topic and whether the evidence presented verifies the points that the author makes.

What text evidence could you cite to support the author's statement that the capabilities of smartphones may be unlimited?

Through access to the Internet as well as by use of third-party software applications (apps), the capabilities of today's smartphones as small computers for personal and business use have expanded tremendously. Smartphone users can browse the Internet for most information that is accessible through a personal computer. Internet access also allows smartphone users to chat via instant messaging services. Users can interact through various social media services. Also, some traditional uses for personal computers, such as viewing and editing documents, can be performed on many smartphones.

Already there are apps for a variety of functions that would have been unthinkable to perform on a smartphone when the IBM Simon appeared. These include GPS navigation capability as well as control of many remote programmable devices such as home electronics and appliances. A smartphone user can set up apps to receive electronic newsfeeds and stay abreast of current events. Apps also allow smartphone users to listen to radio stations or view television programs or videos. Personal banking, including scanning of checks for deposit, can be done through smartphone apps. Also, credit card readers can be attached to smartphones so that vendors or service providers can accept customer payments through a smartphone app. Some smartphones can even display an image to be scanned from the screen as a method of payment for purchases such as concert or movie tickets.

These are just some of the constantly developing uses for today's smartphones. As the operating systems of these devices and the communications networks on which they function improve further, the capabilities of smartphones may be as unlimited as the imaginations of the developers of apps.

Answer the following questions.

1. Which sentence BEST summarizes paragraph 2?

   A. Apple's iPhone was the first smartphone to use touchscreen technology.

   B. Apple dominated the smartphone market when it introduced the iPhone.

   C. Early versions of smartphones required a stylus, keypad, or keyboard.

   D. The smartphone market became highly competitive with the introduction of touchscreen technology.

2. What is the central idea of the passage?

   A. Smartphone technology continues to change rapidly as people develop more functions.

   B. Smartphones can be used for both business and entertainment.

   C. Smartphones now do many of the same things as computers have done in the past.

   D. The ability of smartphones to make purchases of products and services may replace cash money.

3. What text evidence supports the claim that smartphones are important to people for personal entertainment?

   A. "Touchscreen technology allowed a larger screen area because a keypad was no longer necessary."

   B. "Personal banking, including scanning of checks for deposit, can be done through smartphone apps."

   C. "They usually include a digital camera that takes photos and records videos, and they can store these media along with digital music."

   D. "Today's smartphones combine the communication capabilities of the cell phone and the PDA, including voice calling, texting, and e-mail."

4. Which claim does the information in the passage BEST support?

   A. The market for smartphones will peak and begin to decline.

   B. Smartphones will keep changing and become more valued.

   C. Smartphones are limited in the types of functions they can provide.

   D. New devices will replace smartphones.

5. Explain why the functions of today's smartphones would have been unthinkable for the first smartphone in the 1990s. Cite two examples from the passage as evidence.

_____

_____

_____

Duplicating any part of this book is prohibited by law.

As you read, look for the claims that the author makes and think about how you might interpret the claims.

Remember to quote directly from the passage when you cite textual evidence that supports your interpretation.

How would you summarize the first paragraph? Which details most strongly support the central idea?

Driving into the Future

In 1913, Henry Ford changed the "horseless carriage" from a novelty into a practical convenience. With his development of the assembly line, Ford was able to manufacture the Model T in a short period of time at a much reduced cost. This changed the dream of owning a car into a reality for millions of Americans. Little more than wagons with an engine, these cars would be the beginning of America's age of the automobile. By the 1950s, the car had become an integral part of our culture and daily lives. The construction of the interstate highway system, which covered the country in a spreading network of roads, expanded the role of automobile transportation. Since then, the automobile has gone through radical technological changes, but it still represents transportation freedom. With a car, people can travel at their own pace and schedule. With a car, people can go places that are still not accessible by public transportation.

The first technological improvements in automobiles were done to make them more user-friendly. One of the major changes was the electric starter, which was invented by Charles Kettering. With a starter, drivers no longer had to use a hand crank in the front of the vehicle. As the years passed, cars were made to be more comfortable and stylish. People began buying cars not only for their utility, but also for how they looked inside and out and whether they were fun to drive.

As cars became easier to use and capable of greater speeds, people began to become more concerned about safety. As a result, engines were made to be more reliable, rear and side mirrors were added, and seat belts appeared. However, no matter how many safety improvements have been added and laws have been passed to require people to use them, motor vehicle accidents are still a major concern. Although fatalities dropped between 1990 and 2009, nearly 36,000 people were killed in car crashes in 2009, according to government statistics. In that same year, there were nearly 11 million accidents.

Duplicating any part of this book is prohibited by law.

Duplicating any part of this book is prohibited by law.

Based on the passage, what claim might you make about greener cars? What evidence would you use to support this claim?

How do details in paragraph 4 help you to understand safety issues that involve cars?

Remember that textual evidence can be paraphrased or directly quoted in your response. For example, you might decide to paraphrase evidence that is particularly lengthy, but you should directly quote evidence that is stated in an interesting, concise way.

Many of the technological advances in cars over the past ten years have been based on safety concerns as well as on the new demand for cars to be kinder to the environment. Now planned and beginning to appear are cars that can self-park, read traffic signs, keep a safe distance from other vehicles, automatically brake to avoid an accident, and sound an alarm if the driver falls asleep. Possible in the near future are cars that can detect people walking or riding on bicycles and then stop before hitting anyone. There are even plans within the next five years for cars that drive themselves without a human controlling them. Since many cars these days are extensively computerized, cars that drive themselves are a logical next step. Driverless cars will also open up transportation to the disabled and to older people who can no longer drive. There is also an economic benefit since insurance costs will likely go down. Computerized cars don't drive while drunk, talking on the phone, or texting. Some people, of course, think that drivers will not give up control of their vehicles. They say that computers do crash and so will computerized cars.

Environmentally, cars are becoming greener. New cars get many more miles to a gallon of gas. There are also many types of hybrid cars that use a combination of gas and battery power. Some cars don't use gas at all, but instead run on electricity and are charged by plugging into an outlet. Plans are also in the works to develop cars that run on hydrogen, water, or even air.

Most drivers don't understand the technology that resides under the hood of their new cars. They just enjoy the convenience of a built-in phone, push-button and remote starters, advanced brakes, sensors that tell when tires are low, GPS navigation, and enhanced security. People in the future may well look back at our time and wonder how we could ever have driven dirty gas-burning cars or even allowed humans behind the wheel.

Answer the following questions.

6. **Use your answer to Part A to answer Part B.**

    Part A

    What is the central idea of paragraph 3?

    A. Fatalities from car accidents have dropped in the past several years.

    B. Technology has made cars safer, but safety is still a problem.

    C. Most car crashes do not result in fatalities.

    D. Technology in cars has adequately addressed safety concerns.

    Part B

    Which evidence from the paragraph BEST supports the answer to Part A?

    A. ". . . rear and side mirrors were added, and seat belts appeared."

    B. "safety improvements have been added and laws have been passed to require people to use them . . ."

    C. "In that same year, there were nearly 11 million accidents."

    D. "Although fatalities dropped between 1990 and 2009, nearly 36,000 people were killed in car crashes in 2009 . . ."

    E. "As cars became easier to use and capable of greater speeds, people began to become more concerned about safety."

7. **Use your answer to Part A to answer Part B.**

    Below are three claims that one could make based on paragraph 4 of the passage.

	Driverless cars would have many benefits to a variety of people.
Claims	Driverless cars run by computers would be a risk to human drivers.
	Driverless cars are an idea that will likely not be seen in the near future.

    Part A

    Circle the claim that the author has MOST strongly supported.

    Part B

    Circle three facts within paragraph 4 that BEST support the claim you circled in Part A.

Duplicating any part of this book is prohibited by law.

8. Read the following portion of paragraph 1 from the passage.

> By the 1950s, the car had become an integral part of our culture and daily lives. The construction of the interstate highway system, which covered the country in a spreading network of roads, expanded the role of automobile transportation. Since then, the automobile has gone through radical technological changes, but it still represents transportation freedom. With a car, people can travel at their own pace and schedule. With a car, people can go places that are still not accessible by public transportation.

Underline the sentence in the paragraph that states a central idea of the passage.

---

9. Read the passage summary below. Decide which three pieces of text evidence in the box BEST support the summary. Write each piece of evidence in a separate Evidence box.

Summary: Since the age of the automobile began in the early 1900s, technological advances have made cars safer and greener.

"Now planned and beginning to appear are cars that can self-park …"	"Plans are also in the works to develop cars that run on hydrogen, water, or even air."
"… computers do crash and so will computerized cars."	"By the 1950s, the car had become an integral part of our culture …"
"New cars get many more miles to a gallon of gas."	"As the years passed, cars were made to be more comfortable and stylish."
"With a starter, drivers no longer had to use a hand crank …"	

Evidence #1	Evidence #2	Evidence #3

9 Main Idea and Supporting Details

RI.8.1, RI.8.2, RI.8.5, RI.8.10, RH.8.10, RST.8.1, RST.8.2, RST.8.5, RST.8.10

Getting the Idea

The **main idea** is the central message a writer is trying to communicate with a text. The main idea may be directly stated or implied. To figure out the main idea of a passage, first read it all the way through. Then, ask yourself what the passage is mostly about. For example, the main idea of a magazine article might be: *Regular exercise has many health benefits*. Authors develop main ideas with **supporting details**. These include examples, reasons, facts, and descriptions. These details back up the main idea and are presented in the supporting paragraphs that follow the introduction.

Each supporting paragraph contributes to the main idea of the passage. The writer uses these paragraphs to explain the main idea expressed in the first paragraph. Each paragraph has its own central idea, usually expressed in a **topic sentence**. The topic sentence is usually near the beginning of a paragraph, though it may also fall at the end. For example, this is a supporting paragraph in a magazine article on exercise.

> Research indicates that exercise may prevent certain diseases or reduce their symptoms. For example, people who exercise regularly lower their risk of developing heart problems. Arthritis sufferers can reduce their joint damage and pain. Exercise may help people with asthma have fewer attacks and decrease their need for medication.

The first sentence of this paragraph is the topic sentence. It clearly states the main idea of the paragraph, which is that exercise can prevent or lessen disease. The author supports it by providing specific examples of the benefits of exercise: lowered risk of heart disease, less pain for arthritis sufferers, fewer attacks for asthma sufferers.

Sometimes main ideas are not directly stated in a paragraph. For example, read this paragraph.

> First, the walls may need to be primed before painting. The floor areas must be covered with a tarp or plastic to protect them from spills and paint splatter. In addition, wall borders must be taped as necessary, particularly when using different colors in one room. The painter should also wear protective clothing and ventilate the room.

This paragraph does not have a topic sentence. However, based on the supporting details in the paragraph, the implied topic sentence might be something like this: *Painting requires a great deal of preparation.*

Some texts may have more than one main idea. For example, an author may decide to write an article in which she describes the benefits of exercise. In that same article, she may also discuss the importance of a healthy diet.

Thinking It Through

Read the following paragraph, and then answer the question that follows.

> The ancient Romans and Greeks used puppets for entertainment. They did not necessarily look like the puppets we might see today. Some were held on strings, but some were moved with sticks. The rulers of the Ottoman Empire had a favorite puppet with a strange name: Karagiozis. In medieval Europe, puppets were used in plays. Puppets were also popular in Asia. The Japanese called them Bunraku; actors appeared on stage with the puppets, actually controlling them with their hands. In Russia, puppets were so important that a State Central Puppet Theater was started for their performances.

Bunraku puppet

Write a topic sentence for this paragraph.

_____

_____

HINT Think about what the supporting details in the paragraph are mainly about.

Duplicating any part of this book is prohibited by law.

Coached Example

Read the passage and answer the questions.

excerpted and adapted from

The Declaration of Independence

We hold these truths to be self-evident, that all men are created equal, that they are endowed by their Creator with certain unalienable Rights, that among these are Life, Liberty and the pursuit of Happiness. —That to secure these rights, Governments are instituted among Men, deriving their powers from the consent of the governed, —That whenever any Form of Government begins to destroy these rights, it is the further Right of the People to alter or to abolish it, and to institute new Government, laying its foundation on solid principles and organizing its powers in a way that will be most likely to ensure their Safety and Happiness. Caution, indeed, will dictate that long-established Governments should not be changed for small, temporary causes; and accordingly all experience has shown that mankind is more likely to suffer under such evils than to live more correctly and abolish the government with which they have grown too comfortable.

The Declaration of Independence

---

1. What is the main idea of the passage?

   A. All men are created equal and have certain rights.

   B. People have a right to abolish a government that is abusive and violates their rights.

   C. Most people will tolerate injustices as long as they are not excessive.

   D. Governments should not be abolished for minor or passing issues.

   HINT Do not focus on supporting details. Think of what the passage as a whole is mainly about.

2. Which of the following ideas is a supporting detail in the passage?

   A. Some people may not be satisfied with their government.

   B. Established governments should not be replaced by small, temporary ones.

   C. People have the right to elect their leaders.

   D. People may become too comfortable with their government.

   HINT Choose the sentence most directly connected to the main idea.

Duplicating any part of this book is prohibited by law.

Lesson Practice

Use the Reading Guide to help you understand the passage.

Reading Guide

What is the main idea of the passage?

What is paragraph 2 mainly about?

Think about which main ideas in the passage are implied and which main ideas are directly stated.

What do Dr. Jemison's out-of-school activities suggest about her?

Mae C. Jemison: A True Space Pioneer

Space exploration has fascinated people throughout the world for decades. Many children grow up dreaming of becoming astronauts one day. However, only an elite and small group of individuals have ever realized that dream. One of these individuals is Mae C. Jemison. Through hard work and determination, rising above a humble background, she became the first African American woman to travel into space.

The National Aeronautics and Space Administration (NASA) has had many milestones since its establishment in 1958. At first, NASA only admitted white men into their astronaut program. Then, in 1967, Robert H. Lawrence, Jr., became the first African American member of NASA, although he passed away before making it to space. In 1983, Sally Ride was the first American woman in space. Then, in 1987, Jemison became the first African American woman to be selected for the astronaut training program. On September 12, 1992, she launched into space and into history.

Jemison was born in Decatur, Alabama, on October 17, 1956, but was raised in Chicago, Illinois, from the age of three. Her mother was an elementary school teacher and her father was a carpenter and a roofer. One could say that Jemison's journey to her impressive achievements began in kindergarten, when she realized that she wanted to be a scientist. From that day forward, she devoted herself wholeheartedly to science.

After graduating from high school in 1973, she was accepted to Stanford, one of the most prestigious universities in the country. She graduated in 1977 with a degree in chemical engineering and a Bachelor of Arts degree in African and Afro-American Studies. Jemison was then accepted into Cornell University, another prominent school, where she earned a medical degree in 1981.

Although college and medical school demand an enormous amount of time and work from students, Jemison made time for important activities outside of school. She visited Kenya and Cuba and studied there. She also worked at a Cambodian refugee

How does the last paragraph help readers understand the main idea of the passage?

camp in Thailand. In 1979, she organized a citywide health and law fair in New York. Jemison also found time to pursue interests not related to school. She was a trained dancer and performed in stage productions.

After medical school, Jemison worked as a General Practitioner in California. Then, she joined the Peace Corps, acting as the Area Peace Corps Medical Officer for West Africa for two and a half years. Her varied duties included supervising the medical staff, teaching, developing a teaching curriculum for medical students, and implementing the guidelines she invented. In the early 1980s, she worked on preventing the spread of hepatitis in Africa.

When she returned to the United States in 1985, Jemison decided to fulfill a lifelong dream. She applied to the astronaut program. It took two years, but in 1987, Jemison was one of fifteen selected from a field of approximately two thousand applicants. After training for a year, she officially became an astronaut. Her first position was as a representative at the Kennedy Space Center in Cape Canaveral, Florida. In 1992, she was chosen to be one of the astronauts on the space shuttle *Endeavour*. She was responsible for conducting science experiments on the shuttle. On September 12, 1992, the *Endeavour* lifted off, carrying Jemison and six other astronauts. They spent eight days in space, completing 127 orbits of Earth.

Jemison proved that the sky is literally the limit when one has intelligence, ambition, and dedication to one's work. Since retiring from NASA, she continues to add to her long list of professional and personal accomplishments. She is the founder of the Jemison Group, which supports technological research and innovation. One of the Jemison Group's projects is an international youth space camp. She is also a TV host, for the Discovery Channel's *World of Wonders* program. Her life continues to be about encouraging others to follow their dreams.

Answer the following questions.

1. Which sentence in paragraph 1 BEST states the main idea of the passage?

   A. "One of these individuals is Mae C. Jemison."

   B. "Space exploration has fascinated people throughout the world for decades."

   C. "However, only an elite and small group of individuals have ever realized that dream."

   D. "Through hard work and determination, rising above a humble background, she became the first African American woman to travel into space."

2. What is a supporting detail in paragraph 2?

   A. Sally Ride's becoming the first American woman in space

   B. Robert Lawrence's death

   C. the reasons for establishing NASA

   D. NASA's acceptance of white men into the space program

3. What is the implied main idea of paragraph 4?

   A. Astronauts are required to have medical degrees.

   B. It is not easy to be accepted into Stanford or Cornell.

   C. Jemison was an excellent student.

   D. Jemison attended high school.

4. Which supporting detail BEST shows that it is not easy to become an astronaut?

   A. Jemison's first position was at the Kennedy Space Center.

   B. Science mission specialists conduct experiments aboard space shuttles.

   C. In 1986, Sally Ride became the first American woman in space.

   D. Only fifteen applicants out of two thousand were chosen for the astronaut program in 1987.

5. Which is the topic sentence in paragraph 5, and how does the author support it? Use examples from the passage in your response.

   _____

   _____

   _____

   _____

Duplicating any part of this book is prohibited by law.

Reading Guide

How does the title of the passage help you understand its main idea?

Which details in the passage help you understand the advantages of hydraulic fracturing? Which help you understand the disadvantages?

As you read, try to summarize the main idea of each paragraph.

Hydraulic Fracturing: Advantages and Disadvantages

excerpted and adapted from the U.S. Geological Survey and the U.S. Environmental Protection Agency

The pursuit of alternative methods of fuel and energy production in the United States has sparked much controversy. Clearly, technology must be used to discover new ways to harness and harvest our natural resources. But what will be risked in this process, and to what extent will we go to achieve the goal of energy self-sufficiency?

Hydraulic fracturing is also known as hydrofracturing or fracking. Introduced in Kansas in 1947, it is an oil and gas recovery process. The process involves pumping large amounts of water, sand, and chemicals at extremely high pressures into shale rock to fracture it, thereby forming pathways for oil and gas to reach a well. Hydraulic fracturing fluid usually consists of water, proppants, and chemical additives that create and enlarge cracks within the rock formation. The proppants, which are primarily comprised of sand, hold open the newly created cracks. This process also increases the extent and connectivity of existing cracks. It is commonly used in rocks such as sandstone, shale, and some coal beds to increase oil and/or gas flow to a well.

Once the pumping, or injection, process is completed, the internal pressure of the rock formation causes fluid to return to the surface through the drill hole. This fluid, which consists of what is termed "flowback" and "produced water," may contain the injected chemicals in addition to naturally occurring materials such as metals and hydrocarbons. The fluid is typically stored on-site in tanks or pits before treatment, disposal, or recycling. Often, it is injected underground for disposal. In areas where that is not an option, it may be treated and reused or processed by a wastewater treatment facility and then discharged to surface water.

Duplicating any part of this book is prohibited by law.

What concerns do people have about hydraulic fracturing?

What claims do people who support hydraulic fracturing make?

As you read the last paragraph, try to restate the challenge that the text describes.

Some people have concerns about the possible environmental effects of hydraulic fracturing. One of these concerns is the potential for contamination of groundwater used for drinking and surface water that spills from wells. Both can impact public health negatively. The contamination can come from either the petroleum being produced or from the chemicals introduced in the fracturing process. The U.S. Geological Survey (USGS) is currently studying well water quality in several states where hydraulic fracturing is being practiced. These states include Arkansas, New York, Pennsylvania, and Wyoming. Air pollution is another known risk. Such pollution can result from the release of unstable organic compounds and greenhouse gases into the atmosphere.

Also, research by the USGS has demonstrated that deep-well fluid injection can trigger earthquakes. This injection process is sometimes used to dispose of flowback or produced waters from hydraulic fracturing and gas production. Problems can arise when fluid is injected back into the Earth for storage. Earthquakes may occur when the fluid reaches a critically stressed fault.

Advocates of hydraulic fracturing support their cause with reasons unconnected to environmental issues. Hydraulic fracturing allows countries to use their own available resources instead of relying on other nations. Financially, this is sound because it creates jobs and stimulates the economy. Hydraulic fracturing is also much less expensive than importing such resources. It is important to understand that a country's abundance or lack of energy resources also affects political issues. Wars are sometimes fought because one nation wants to possess the natural resources of another. Some countries use these resources as leverage in their relations with the rest of the world.

Hydraulic fracturing has the potential to help meet our country's energy needs, but the safety and efficacy of this method of obtaining fuel materials is being debated. Disagreement will always exist between people who are concerned about environmental issues and those who prioritize economic factors. Can these opposing parties meet halfway? That is where the challenge lies.

Answer the following questions.

6.   Circle the letter of the box on the left that contains a main idea of the passage. Then draw a line to each box on the right containing details that support that main idea.

A. | Once the pumping, or injection, process is completed, the internal pressure of the rock formation causes fluid to return to the surface through the drill hole.

1. | Introduced in Kansas in 1947, it is an oil and gas recovery process.

2. | Air pollution is another known risk.

B. | Some people have concerns about the possible environmental effects of hydraulic fracturing.

3. | Hydraulic fracturing is also much less expensive than importing such resources.

C. | Hydraulic fracturing is also known as hydrofracturing or fracking.

4. | The proppants, which are primarily comprised of sand, hold open the newly created cracks.

5. | Also, research by the USGS has demonstrated that deep-well fluid injection can trigger earthquakes.

7.   Read paragraph 5 from the passage. Underline the sentence that states the main idea of the paragraph.

8. **Use your answer to Part A to answer Part B.**

    Part A

    Which of the following BEST states the main idea of the entire passage?

    A. The need for alternative energy sources is great.

    B. Hydraulic fracturing is a dangerous method of obtaining oil and gas.

    C. Hydraulic fracturing is a controversial method of obtaining oil and gas.

    D. Hydraulic fracturing is an economical method of obtaining oil and gas.

    Part B

    Which detail from the passage BEST supports the answer to Part A?

    A. "Hydraulic fracturing fluid usually consists of water, proppants, and chemical additives that create and enlarge cracks within the rock formation."

    B. "Disagreement will always exist between people who are concerned about environmental issues and those who prioritize economic factors."

    C. "Clearly, technology must be used to discover new ways to harness and harvest our natural resources."

    D. "But what will be risked in this process, and to what extent will we go to achieve the goal of energy self-sufficiency?"

---

9. Based on evidence from the text, choose supporting details that indicate why some people favor hydraulic fracturing. There is more than one correct choice listed.

    A. makes countries more independent

    B. increases existing cracks in rock

    C. may contaminate surface water

    D. creates controversy

    E. stimulates the economy

    F. might reduce the chances of war

    G. can trigger earthquakes

    H. is less expensive than importing oil

    I. was introduced in 1947

10 Summarize

RI.8.1, RI.8.2, RST.8.2

Getting the Idea

A **summary** is a short restatement of a longer text in the reader's own words. You might summarize for various purposes, but the underlying reason will always be the same: to communicate information as concisely and as directly as you can. A summary should contain only the main idea and the most important supporting details of a passage. A summary's content should also be as similar as possible to the original source. If you present a fact or idea out of context, it might mislead a reader about the meaning of the passage being summarized. Here is a paragraph that could be summarized:

> Sometimes called the "stinking rose," garlic is a bulbous plant of the genus *Allium*. Garlic has been used for centuries to flavor food. However, it is also valuable for its medicinal properties. There is evidence that it may cure colds, viral infections, and reduce blood cholesterol levels. It may even lower the risk of certain cancers.

Now read a summary a student wrote:

> Garlic is a bulbous plant similar to a rose. It has been around for centuries and has been proven to cure some cancers.

This summary misrepresents the information in the original. Garlic is not similar to a rose. The original also does not say that there is proof of garlic's power to cure cancers. Here is a more accurate summary.

> Garlic is a bulbous plant that is prized for both its flavor and for its possible medical benefits.

This summary communicates the content of the original passage, and it relies on its main points: garlic's appearance, its value, its flavor, and its potential benefits. It does not include specific information, such as garlic's genus name or the names of diseases it might cure, because these are not the passage's primary points. Including them might also make a reader think they were more important to the passage than they actually were.

For a brief paragraph, a one- or two-sentence summary is enough. Longer works may require longer summaries. Notice, as well, that the second summary on the previous page did not use the same words as the original. It is very important that a summary be in your own words.

Deciding what to leave out of a summary may require careful judgment. After all, you wouldn't want to leave out information crucial to understanding a writer's point. A passage may list the titles of every song a singer recorded, but the summary should not. If you are summarizing a biography of a famous inventor, choose only the events that are most significant to the inventor's life and work. If the writer mentions that his favorite food is chicken, this probably should not be included in the summary. Finally, never add information that does not appear in the original just because it happens to be your own prior knowledge. A summary of the text must be just that: a summary of the text in front of you.

Thinking It Through

Read the following paragraph, and then answer the question that follows.

To all staff: Please be advised that all requests for office supplies must be submitted by 2:00 p.m. on Thursdays. Only requests submitted on the official office supply form will be accepted. Forms may be obtained from Beth Goldstein. Her office is on the second floor by the water cooler.

Write a summary of this paragraph.

_____

_____

 HINT In a summary, you should leave out the nonessential details.

Duplicating any part of this book is prohibited by law.

Coached Example

Read the passage and answer the questions.

In certain parts of the world, at certain times, a remarkable light display appears in the night sky. Aurora borealis is its scientific name; since it occurs in the Northern Hemisphere, this phenomenon is more commonly known as the northern lights. The northern lights occur when electromagnetically charged particles from the sun are pulled toward Earth's two magnetic poles, in the North and the South. This causes molecules in the air to glow.

The northern lights take various forms, including rays, arcs, bands, and patches of light. The lights appear in striking and beautiful shades of red, blue, green, yellow, and violet. The farther north they appear, the brighter they are. While you could easily find a picture or a video of the northern lights, you would have to see them for yourself to truly appreciate them.

---

1. Which sentence BEST summarizes paragraph 1?

   A. It happens in the Northern Hemisphere, and this is the reason that the aurora borealis is also known as the northern lights.

   B. The aurora borealis is a natural phenomenon that occurs near the sun at certain times of the year.

   C. The aurora borealis, or northern lights, is caused by electromagnetic activity between the sun and Earth.

   D. More commonly known as the northern lights, the aurora borealis appears in the sky when the sun is magnetic.

   HINT Eliminate any answers that change the facts of the original.

2. What is the BEST summary of paragraph 2?

   A. The northern lights appear in shades of red, green, violet, yellow, and blue.

   B. The northern lights appear in a variety of forms and beautiful colors.

   C. In order to truly appreciate the beauty of the northern lights, people should see them in person.

   D. The northern lights have many forms, including bands and rays, and they have striking colors that look beautiful in pictures.

   HINT Look for the summary that best captures the main idea of the paragraph.

Duplicating any part of this book is prohibited by law.

Lesson Practice

Use the Reading Guide to help you understand the passage.

Reading	Guide

Remember that a summary should restate only the main idea and most important details.

Which details from paragraph 4 belong in a summary of that paragraph?

The Great Nile

Today, we know that the Nile River is the longest river in the world. It covers over four thousand miles as it flows from Burundi in east-central Africa to the Mediterranean Sea in northeast Egypt. We know a great deal about the native people who have depended on the Nile for their survival for centuries. For instance, we know that it supports almost all of the agriculture of Egypt. We have also studied the abundant and varied wildlife in and around the Nile.

Centuries ago, however, much about the Nile was a mystery. People knew almost nothing about it. They didn't even know where it started and where it ended. A Greek astronomer and mathematician named Ptolemy wrote that the source of the Nile was "the Mountains of the Moon." Historians believe that Ptolemy was referring to a mountain range in east-central Africa whose peaks are shrouded in an eerie mist. Unfortunately, Ptolemy's research sources were incorrect. The origin was elsewhere.

In the first century CE, Roman explorers attempted to find the source of the Nile. However, they only reached the swamplands of modern-day southern Sudan. Later explorers would also be unsuccessful.

Two of the most ambitious explorers were Richard Burton and John Hanning Speke. They both served in the British Indian Army. Burton was known to be adventurous and unpredictable. He was also highly skilled and adept at learning foreign languages. Although Speke loved adventure and exploration as well, he was different from Burton. He did not want to adopt the local customs when exploring. Speke could be arrogant, at times; he was known to treat the people working for him harshly. Burton, on the other hand, enjoyed learning native languages and practices.

In 1856, the Royal Geographical Society commissioned Burton and Speke to find the source of the Nile. They set off in 1857 on a long and grueling journey. They endured illness, pain, attack by a native tribe, and great hardship, but in 1858 they reached Lake Tanganyika. However, the difficulty of the trip had caused many of the men they had hired to desert them. The men that were left, including Burton and Speke, were also ill and running out of money. At the time, some considered Lake

What is paragraph 6 mainly about?

Which details from this passage belong in a summary of that passage?

Tanganyika a possible source of the Nile. However, the explorers were unable to complete their exploration of the lake.

After Burton determined that he was physically unable to continue, Speke went on alone, reaching Lake N'yanza in 1859. After checking his notes and other research, Speke convinced himself that this lake was the source of the Nile. He renamed it Lake Victoria, after the British queen. Speke then returned home and publicly announced his discovery. However, Burton questioned Speke's findings. He argued that Speke had not followed the course of the river far enough to be certain. And, upon examining a map, Burton found that the river, in fact, probably ended elsewhere.

Their disagreement started a prolonged and heated public debate. In 1864, the two explorers agreed to present their theories before the British Association for the Advancement of Science. The members of the Association would decide who was correct. However, in a tragic incident that still causes controversy, Speke accidentally shot himself while hunting on the day before the debate.

Today, the Nile's source is still a bit of a mystery. The complex geography still causes debate about the true source. In 2006, a group of explorers claimed that they had reached the true source of the Nile: a stream in the Nyungwe forest in Rwanda. Lake Victoria, which is fed by a number of rivers, is not considered the source currently. However, it is one of the main reservoirs the Nile feeds near its beginning, so Speke was not so far off.

The Nile is truly one of the great rivers of the world. As we continue exploring it, we will continue to make remarkable discoveries.

Answer the following questions.

1. What is the BEST summary of paragraph 1?

   A. The people and wildlife of the Nile River region have taught us a great deal.

   B. Today, the Nile River flows from east-central Africa to the Mediterranean Sea.

   C. We have learned a lot about the Nile River and the people and wildlife connected to it.

   D. We now know that the Nile River is the longest river in the world.

2. Which detail from paragraph 4 should NOT be included in a summary of the paragraph?

   A. Burton was skilled and learned languages easily.

   B. Speke and Burton had different personalities.

   C. Burton and Speke were English explorers.

   D. Burton and Speke served in the British Indian Army.

3. Which summary of paragraph 5 contains inaccurate information?

   A. Burton and Speke's long and difficult journey to find the source of the Nile was made worse by illness and lack of money.

   B. Burton and Speke joined the Royal Geographical Society in 1856 before leaving to find the source of the Nile.

   C. Due to various unfortunate circumstances, Speke and Burton were unable to fully explore Lake Tanganyika.

   D. Speke and Burton traveled to Lake Tanganyika, a candidate for the source of the Nile.

4. What information belongs in a summary of paragraph 7?

   A. Speke's death before the debate

   B. the reason Speke was hunting

   C. how Burton felt about Speke's death

   D. the history of the Science Association

5. Write a summary of paragraph 6.

   _____

   _____

   _____

   _____

Use the Reading Guide to help you understand the passage.

Reading Guide

As you read, reflect on the big ideas that help you understand what the passage is mainly about.

What details from paragraph 2 would you include in a summary describing the black rhino?

Which details in paragraph 3 would you leave out of a summary?

The Black Rhino

Once seriously threatened, the black rhinoceros, or black rhino, is an example of how the hunting and poaching of animals for money can lead to possible extinction. Many people who live in areas with black rhinos believe that the rhino's horns can cure diseases. The rhinos are hunted, and their horns are sold for a lot of money. But conservationists are working to help save the black rhino and increase its population. This is welcome news because the black rhino is a unique animal with many interesting characteristics.

A very large animal, the black rhino can weigh between 1,500 and 2,900 pounds and can measure five feet high at its shoulders. When you look at black rhinos, you'll notice that they are really gray, not black. It isn't clear why they have the name "black" rhino, though some think it is because their skin looks very dark after they have bathed in water or mud. They have two horns, which are used for protection or defense.

Interestingly, black rhinos can live in areas where water doesn't flow, such as areas with standing ponds or lakes. Because they don't depend on flowing water, black rhinos live in various habitats, such as forests, in low and high altitudes. They mostly live on plains, which are large land areas with few trees, or in savannas, which are flat, grassy areas in tropical or subtropical regions.

Though they call grassy lands home, black rhinos do not typically rely on grass for their nutritional needs. Instead, they are picky eaters and choose to browse for plants that grow in dry areas, eating leaves and twigs from trees and bushes. They prefer to eat in the near-darkness, grazing at dusk or dawn. They search for water in dry riverbeds and ponds, digging underground. They prefer to spend the sunny days in water holes or mud holes. The water and mud cool them and keep insects away.

As you read a detail, think about whether or not it belongs in a summary of the text. It may not belong—even if the detail is more interesting than other details in the text.

What is paragraph 6 mainly about?

Would you include your own feelings about black rhino conservation in a summary of paragraph 7? Why or why not?

Black rhinos are solitary, which means they don't travel in packs or groups. Of course, female rhinos stay with their young until the baby rhinos are about three years old. Rhinos do socialize regularly in small groups for a short time. They communicate by movements of tails and ears, as well as by a variety of snorts. Another interesting trait of the black rhino is its incredibly strong senses of hearing and smell. It is easily angered and will often charge when it encounters a strange noise or an unfamiliar smell it finds threatening. As you can imagine, their size makes them formidable opponents. You wouldn't want to be facing a black rhino charge.

Around 1900, the black rhino populations were calculated at more than one million. These large animals roamed through a majority of savannas and plains in sub-Saharan Africa, which is the area south of the Sahara Desert. However, poachers—people who hunt illegally for profit—have reduced the numbers of black rhinos dramatically. By 1995, some calculated the black rhino population at a little more than 2,400. The result was an increase in conservation efforts.

Today, though the black rhino is still classified as endangered, its population is on the rise. The black rhino used to cover an enormous range of land, but now the animals live in much smaller areas designated as parks and reserves. These areas are protected, and the black rhinos are guarded from hunters. While these controlled populations are safe, conservationists still worry about the wild black rhinos that live in larger reserves in South Africa and Namibia. Though population levels are around 4,800 today, there is still a lot of work to be done to safeguard the black rhino from extinction.

Answer the following questions.

6. Read paragraph 1 of the passage. Which detail would be BEST to omit from a summary of the paragraph? Underline the sentence containing the detail.

---

7. **Use your answer to Part A to answer Part B.**

Part A

Which of the following BEST summarizes paragraph 5?

A. Black rhinos prefer to live alone and are quick to defend themselves.

B. Female rhinos raise their young until the babies are three years old.

C. A strong sense of smell and hearing helps black rhinos locate each other.

D. One reason that the black rhino is in danger is that it does not defend itself well.

Part B

Circle the two details from the paragraph that BEST support the answer to Part A.

A. "Of course, female rhinos stay with their young until the baby rhinos are about three years old."

B. "Black rhinos are solitary, which means they don't travel in packs or groups."

C. "It is easily angered and will often charge when it encounters a strange noise or an unfamiliar smell it finds threatening."

D. "Another interesting trait of the black rhino is its incredibly strong senses of hearing and smell."

E. "They communicate by movements of tails and ears, as well as by a variety of snorts."

F. "As you can imagine, their size makes them formidable opponents."

8. **Use your answer to Part A to answer Part B.**

Below are three ideas from the passage.

Ideas	Black rhinos are solitary creatures that can live in a variety of areas.
	Although considered endangered, the black rhino is a unique animal with interesting traits and characteristics.
	Today, conservationists are protecting rhino populations within parks and reserves.

Part A

Circle the idea that would be MOST important to include in a summary of the passage.

Part B

Circle three details within the passage that BEST support the idea you circled in Part A.

---

9. **Use your answer to Part A to answer Part B.**

Part A

Which of the following presents the LEAST objective summary of paragraph 7?

A. Although conservations are still worried, they believe that they have begun to increase at least some of the black rhino population.

B. The black rhino population is on the rise, thanks to the work of conservationists who have protected the rhino in controlled environments.

C. For the most part, black rhino populations are concentrated into smaller, controlled areas.

D. People should worry about the rhino population because there is still much to be done before conservationists consider the animal to be no longer endangered.

Part B

Revise the summary you chose in Part A so that it is stated objectively.

_____

_____

_____

11 Arguments and Author's Point of View

RI.8.1, RI.8.2, RI.8.5, RI.8.6, RI.8.8, RI.8.9, RI.8.10, RH.8.6, RH.8.10, RST.8.5, RST.8.10

Getting the Idea

An **argument** is an attempt to persuade someone on a topic open to debate. When authors write arguments, they try to convince readers to think or act in a certain way. An argument reflects the author's **point of view**, or attitude toward the subject. Arguments are based on opinions supported with facts and evidence. Each part of the argument should support the main purpose of the text.

Arguments typically begin with a claim. The **claim** is a statement of the author's point of view. Although it may be presented as a fact, it is an opinion that the author must prove in his or her argument. The claim must be based on solid reasoning; it must be clear that the writer has thought through the reasons for making a particular claim. Further, the evidence an author uses should be directly connected to the claim; there should also be enough evidence to offer support. Evidence that does not support a claim or is irrelevant can hurt an argument. For example, an author writes the following:

Watching too much television is harmful to children.

The author would then write the paragraph below to back up this claim.

Studies indicate that children who watch too much television earn lower grades in school. Television reduces their homework and study time. In addition, other research shows that kids tend to eat unhealthy snacks when they watch television, so their health is also at risk. Many kids like cheesy snacks—who would possibly know why? Lower grades can hurt a student's future, and we all know what kind of adults television lovers turn into.

You should notice two things. Go to the third sentence first: the author explains why lower grades and poor health, possible effects of too much television, are problems. Before that sentence, though, he supports this explanation with facts from studies. The sentence about cheesy snacks is an example of irrelevant evidence; the author doesn't, and can't, connect it with the main claim. Also, the phrase beginning "we all know" in the last sentence is called **loaded language** because it reveals the author's feelings.

Good writers will also acknowledge arguments that oppose their claims. This might seem strange—after all, why would you want to include an opinion that differs from yours? Writers include conflicting arguments because they know that readers might think of opposing arguments as they read, and they want to address those points. The writer from the earlier paragraph might have gone on to say this:

> Some would say that students can learn quite a bit by watching high-quality television shows and that it is unfair to assume that any student-age person who watches television is watching trash. These points might be true. This, however, is not the point. No one could argue that focusing on your schoolwork doesn't help academic performance or that reading in a focused way isn't good for your mind.

Notice that the writer acknowledges that opposing arguments are valid and then introduces a similarly valid argument in response. A bad writer would simply insult the opposing argument—which automatically weakens his or her position.

Thinking It Through

Read the following paragraph, and then answer the question that follows.

> Our school should offer more rigorous science classes. The biology unit of our class only includes one dissection. The chemistry section teaches very little about subjects like microbiology or genetics. Additionally, the way it's taught is very dull. The teacher simply reads the book, and there is never any discussion of how science relates to the real world. Also, we're missing the opportunity to mix skills in our science classes. To really learn biology or chemistry, you have to use reading skills to analyze what's on the page in the textbook. You also have to use math skills for areas like chemistry. A change to our science class would be very beneficial for me and for other students.

Write a specific reason or example the author supplies to support his claim.

_____

_____

HINT   There are two main points the author uses as supports—can you find them?

 DISCUSS   Do you think the author's argument is convincing?

Coached Example

Read the passage and answer the questions.

The Inca Empire was one of the greatest empires the world has ever seen. Scholars believe that these South American Indians migrated to the Cuzco Valley in southeastern Peru around 1200 CE. The Incas were organized and had great leadership. They were excellent farmers. They built an irrigation system in the desert. They even built paved roads. They formed a powerful army and conquered nearby villages. The Incas expanded their territory, at one point controlling most of South America.

Despite the vastness and strength of their empire, the Incas were no match for the Spanish conquistadors. The conquistadors came to the Americas in search of fortune. Their greed, ruthlessness, and contempt for native cultures proved deadly for the Incas. However, nothing was more deadly than the smallpox with which the conquistadors infected the Incas. By 1535, the conquistadors had wiped out the Inca Empire, needlessly destroying a grand civilization.

---

1. Which sentence from the passage is a claim by the author?

   A. "Scholars believe that these South American Indians migrated to the Cuzco Valley in southeastern Peru around 1200 CE."

   B. "The Incas expanded their territory, at one point controlling most of South America."

   C. "The conquistadors came to the Americas in search of fortune."

   D. "The Inca Empire was one of the greatest empires the world has ever seen."

   HINT Look for the sentence that contains an opinion the author must prove.

2. Which sentence BEST states the author's point of view?

   A. The Incas were even worse conquerors than the Spanish.

   B. The Incas were not efficient in managing their empire.

   C. The Spanish conquistadors were cruel and selfish.

   D. The Spanish conquistadors respected the Incas.

   HINT Check each answer choice against the passage.

Lesson Practice

Use the Reading Guide to help you understand the passage.

Reading Guide

How is the author's viewpoint revealed in paragraphs 1 and 2?

Where in the passage does the author state opinions?

Don't Touch That Dial!

Where would we be without our remote controls? Today, it seems that almost every electronic device comes with a remote. TVs, DVRs, audio systems, even air conditioners can be controlled from across the room. All we have to do is put in the batteries—and sometimes they're included when you purchase the product!

Most of us can't imagine watching TV without being able to change the channel from the comfort of our seat. The invention of the remote control revolutionized the way we watch television. Sadly, the remote control is also a small symbol of the general laziness of modern society.

How did we get here? Our path to laziness began more than one hundred years ago, with the work of Nikola Tesla. Tesla invented one of the earliest versions of the remote control in 1898, though he wasn't intending it for lazy people. Tesla built a pair of radio-controlled six-foot iron boats, powered by an electric battery Tesla designed himself. He sent commands to a radio-mechanical receiver on the boats with a wireless transmitter. The boats' features, including diving rudders and electric lights, were remotely controlled. When people first heard about the boat, they didn't believe such a thing could exist. Tesla then did a demonstration of the remotely controlled boat in New York City. Who knew his discovery would lead to hours on the couch?

In 1950, the Zenith Radio Corporation invented the first television remote control. Correctly called "Lazy Bones," the device turned the television on and off and changed the channel. Although TV viewers could do this from the couch, the remote control was not wireless. The Lazy Bones was attached to the TV by a cable. Unfortunately, people often tripped over the thick cable. Also, Lazy Bones was awkwardly shaped and difficult to handle. Therefore, even though the Lazy Bones was convenient, it was not popular. If it took so much work to use, clearly the people likely to buy it wouldn't be interested!

In another five years, our fate as a world of couch potatoes was sealed. This is when Eugene Polley, an engineer for Zenith, invented the first wireless remote control. It was called the

As you read this passage, look for words that state or overstate the author's feelings. We typically call this loaded language.

Which facts in the passage support the claim that early remote control devices were not very effective?

"Flashmatic." The Flashmatic was basically a flashlight, which a viewer would shine on photocells in the corners of the TV screen. These activated the picture, sound, and channel controls. Like the remote that preceded it, the Flashmatic had flaws. Since the TV responded to light, sunlight sometimes changed the channel. Additionally, the light beam had to be pointed very precisely. So, it was not a workable design. However, we kept searching for a solution. What would our weekends and vacations be without it?

Finally, in 1956, Robert Adler, another Zenith engineer, invented a wireless remote control that worked. Adler's invention has made a significant difference in the way we live, though it might not be a positive difference. His invention was called the "Zenith Space Command." Adler's remote worked with ultrasound waves and used no batteries. It was powered by four aluminum rods inside the remote. When a viewer pressed one of the remote's buttons, a rod was struck. When struck, the rods emitted high-frequency sounds. The sounds traveled through the air to a receiver in the TV. When the receiver "heard" the sounds, it interpreted them as basic commands, such as on/off, change channel, etc. The downside to the Space Command was that it was big and raised the price of a television set by 30 percent. Of course, this may have been a slick way for the company to make money. Transistor technology eventually enabled the development of battery-operated, handheld remotes.

Today's remote controls usually use infrared technology. They work with low-frequency light beams that the human eye cannot see. There is no denying that they are convenient. The problem is that they are yet another way for people to avoid physical activity. Think about it. Is it so hard to get up and change the channel? Surely we don't want our precious children to become couch potatoes like us. It is no coincidence that the first remote control was called "Lazy Bones." We can sit for five hours in front of the TV set without ever getting up.

The remote control changed the way we watch television. Unfortunately, this device proves that change is not always a good thing.

Answer the following questions.

1. What is the author's main argument?

   A. TV remote controls make it easier for people to change the channel.

   B. TV remote controls contribute to people's lack of physical activity.

   C. People find it impossible to function without their electronic devices.

   D. Today's TV remote controls are a huge technological improvement over early models.

2. Read this sentence from the passage.

   Of course, this may have been a <u>slick</u> way for the company to make money.

   The author uses the word <u>slick</u> to suggest that the company

   A. may have tried to take advantage of consumers.

   B. was actually losing money on the product.

   C. found a creative way to raise profits.

   D. handled financial matters honestly.

3. Which sentence would NOT support the author's argument?

   A. Universal remote controls are the worst because they can control most electronic devices regardless of the model.

   B. Laziness is often learned at a young age, and remote controls must share the blame for that.

   C. Some studies show that the average American household spends at least eight hours a day in front of the television set.

   D. Remote controls make it easier for people to run on the treadmill or ride a stationary bike and watch TV at the same time.

4. Which sentence from the passage is an example of loaded language?

   A. "Surely we don't want our precious children to become couch potatoes like us."

   B. "There is no denying that they are convenient."

   C. "The problem is that they are yet another way for people to avoid physical activity."

   D. "The Flashmatic was basically a flashlight, which a viewer would shine on photocells in the corners of the TV screen."

5. Write a summary of paragraph 6.

   _____

   _____

   _____

Use the Reading Guide to help you understand the passage.

Reading Guide

What claim does the author express in the first sentence in paragraph 2?

How does the author support that claim with evidence?

As you read, look for loaded language that reveals the author's feelings. How does it make you respond emotionally? How does it affect your evaluation of the author's argument?

Genetically Engineered Foods? Not So Fast!

Americans today are more concerned than ever with food safety. The focus is now on foods that contain ingredients from genetically engineered crops. Are these foods dangerous or safe? On one side of the debate are corporations with a stake in genetically modified foods. These corporations have spent millions of dollars to stop the passing of laws restricting the industry. On the other side: those who claim that the foods have the potential to make millions sick. Look past both sides, however, and one argument is clear: Genetically engineered foods are not safe because they are not well regulated and because the public is woefully uninformed about them.

Produced since the 1990s, genetically modified foods are now a major part of the American food supply. Between 60 percent and 70 percent of the processed foods sold in grocery stores in the U.S. have some ingredients that are genetically modified. These frankenfoods include cereals, snack foods, soda, and foods containing soy or cottonseed and canola oils. But only 52 percent of Americans know about these foods, and only 26 percent think they have eaten them.

To create these foods, plants are modified in the laboratory. Genes from other species are inserted to make the plants more resistant to disease, pesticides, and drought. Admittedly, the process is beneficial in a number of ways. Farmers who use modified seeds from these plants don't have to treat their fields with as much pesticide. As a result, the environment is cleaner, and the plants produce more. More crops means more food to feed the world's growing population.

All of this sounds great, but who is watching over this process to make sure there are no mistakes or accidents? Strangely, the corporations that control—and profit from—this technology also administer the safety tests. That's not much of a motivation to admit there are problems. A study done in 2003 also showed that biotech companies don't always follow the rules for testing their own products.

Remember that one way
to evaluate the author's
argument is to look for
acknowledgment of and
response to opposing
claims.

As you read, think about
the relevance of the
evidence that the author
includes. Does each piece
of evidence support a
specific claim or reason?

After you've read the
argument, think about how
well the author supported
the overall claim. Are you
convinced that the claim
is valid?

And clearly testing is needed, as there are real risks associated with eating foods that have been genetically modified. One risk is that allergens and toxins will be added to the food supply. For example, if a fish gene is introduced into a plant to create resistance to frost, someone who is allergic to fish could have a severe reaction.

Another fear is contamination of nongenetically modified foods and crops, resistance to antibiotics, and negative effects on nutrients. In 2000, a protein linked to dangerous allergic reactions turned up in food products on store shelves. One of these products was corn taco shells, which many people enjoy. Many people became ill when corn crops were accidentally contaminated by genetically modified seed. Many scientists also admit that the long-term effects are not known. There are still a lot of questions and no answers.

The U.S. government says these foods are safe. It supports the claim that genetically engineered crops resist disease better and have higher yields. Not surprisingly, however, the U.S. also happens to be the largest producer of these modified crops. Europe doesn't want these foods. They believe the risks are too great. They say that the big biotech companies are the only ones that benefit in their goal to dominate the world's food supply. The ones who lose are the regular farmers who grow food the old-fashioned way.

Europe has taken the step of requiring that all products with genetically modified ingredients say so on the label. Over half of Americans surveyed want labels in the U.S. as well. So far, the corporations have resisted. If these foods are so safe, why won't the corporations say so on a food box? By being truthful, companies may encourage people to try these products and not reject them as corporations fear. Changes may be coming in the future as public protests have encouraged some companies to not use modified crops. Some stores now won't sell modified products without labels. But at the moment, it seems that for the makers of these foods, it's more about the money and less about nutrition, health, or public safety.

Answer the following questions.

6. **Use your answer to Part A to answer Part B.**

   Part A

   Below are claims the author makes about genetically modified foods. Circle the claim that BEST expresses the author's overall point of view within the passage.

Claims	Genetically modified foods are now a major part of the American food supply.
	Biotech companies are the big winners in the race to dominate the world's food supply.
	Lack of regulation and an uninformed public are two big issues concerning genetically modified foods.

   Part B

   Underline two pieces of evidence in the passage that the author includes to support the claim you circled in Part A.

   _____

7. **Use your answer to Part A to answer Part B.**

   Part A

   Read paragraph 2 from the passage. Circle an example of loaded language in the paragraph.

   Part B

   On the lines, explain why the language you circled might produce an emotional response in readers.

   _____

   _____

   _____

   _____

   _____

8. Read paragraph 6 of the passage. Circle one example of irrelevant evidence in the paragraph.

_____

9. **Use your answer to Part A to answer Part B.**

Part A

Read each sentence from the passage. Decide whether it supports the author's point of view or a conflicting viewpoint. Write the sentence in the correct column.

The U.S. government says these foods are safe. / More crops mean more food to feed the world's growing population. / If these foods are so safe, why won't the corporations say so on a food box? / Strangely, the corporations that control—and profit from—this technology also administer the safety tests.

Author's Point of View	Conflicting Viewpoint
_____	_____
_____	_____
_____	_____
_____	_____

Part B

Choose one sentence you included in Conflicting Viewpoint. On the lines below, explain how the author responded to that conflicting point of view.

_____

_____

_____

_____

_____

12 Compare and Contrast

RI.8.1, RI.8.3, RI.8.5, RI.8.6, RI.8.9, RI.8.10, RH.8.1, RH.8.2, RH.8.5, RH.8.9, RH.8.10, RST.8.9, RST.8.10

Getting the Idea

Most of the time, you read and respond to texts individually. Sometimes you need to analyze how different texts relate to each other. When you **compare** texts, you study their similarities. When you **contrast** texts, you evaluate their differences.

Authors often write about the same topic. Think, for example, of how many books and articles have been written about the civil rights movement. Obviously, these texts will have elements in common. Most of the basic facts, dates, and events will be the same. These are points of comparison. However, different authors will approach this topic differently, and this is where the contrast comes in. For instance, one author might focus on certain people who played key roles in the movement. Another author might analyze the effects of the movement on modern society. So, even though the authors' topics are both connected to the civil rights movement, their texts are substantially different.

In fact, an author's **point of view**, or opinion about a subject, can have a major influence on his or her interpretation of the facts. This is especially true when the topic is controversial. For example, some historians credit the atomic bomb with ending World War II and saving lives. Other historians believe that dropping the bomb on Japan was unnecessary and excessive. These different views will be reflected in the authors' texts. Hopefully, the authors will address points of view that are different from their own, as well; this helps to make a discussion more believable and lets readers know that an author has thought deeply about a subject.

Another point of comparison and contrast is the **author's purpose**. Read the two paragraphs below.

> The United States Supreme Court was established in 1789. It consists of one chief justice and eight associate justices. It hears cases that involve constitutional matters.

> The United States Supreme Court has too much power. They hear some cases while ignoring others. Nine people should not make rulings that affect millions.

The purpose of the first paragraph is to inform, with facts. The purpose of the second paragraph is to persuade. It expresses opinions.

Authors might also compare and contrast within a text. For example, in an article comparing Civil War generals Robert E. Lee and Ulysses S. Grant, the author's point of view and purpose shape the article. She might use several approaches: for example, she might make an analogy showing their historical relationship to each other.

As a student, you read **primary** and **secondary sources**, comparing and contrasting as you work with them. A letter written from a Civil War hospital by a nurse is a primary source, written at the time an event occurred; an article about the hospital by a historian is a secondary source, written after the fact. A biography of Benjamin Franklin, for instance, might describe his experiments with electricity one way, while his autobiography might describe them differently. The autobiography is a primary source, and the biography is a secondary source.

Thinking It Through

Read the following paragraphs, and then answer the question that follows.

People sometimes confuse dolphins with porpoises. Both dolphins and porpoises are mammals, meaning that they produce milk to feed their young. Both have lungs and breathe air. Both animals have streamlined bodies and blowholes.

One of the biggest differences is their size. Porpoises are rarely longer than seven feet long, whereas dolphins can be longer than ten feet. Dolphins also have a prominent rostrum, or beak, and porpoises don't. Dolphins live longer than porpoises, as well.

dolphin

porpoise

How does the author organize the two paragraphs in order to compare dolphins and porpoises?

_____

_____

_____

 Look at how each paragraph is structured.

💬 **DISCUSS**   Is this passage a primary or secondary source? Explain.

Coached Example

Read the passages and answer the questions.

The Black Death

During the 1300s, a deadly plague known as the Black Death wiped out approximately one-third of the European population, or about twenty-five million people. Although there is some debate as to the source of the epidemic, many think the disease was carried by fleas on the bodies of diseased rats. The plague was highly contagious, a situation made worse by the crowded living conditions and poor sanitation in much of medieval Europe.

Once infected, a person experienced painful and terrible symptoms and died within days. Because it was so contagious, entire families became sick with the illness. People soon learned that even casual contact with an infected person could be deadly. Even the mention of the plague could fill people with terror.

While no one was immune to the plague, wealthy people were sometimes able to escape its reach by retreating to secluded country estates. For the rest of medieval society, staying healthy was mostly a matter of luck. At the time, there was no cure, no explanation of its causes—the plague simply swept over the land, terrifying the population.

excerpted and adapted from

The Black Death of 1348 and 1349
by Francis Aidan Gasquet

A most deadly pestilence sprang up over the entire island. It happened that in the month of October…1347… twelve Genoese ships… put into the port of Messina, bringing with them such a sickness clinging to their very bones that, did anyone speak to them, he was directly struck with a mortal sickness from which there was no escape. …Seeing what a calamity of sudden death had come to them by the arrival of the Genoese, the people of Messina drove them in all haste from their city and port. But the sickness remained and a terrible mortality ensued. The one thought in the mind of all was how to avoid the infection. The father abandoned the sick son; magistrates and notaries refused to come and make the wills of the dying. …The houses of the dead were left open and unguarded with their jewels, money, and valuables; if anyone wished to enter there.

1. The authors' main purpose in BOTH passages is to

    A. inform the reader about the causes of the plague.

    B. explain the impact of the plague on the people.

    C. persuade the reader to learn more about the plague.

    D. describe the physical symptoms of the plague.

    HINT The correct answer is true for both passages.

2. Which idea is mentioned in BOTH passages?

    A. possible treatments for the plague

    B. officials refusing to do their jobs

    C. people's attempts to avoid infection

    D. the number of people who died

    HINT Check each answer choice to see which idea appears in both passages.

3. Explain how the primary source approaches the same topic differently from the secondary source.

    _____

    _____

    _____

    _____

    HINT Think about the details that the authors chose to include.

Lesson Practice

Use the Reading Guides to help you understand the passages.

Reading Guide

Think about the author's purpose for writing this passage.

What is the author's point of view on Albert Lutuli?

How does Lutuli compare to other political leaders you have read about?

A Life Well Lived: Albert John Lutuli

Many people may not have heard of Albert John Lutuli, but he was a modern-day hero worthy of recognition.

Lutuli was born in the African country of Rhodesia in 1898. His father, a missionary, died when Lutuli was a young boy. His mother took him to live in the Groutville region of South Africa, with Lutuli's uncle, who was the chief of Groutville. Lutuli's mother made sure he received an education. Eventually, Lutuli became a teacher at Adams College. He had a strong belief in the value of education and that all children should be educated equally, regardless of color. In 1933, he was elected president of the African Teacher's Association.

When Lutuli's uncle died, Lutuli was next in line to become chief of Groutville. Lutuli wasn't sure he wanted to assume the responsibility. It would mean giving up his job and the regular income that came with it. But in 1936, he accepted his role as chief of a tribe of five thousand people.

In that same year, the South African government imposed severe restrictions on nonwhites. Many of their freedoms were taken away from them, including their right to vote. The government adopted the policy of apartheid, or racial segregation, in 1948. In the process, discriminatory laws were enacted. Lutuli joined the African National Congress (ANC), an African liberation movement, hoping to reestablish the rights of his people.

In the years that followed, Lutuli led nonviolent campaigns against apartheid. Although Lutuli was deeply religious and a man of peace, his compaigns were effective and he was a threat to the government. In 1952, the government demanded that he leave the ANC or resign as tribal chief. When Lutuli refused to do either one, the government fired him from his chieftainship. Later that year, Lutuli was elected president-general of the ANC. The government imposed a series of restrictions on Lutuli, in the hopes of limiting his popularity. He was arrested multiple times and charged with treason, but he never gave up his fight for freedom.

In 1960, Albert Lutuli was awarded the Nobel Peace Prize. He died six years later, having helped lay the groundwork for the end of apartheid.

A Man of Peace

Reading Guide

When did Gandhi experience an awakening?

What qualities did Gandhi share with Lutuli?

His name will always be associated with nonviolence, and he was an inspiration to Martin Luther King Jr. His quiet yet forceful fight for justice remains one of the great stories of our time. His name, of course, was Mohandas Gandhi.

Gandhi was born into a wealthy family in Porbandar, India, on October 2, 1869. Although he wanted to be a doctor, his father pushed him to study law. In 1888, Gandhi left for England to pursue his studies. Upon returning to India, he briefly served as lawyer for the prince of Porbandar.

In 1893, Gandhi traveled to South Africa, where he had accepted a job offer. While sitting in the first-class compartment of the train, Gandhi suffered a humiliating experience. A white man complained about sharing the compartment with a man of color, and Gandhi was forced off the train.

This moment would have a significant impact on Gandhi's life. He became determined to end racial discrimination. Soon after this incident, Gandhi organized a meeting with other Indians in South Africa, where he spoke against racial injustice and the treatment of Indians by whites. Thus began his campaign to improve the legal status of Indians in South Africa. This cause would keep him in South Africa until 1914.

During this period, Gandhi changed greatly and learned much about himself. He got rid of his expensive possessions and adopted a simpler life, doing menial chores and serving others. He developed the concept of *Satyagraha*, or soul force, which he described as "a quiet and irresistible pursuit of truth." He would come to live by this concept, even when his work led to his arrest.

Gandhi's social activism grew in power and scope. In 1907, he urged Indians in South Africa to disobey the law that required all Indians to be registered and fingerprinted. He returned to India in early 1915, where he began his struggle to liberate India from British control. In 1930, to protest a British tax on salt used by Indians, Gandhi led his famous salt march to the sea. Thousands of marchers walked nearly 250 miles to the ocean, where Gandhi broke the law by picking up salt crystals from the beach and boiling them to make salt grains.

Gandhi's fight for social justice lasted until his assassination in 1948. Remarkably, although Gandhi was nominated for the Nobel Peace Prize five times, he was never selected. Still, his impact on India would live forever.

Answer the following questions.

1. A key similarity between Lutuli and Gandhi is that they BOTH

   A. fought for racial equality in South Africa.

   B. organized protest marches in India.

   C. were born into wealthy families.

   D. adopted a totally new way of life.

2. A central difference between Lutuli and Gandhi was their

   A. sense of justice.

   B. determination.

   C. beliefs.

   D. race.

3. Based on both passages, which statement is true?

   A. Gandhi and Lutuli were elected chief of their tribes.

   B. Neither Gandhi nor Lutuli were a threat to the government.

   C. Like Gandhi, Lutuli pursued studies in law.

   D. Lutuli and Gandhi were both arrested for their activism.

4. Both Gandhi and Lutuli

   A. were presidents of organizations.

   B. won the Nobel Peace Prize.

   C. were educated men.

   D. traveled to England.

5. Based on the passages, explain why both Lutuli and Gandhi would be an inspiration to civil rights leader Martin Luther King Jr. Use examples from the passages in your response.

   _____

   _____

   _____

   _____

Reading Guide

What information is presented in these resolutions?

Consider how IAU Resolution B5 compares and contrasts planets and dwarf planets.

Are these primary or secondary sources? How do you know?

excerpted from

IAU Resolution B5:
Definition of a Planet in the Solar System

submitted by the International Astronomical Union, August 2006

Contemporary observations are changing our understanding of planetary systems, and it is important that our nomenclature for objects reflect our current understanding. . . . The word "planet" originally described "wanderers" that were known only as moving lights in the sky. Recent discoveries lead us to create a new definition, which we can make using currently available scientific information.

The IAU therefore resolves that planets and other bodies, except satellites, in our Solar System be defined into three distinct categories in the following way:

(1) A planet[1] is a celestial body that
  (a) is in orbit around the Sun,
  (b) has sufficient mass for its self-gravity to overcome rigid body forces so that it assumes a hydrostatic equilibrium (nearly round) shape, and
  (c) has cleared the neighbourhood around its orbit.

(2) A "dwarf planet" is a celestial body that
  (a) is in orbit around the Sun,
  (b) has sufficient mass for its self-gravity to overcome rigid body forces so that it assumes a hydrostatic equilibrium (nearly round) shape[2],
  (c) has not cleared the neighbourhood around its orbit, and
  (d) is not a satellite.

(3) All other objects[3], except satellites, orbiting the Sun shall be referred to collectively as "Small Solar System Bodies."

[1] The eight planets: Mercury, Venus, Earth, Mars, Jupiter, Saturn, Uranus, and Neptune.

[2] An IAU process will assign borderline objects to the dwarf planet or to another category.

[3] These currently include most of the Solar System asteroids, most Trans-Neptunian Objects (TNOs), comets, and other small bodies.

IAU Resolution B6: Pluto

The IAU further resolves:

Pluto is a "dwarf planet" by the above definition and is recognized as the prototype of a new category of Trans-Neptunian Objects.

Dwarfing Pluto

Reading Guide

What is the author's point of view about Pluto's reclassification?

What similar ideas appear in this passage and the previous passage?

Pluto's demotion to dwarf planet status in 2006 through the International Astronomical Union (IAU) resolutions created a backlash among many interested in the classification of planets. The IAU is an organization of professional astronomers who meet regularly to support the science of astronomy. The group had reclassified Pluto on the basis of criteria that include its mass, its orbit, and its gravitational power. However, some people believe that these standards are misapplied or that the same criteria should be applied to other bodies in space.

When comparing its mass to the mass of objects around it, many agree that Pluto is worthy of reclassification. Its mass is less than one-tenth of the total mass of the other objects near its orbit. In comparison, Earth's mass is 1.7 million times the combined mass of all other objects in its neighborhood. This value is known as the planetary discriminant. Other objects in the solar system that have been classified as dwarf planets also have fractional planetary discriminants like Pluto's. Their mass is not significant enough to qualify as a planet. Neptune's discriminant value of 24,000 is the lowest of the eight planets.

Another reason the IAU reclassified Pluto is that it had not "cleared the neighborhood around its orbit." Pluto doesn't follow the same path around the sun as the planets. Instead, it follows the path of the Kuiper belt, an area of freezing objects that are billions of kilometers from our sun. Another dwarf planet, Eris, follows this same orbit. Scientists think there are hundreds of other dwarf planets circling the Kuiper belt that have yet to be identified.

When discussing Pluto's capability of moving other space objects in its orbit, such as asteroids, there is some disagreement. It is true that Pluto doesn't have a strong enough gravitational pull to drag other space bodies within its orbit. However, Earth, Mars, Jupiter, and Neptune don't have strong enough gravitational pulls either. These planets all have thousands of asteroids or other bodies in the area of their orbits that they have not pulled in. In fact, Neptune's and Pluto's orbits actually intersect, and Neptune has not influenced Pluto's orbit. Perhaps this will convince people that if Pluto is correctly categorized as a dwarf planet, other planets may need to be dwarfed as well.

Answer the following questions.

6. **Use your answer to Part A to answer Part B.**

    Part A

    Read paragraph 1 of "Dwarfing Pluto." Underline words or phrases that help you identify whether the passage is a primary or a secondary source.

    Part B

    On the lines below, identify the type of source and explain your reasoning.

    _____

    _____

    _____

7. Decide whether each item in the box refers to IAU Resolution B5/B6, to "Dwarfing Pluto," or to both sources. Write each item in the correct area on the diagram.

calls for further planetary classification	bodies are planets or dwarf planets
primary source	Neptune classified as a planet
secondary source	Neptune might not be a planet
Earth meets all classification criteria	criteria for planet classification

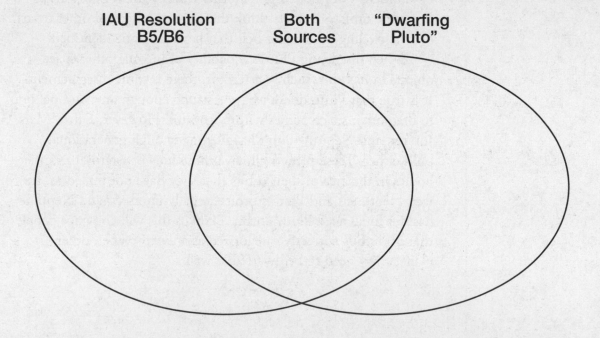

IAU Resolution B5/B6   Both Sources   "Dwarfing Pluto"

8. **Use your answer to Part A to answer Part B.**

    Part A

    Which of the following BEST states the author's point of view in "Dwarfing Pluto"?

    A. The reclassification of Pluto is the beginning of identifying other dwarf planets.

    B. The International Astronomical Union encourages the science of astronomy by professional astronomers, so reclassification is accurate.

    C. The standards used to reclassify Pluto may need to be applied to other planets that meet some of the same standards and were not reclassified.

    D. The criteria used to reclassify Pluto should be expanded upon to include the mass of space objects.

    Part B

    Which detail from "Dwarfing Pluto" BEST supports the answer to Part A?

    A. "However, Earth, Mars, Jupiter, and Neptune don't have strong enough gravitational pulls either."

    B. "It is true that Pluto doesn't have a strong enough gravitational pull to drag other space bodies within its orbit."

    C. "The group had reclassified Pluto on the basis of criteria that includes its mass, its orbit, and its gravitational power."

    D. "Pluto's demotion to dwarf planet status in 2006 through the International Astronomical Union (IAU) resolutions created a backlash…"

9. Which of the following ideas are presented in BOTH passages?

    A. The fact that there are no new or modern observations of the universe and space bodies has led to reclassifications of planets.

    B. The criteria presented by the IAU distinguishes the difference between a dwarf planet and a planet mostly on the basis of mass.

    C. Reclassifying all of the planets as dwarf planets will be the outcome of the IAU's resolutions.

    D. The IAU is an influential organization within the science of astronomy.

    E. Accurate standards applied to all space bodies will help astronomers classify space bodies correctly and lead to a better understanding of the universe.

    F. Three classifications for space bodies are unnecessary and should be modified so it is simpler to categorize objects in space.

13 Text Structures

RI.8.1, RI.8.5, RI.8.10, RH.8.3, RH.8.5, RH.8.10, RST.8.3, RST.8.6, RST.8.10

Getting the Idea

Authors arrange their texts using various **structures**, or patterns of organization. They choose a structure according to the content of the text. Sometimes authors present information sequentially. **Sequence** is the organization of information or events in the order in which they happen. For example, the experiment below tests the density of water.

1. First, fill two glass jars with three cups of water.

2. Place an egg in each jar. Record whether the eggs sink or float.

3. Next, add a teaspoon of sugar to one jar. Record whether this makes the egg float or sink. Then, add more sugar and record the results.

4. Add a teaspoon of salt to the other jar. Record whether this makes the egg float or sink. Add more salt and record your results.

5. Finally, compare the results when you add salt and sugar to the water.

The numbered steps in this experiment help the reader follow the instructions. In fact, sequence is the standard structure for texts like instruction manuals and cookbooks. After all, the author's purpose is usually to help readers perform the experiments themselves. Therefore, a clear sequence is important. Note that texts written in sequence often use key words like *first, then, next, after, last,* and *finally*.

Other texts use sequence as well. Read the following passage about Albert Einstein.

> Albert Einstein was born March 14, 1879, in Germany. He graduated from the Swiss Federal Polytechnic School in 1900 and married Mileva Maric in 1903. In 1905, he published his first paper on relativity. In 1915, he published his second paper on relativity, which established his worldwide reputation as a great scientist. In 1921, he was awarded the Nobel Prize. He died in the United States on April 18, 1955.

The author uses sequence in this passage because it is a biography, listing the events in Einstein's life in the order in which they occurred. A passage explaining how a bill becomes a law, for instance, would also be written in sequence.

Another text structure is cause and effect. A **cause** is the reason something happens, such as an event or action. An **effect** is what happens as a result of the event or action. Read the paragraph below.

> On January 10, 1901, the most powerful geyser of oil ever seen in the world gushed out of a drilling site at Spindletop Hill in southeastern Texas. It reached a height of over 150 feet and produced nearly one hundred thousand barrels of oil a day. This led to an oil industry boom in the area and the founding of many American oil companies.

The event, or cause, was the geyser of oil in Texas. The effects were an oil industry boom and the establishment of many American oil companies. Authors often use the cause-and-effect structure to analyze historical events or to explain the impact of technology on society.

Thinking It Through

Read the following paragraph, and then answer the question that follows.

When the U.S. stock market crashed in October 1929, the impact was immediate and devastating. Many banks closed. Investors lost all of their money. Massive numbers of people lost their jobs, leading to poverty, hunger, and homelessness. The economy was in shambles. To try to improve the desperate situation, the federal government established relief programs and created temporary public works employment. One of the programs created was the Works Progress Administration. The WPA's many projects, such as their public murals, made a lasting mark on our country and supported our economy.

List two effects of the stock market crash.

_____

_____

HINT   Think about what happened as a result of the crash.

Coached Example

Read the passage and answer the questions.

Static Electricity Experiment

Materials Needed:

a hard rubber or plastic comb

thread

small pieces of dry, O-shaped cereal

Steps:

1. Tie one piece of cereal to the end of a foot-long piece of thread.

2. Attach the other end of the thread to something that is not close to anything else.

3. Next, clean the comb well and dry it.

4. Now run the comb through long, dry hair a couple of times or rub the comb on a wool sweater or rug.

5. Gently and slowly, pass the comb near the cereal. It should move toward the comb to touch it. Hold the comb still until the cereal moves away on its own.

6. Finally, try to touch the comb to the cereal again. This time, it should move away as the comb comes near.

---

1. Which of these would likely cause the experiment to fail?

   A. passing the comb near the cereal

   B. using a supermarket brand cereal

   C. using a wet, dirty comb

   D. using colored thread

   HINT The steps in the experiment are very specific about how the materials are used.

2. AFTER cleaning and drying the comb, you should

   A. tie the cereal to the thread.

   B. move the comb near the cereal.

   C. run the comb through your hair.

   D. attach the thread to something not close to anything else.

   HINT Think about where you find static as you look for the answer to this question.

Lesson Practice

Use the Reading Guide to help you understand the passage.

Reading Guide

How do the different paragraphs use different text structures in this passage?

Why was it sometimes difficult to send messages from the battlefield?

Think about how actions cause effects in this passage.

Heroes with Wings

Pigeons aren't really very interesting to most people. Sure, some people like to sit in the park and feed them. But for the most part, there's just nothing special about the ordinary pigeon. Did you know, though, that pigeons played a key role in World War I? In fact, the pigeons of that war were far from ordinary. They actually saved lives.

Imagine being a soldier in the middle of a battle. You're running out of supplies, the enemy is approaching, and you need military backup—now! You don't have a two-way radio because that technology is not available yet. You're in the middle of nowhere, and you can't send a message by telegraph because the difficult terrain makes it impossible to set up a telegraph wire. To put it mildly, you are in a bad situation. During World War I, soldiers sometimes found themselves in situations like this. What did they do? They used their secret weapon—carrier pigeons.

Back then, the Army Signal Corps was responsible for making sure that messages between military units, or between the Army and the Navy, were delivered. Many of these messages were delivered in code, but some were delivered in other ways. When the United States entered World War I, British bird breeders donated six hundred pigeons to the Army Signal Corps. The birds would be used to deliver messages when it was not possible to do so by flag or field phone.

The system was simple but effective. When a field commander needed to send a message, he wrote it down on a piece of paper. Then, a Signal Corps officer brought over one of the trained carrier pigeons that accompanied soldiers into battle. They put the message into a small capsule, and then they tied the capsule to the bird's leg. Then, they tossed the bird into the air to fly home.

When Whittlesey gave a group of pigeons the wrong coordinates, what was the most likely effect?

Note the sequence of events in the last two paragraphs.

"Home" was a pigeon coop set up behind the lines. The pigeons were able to find the coop because they had a homing instinct. Animals that have a homing instinct know how to find their homes, no matter how far away those homes might be. When the pigeon landed in the coop, a bell would ring or a buzzer would sound, announcing the bird's return. Another Signal Corps officer would retrieve the message from the canister and then forward it via messenger, field phone, or telegraph to the appropriate people.

It was dangerous work being a carrier pigeon. Since enemy soldiers knew the birds carried important messages, they tried to shoot them down to keep the messages from being delivered.

The heroic actions of a carrier pigeon named "Cher Ami" (French for "dear friend") are the most well-known. On October 3, 1918, Major Charles Whittlesey and his men were in a battle with Germans in the Argonne Forest. Whittlesey and his American battalion had gone to Europe to aid France in the war. They were surrounded, running out of supplies, and under fierce attack. Their only way of getting help was to send a message by carrier pigeon. Major Whittlesey sent out several pigeons, but they were given the wrong coordinates. They went where they were told, but it was the wrong location. To make things worse, since the American commanders were unaware of the battalion's location, they were unintentionally firing on Whittlesey and his men. Whittlesey sent a desperate message with the only pigeon he had left—Cher Ami.

This time the bird was given the right coordinates. Cher Ami took off, bullets flying all around him. He flew twenty-five miles to deliver the vital message, even though he was badly wounded. He lost a leg but saved nearly two hundred men. The French gave the brave carrier pigeon the *Croix de Guerre*, a medal that is one of the country's highest honors. Cher Ami became an international hero—and proof that sometimes a pigeon is more than just a pigeon.

Answer the following questions.

1. Why did the British bird breeders MOST LIKELY donate six hundred pigeons to the U.S. Army Signals Corps?

    A. The British and Americans were allies in the war.

    B. The breeders did not have the room to keep so many birds.

    C. The pigeons were a symbol of peace in a time of war.

    D. The British no longer had to send messages by carrier pigeon.

2. What was the effect of the bell or buzzer sounding in the pigeon coup?

    A. The men knew it was time to feed the pigeon.

    B. An officer knew a pigeon had delivered a message.

    C. The infantrymen realized the enemy was nearby.

    D. The pigeons knew it was time to come home.

3. What happened before Major Whittlesey sent off Cher Ami with the message?

    A. Other pigeons were given the wrong coordinates.

    B. Cher Ami was wounded and lost a leg.

    C. Nearly two hundred men were saved.

    D. Cher Ami received a medal.

4. According to the passage, which of these was invented after World War I?

    A. the airplane

    B. the telegraph

    C. the two-way radio

    D. the field phone

5. Explain the effects of the use of carrier pigeons during World War I. Use examples from the passage in your response.

    _____

    _____

    _____

    _____

Duplicating any part of this book is prohibited by law.

Reading Guide What information does this passage provide readers? How does text structure help the author organize the information? Why is it important that a blogger understand his or her audience? As you read, look for keywords that signal a specific text structure. What signal words do you notice in paragraph 2?	## So, You Want to Start a Blog? Blogs have become one of the biggest and most popular forms of social media. There are many reasons why people create blogs. Many business owners have found that keeping a professional-looking blog helps them obtain customers and make money. Other people are more interested in writing conversationally and sharing information about things they enjoy or issues they feel strongly about. Still others blog to keep in touch with friends and family. Blog posts can be long or short, serious or funny, friendly or businesslike. In fact, blogging can be very much like sending e-mail. But before you can share your thoughts with the world of cyberspace, you have to create a blog. You might be surprised at just how easy it is to do! Before you begin to design your blog, you will need to think about why you are blogging. Businesses want to create a brand and earn money. For a social blog, decide whether your content will be light or serious, humorous, or about a specific topic. Figure out who you want your audience to be. Focusing your blog on a specific concept or idea will allow you to more easily choose a design that reflects your content. Once you know what you are blogging about, it's time to decide *how* you'll blog—and that means choosing a platform. A platform is the software application that allows you to create your blog site. It also maintains your blog. There are many platforms to choose from, such as Blogger, Tumblr, WordPress, SquareSpace, or TypePad. Choosing the right platform is an essential step in establishing yourself as a blogger. Since there are so many platforms out there to choose from, and since some are more challenging to use than others, you'll need to find a platform that will work for you and be appropriate for the content you want to create. Next, you need to create the perfect name for your blog. It is important to get the name right because it will become part of your domain name; once you have selected a name, it can be difficult to change. A domain name looks like this: www.mygreatblog.com. It will be the Web site address of your blog, so make sure it's something that is clear and easy for your readers to remember and access.

Remember that events in a series are not always described in the order in which they happen. As you read, use signal words to keep the order of the steps clear.

What causes and effects are described in paragraph 9?

You are almost ready to design your blog! But first, you need to choose a host, or area on the Web where you will store all your content. There are many hosts to choose from. Some are free, but you might have to put up with advertising in exchange. Others charge a monthly hosting cost ranging from $0.99 to about $5.00.

If you don't know much about Web design, one thing you can do is to use a theme, or existing blog template. The Internet is practically bursting with sites where you can select a theme. You may also be able to buy one through the platform application you have selected. You will be able to customize your theme as much as you like. You might also want to think about creating a logo.

Congratulations! You are now ready to create the content and launch your blog. You'll want to attract as many people as possible to read your blog, so engaging, well-written blog posts are a must. Think about what your audience will want to read. Once you have begun blogging, it's a good idea to keep to a schedule so you can publish posts at regular intervals and keep your readers coming back for more. That way, your blog has a better shot at becoming popular.

After your blog is established, you might want to work on bringing in new readers. Creating a profile on a social media site such as Facebook or Twitter can help you attract potential readers who share your interests.

All that is left now is to keep writing interesting posts to make visitors want to keep coming back. Writing great posts and generating readers are the keys to a fun and successful blog!

Answer the following questions.

6. **Use your answer to Part A to answer Part B.**

    Part A

    Read paragraph 1 of the passage. Then circle the text structure in the box below that BEST describes the text structure of the paragraph.

Text Structures	sequence
	cause and effect
	compare and contrast

    Part B

    Underline three details in the paragraph that support your answer to Part A.

---

7. **Use your answer to Part A to answer Part B.**

    Part A

    Which purpose for writing is BEST reflected in the passage?

    A. to help readers understand what they need to do to create a blog

    B. to explain what a blog is and why someone should start a blog

    C. to reassure readers that creating a blog is not difficult

    D. to detail problems bloggers might encounter and explain how to solve them

    Part B

    Which text structure BEST helps the author accomplish the purpose you selected in Part A?

    A. compare and contrast

    B. descriptive

    C. cause and effect

    D. problem and solution

    E. sequential

8. The following are steps in creating a blog. In each box, write the number 2, 3, 4, or 5 so that the steps are in the correct order.

| 1 | Decide what to blog about. |

| | Select a Web host. |

| | Design the blog's appearance. |

| | Determine a schedule for posting blog entries. |

| | Choose a blogging platform application. |

| 6 | Attract new readers to the blog. |

9. Read this paragraph from the passage.

> **You are now ready to create the content and launch your blog. You'll want to attract as many people as possible to read your blog, so engaging, well-written blog posts are a must. Think about what your audience will want to read. Once you have begun blogging, it's a good idea to keep to a schedule so you can publish posts at regular intervals and keep your readers coming back for more. That way, your blog has a better shot at becoming popular.**

Based on the paragraph, which of the following are effects of keeping to a blogging schedule? More than one correct answer choice is listed.

A. posts published at regular intervals

B. posts appeal to readers' tastes

C. blog becomes popular

D. readers return to the blog

E. blog posts are easier to write

F. blog posts are engaging

Duplicating any part of this book is prohibited by law.

14 Graphics

RI.8.1, RI.8.8, RI.8.10, RH.8.7, RH.8.10, RST.8.7, RST.8.10

Getting the Idea

Graphics are visual representations of information and ideas. In other words, they show information instead of just communicating it with words. Authors use graphics in texts in order to make information easier to understand. For instance, if a writer is trying to explain how a dynamo works, a diagram makes it much easier to grasp. If someone wanted to illustrate the path Paul Revere took when he warned his fellow patriots that the British were coming, a map would be very helpful.

If you look through your science or history book, you will see many examples of graphics that illustrate complex ideas. The most common kind of graphic is an **illustration**, of course, which would be a photograph or drawing used to help understanding of a text. A **table** is an arrangement of information in columns and rows. A **timeline** is a representation of events in chronological order. Some online sources might contain links to **videos**, or short films about a subject which you could watch on the Internet. In some cases, print isn't the best way to communicate. For instance, many people find they learn more about exercise from exercise videos than from books. This is why many exercise books use photos as video substitutes.

The list below defines some other commonly used graphics.

- **diagram:** an illustration with labels that describes something or shows how it works

The Human Ear

- **flowchart:** a graphic that shows the sequence of steps in a process, typically with boxes, circles, and arrows

- **graph:** a diagram that shows relationships between sets of data, such as a bar graph or line graph
- **map:** a graphic representation of regions on Earth and their geographical features

Look at the two graphics below.

The stock market crash of 1929 had a devastating effect on the economy. The line graph illustrates the sharp decline of the gross national product in the years following the crash. The map of Australia allows the reader to see at a glance the major regions of the continent and their relative size.

Thinking It Through

Read the following paragraph, and then answer the question that follows.

> Thomas Edison was a productive inventor. His many inventions include the electric pen (1875), a new type of dictating machine (1905), and the talking motion picture (1912). In 1907, he invented the universal electric motor. He invented the incandescent lamp in 1879 and the phonograph in 1877.

Which type of graphic would best present the ideas in this passage? Explain your answer.

_____

_____

HINT   The passage includes a lot of dates out of order.

Coached Example

Read the passage and answer the questions.

The graphic below represents information gathered by the U.S. Census for the year 2008. It is based on responses to a survey.

Health Insurance Coverage

Age	Not Covered at Any Time during the Year	Covered by Private Insurance	Covered by Government Health Plan
under 6	2,209	14,828	9,969
6 to 11	2,211	15,456	7,898
12 to 17	2,929	16,998	6,900
18 to 24	8,200	16,947	4,741
25 to 34	10,754	25,879	5,086
35 to 44	8,035	29,780	4,685
45 to 54	7,054	33,234	5,797
55 to 64	4,301	25,584	6,901
65 and over	646	22,287	35,434

1. What type of graphic is illustrated in the example?

   A. table

   B. timeline

   C. diagram

   D. flowchart

   HINT The graphic has rows and columns.

2. Which age group had the most number of people covered by private health insurance in 2008?

   A. under 6

   B. 25 to 34

   C. 35 to 44

   D. 45 to 54

   HINT Find the highest number in the column for private insurance, and then find the age group that is in the same row.

Lesson Practice

Use the Reading Guide to help you understand the passage.

Reading Guide

Look for connections between the passage and the graphic on page 114.

Look at the graphic for this passage. How does it help you understand difficult concepts?

The Human Respiratory System

The human respiratory system is the system of organs that allows people to breathe in oxygen and breathe out carbon dioxide. Because it is a system, it is made up of individual parts. Each plays an important role in keeping the system functioning efficiently.

In the respiratory system, the biggest part is played by the lungs. These are the two large and spongy organs located in the chest, behind the rib cage. The left lung is usually smaller than the right lung. The lungs are divided into lobes, or sections. Think of the lobe as a balloon filled with spongelike tissue through which air moves in and out. The right lung is divided into three lobes and the left lung into two. Each lobe is surrounded by the pleura, membranes that separate the lungs from the chest wall.

There is a band of muscle called the diaphragm that stretches across the rib cage. The diaphragm contracts, or tightens, when we inhale. The muscles beneath the ribs then draw air into the lungs through a thin tube called the trachea. The trachea splits into two branches. These branches, called bronchial tubes or bronchi, are the main air passageways to the lungs.

When the air enters the lungs through the bronchial tubes, it makes its way down through the bronchioles, subdivisions of the bronchial tubes. The bronchioles are very small. At their biggest, they would be three millimeters in diameter; at their smallest, they would be less than one millimeter in diameter. At the end of the bronchioles are the alveoli, the small elastic cavities where the air we breathe ends up. When air is taken into the body and reaches the alveoli, they expand.

When we exhale, we expel a waste gas called carbon dioxide. When carbon combines with oxygen in the blood to make energy for the body, carbon dioxide is produced. Releasing the carbon dioxide cleans the blood.

Breathing is considered both a voluntary and involuntary process because, although most of the time we breathe without thinking about it, we can also regulate it, as we do when we hold our breath, for example.

Duplicating any part of this book is prohibited by law.

Can you find the title of this graphic?

Follow the lines on the diagram to see what each label describes.

The respiratory system gives us the oxygen we need to keep our bodies functioning. When we are healthy, the respiratory system works like a well-oiled machine. For the respiratory system to work properly, the circulatory system, which moves blood through the body, and the metabolic system, which turns the food and drink we consume into energy, must be functioning correctly. If there is a problem with one system, the other systems are affected.

Respiratory System

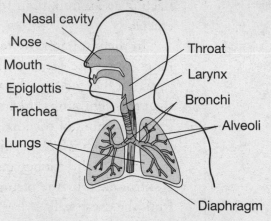

Answer the following questions.

1. The graphic in the passage is called a

    A. model.

    B. graph.

    C. diagram.

    D. flowchart.

2. The graphic helps readers understand that the trachea

    A. is wider than the lungs.

    B. leads to the heart.

    C. is part of the mouth.

    D. is in the throat.

3. What does the graphic show about the alveoli?

    A. They are small air sacs.

    B. They are outside of the lungs.

    C. They are next to the pharynx.

    D. They are part of the thyroid.

4. If the author wanted to illustrate the steps involved in breathing, the BEST graphic to use would be a

    A. flowchart.

    B. model.

    C. table.

    D. graph.

5. What other kind of graphic might you use with this passage? What would it show?

    _____

    _____

    _____

    _____

Use the Reading Guide to help you understand the passage.

Reading Guide

Look for connections between paragraph 3 and the map on page 177.

How does the map help you understand complex text ideas such as the role of geography in battle events?

The Battle of Gettysburg

A turning point in the American Civil War, the Battle of Gettysburg was waged from July 1 through July 3, 1863. The battle took place in Gettysburg, Pennsylvania. This battle has the distinction of being one of the bloodiest ever fought on U.S. soil. During those three days, there were close to 10,000 fatalities and 30,000 wounded on the Union (North) and Confederate (South) sides combined. Although the war would last another two years, the South and General Robert E. Lee suffered a demoralizing defeat. This defeat would haunt them well beyond the surrender at Appomattox.

The battle began west of Gettysburg on July 1, when General John Buford and the Union cavalry locked horns with Confederate General Henry Heth and his men. Buford held against overwhelming opposition until General Reynolds and the 1st Corps arrived in relief. Intense fighting ensued on both sides of the Chambersburg Pike. Although the South succeeded in pushing the Union troops back to Seminary Ridge, at the end of the day, the Union was in control of the high ground.

Most of day two of the battle focused around Devil's Den and Little Round Top. Devil's Den was a natural fortress whose tremendous boulders provided excellent protection for snipers. Little Round Top proved a formidable opponent to troops attempting to move uphill over its rocky slope. The South held Devil's Den for a considerable portion of the day, only to lose it to the Union by nightfall. The battle at Little Round Top proved a key skirmish that prevented the Confederate army from flanking the Union troops on all three sides. Outnumbered, out of ammunition, and faced with imminent attack, the 20th Maine regiment led by Colonel Joshua Chamberlain charged down the hill with bayonets fixed. This move was so unexpected that the Confederate soldiers fled in panic, leaving Little Round Top to what remained of the Union troops. This battle is often recognized as the decisive factor in the Union victory at Gettysburg and likely set in motion events that led to the outcome of the Civil War.

Read the map labels. What locations from the text are shown on the map?

Check the legend. What do the arrows on the map represent?

How are you able to tell the difference between Union and Confederate troops on the map?

Day three became notorious for one battle in particular, Longstreet's Assault, or as it is more commonly known, Pickett's Charge. That morning, Confederate forces lost control of strategically important Culp Hill. Consequently, General Lee decided to concentrate all of his might on the direct center of the Union line at Cemetery Ridge. Heavy artillery was directed there in an effort to clear Union troops from the hill. At first, the artillery appeared to have done considerable damage to the Union line, but reinforcements were brought forward to fill the gaps. As Confederate forces advanced three-quarters of a mile across an open field and uphill toward the Union army, they suffered severe casualties. Of the 15,000 Confederate soldiers sent into the fray, General George Pickett's division was the largest. His division lost a majority of its men, and so his name is most often associated with this bloody final battle at Gettysburg. The next day, Lee withdrew his troops and headed back to Virginia.

Answer the following questions.

6. **Use your answer to Part A to answer Part B.**

Part A

Which text detail does the map help readers understand?

A. the location of soldiers at Pickett's Charge

B. where the second day of fighting took place

C. the number of soldiers that fought at Gettysburg

D. Lee's route back to Virginia

Part B

Choose all ways the map aids readers. There is more than one correct choice listed below.

A. adds facts to the text

B. identifies Confederate and Union generals

C. demonstrates troop movement

D. displays causes of the Civil War

E. indicates importance of events

F. illustrates a complex idea

G. shows battle locations

H. demonstrates effects of the battle

I. shows information visually

J. suggests how geography impacted the battle

7. Use the text and map to determine the correct sequence of the movements listed in the box. Write the movements in the correct order in the sequence chart below.

| Union troops down the hill at Little Round Top | Confederate troops away from Little Round Top | Confederate troops toward Little Round Top |

Movement of _____ → Movement of _____ → Movement of _____

8. Read the following sentence from the passage.

Little Round Top proved a formidable opponent to troops attempting to move uphill over its rocky slope.

Underline two details in the sentence that can be found on the map. Then circle areas on the map that display the corresponding information.

---

9. **Use your answer to Part A to answer Part B.**

Part A

If the author wanted to illustrate the series of events that took place during the Battle of Gettysburg, the BEST graphic to use would be a

A. timeline.

B. graph.

C. table.

D. map.

Part B

Which detail from the passage might appear on the graphic you chose in Part A?

A. "was a natural fortress"

B. "war ended two years later"

C. "provided excellent protection for snipers"

D. "Confederates lost control of strategically important Culp Hill"

E. "has the distinction of being one of the bloodiest ever fought"

15 Fact and Opinion

RI.8.1, RI.8.10, RH.8.8, RH.8.10, RST.8.8, RST.8.10

Getting the Idea

Writers include different types of statements in their texts. Learning to tell the difference between statements can help you evaluate whether the content is valid and reliable. It can also help you determine an author's purpose for a passage. When you read, you should distinguish between facts, opinions, and reasoned judgments.

A **fact** is a statement that can be verified, independently and objectively. For example, all of the statements below are facts.

- Although penguins have wings, they cannot fly.
- Zachary Taylor was the twelfth president of the United States.
- Earth is the fifth largest planet in our solar system.
- All spiders have eight legs.
- Istanbul was once known as Constantinople.

An **opinion** is a personal belief, a statement that cannot be proven true. Authors often state their opinions strongly, particularly when they are writing arguments. But no matter how persuasive these statements may be, they are still opinions. Do not confuse them with facts. Evaluate authors' opinions based on the facts they use to support them. The statements below are opinions.

- Broccoli is healthy for you, but it doesn't taste very good.
- The best place to spend winter vacation is on a tropical island.
- Teenagers should not be allowed to drive before they turn eighteen.
- These days, Hollywood is producing terrible movies.
- No one with any sense owns a Saint Bernard.

A **reasoned judgment** is a statement based on an issue for which there is more than one standard of judgment. A standard is a law or rule with which a group of people agree. However, people have different standards, and that's why a reasoned judgment can be a source of disagreement. It can be tricky to distinguish between an opinion and a reasoned judgment because there is a fine line between them. Just remember that a reasoned judgment is usually weighed more carefully, as a person considers the pros and cons of the issue. Also, reasoned judgments are statements which people like to repeat—so such a statement might already be familiar to you. The statements below are examples of reasoned judgments.

- Corrupt politicians should be removed from office.
- Students should not be allowed to disrupt class.

Neither of these statements are facts that can be proven. But they are more than opinions. There is a certain standard of judgment that makes these statements logical and reasonable.

Thinking It Through

Read the following paragraph, and then answer the question that follows.

My Pal, Brian is the funniest show on television. It is about a boy named Brian who always gets other people in trouble but then figures out a way to make things right. They've had some very funny episodes this season. The funniest so far was the one where Brian ran his big brother's high school diploma through the washer!

Write down the type of statement that BEST describes each sentence in the paragraph.

_____

_____

_____

 Decide whether each sentence can be proven to be true.

Coached Example

Read the passage and answer the questions.

An artesian well is a well into which water is forced by pressure under Earth's surface. Artesian wells are possible only under specific geologic conditions. An aquifer, or underground layer of very porous rock or sand, is buried between two layers of solid rock through which water cannot pass. At some point, water falling as rain or snow passes through the top layer of solid rock and is trapped between the two layers of solid, watertight rock. The water remains there, held in place by great pressure on all sides. In order to create the well, a deep hole only a few inches wide is drilled so that it reaches the sandy layer. The freed water gushes to the surface like a geyser. The practice of drilling artesian wells is ancient. The Chinese and Egyptians did it, although it took them years. Today's drilling methods make it a much easier and quicker task. Aquifers provide more than half the water Americans drink. People don't need to waste money on bottled water.

1. Which sentence from the passage is an opinion?

   A. "People don't need to waste money on bottled water."

   B. "Aquifers provide more than half the water Americans drink."

   C. "The Chinese and Egyptians did it, although it took them years."

   D. "The practice of drilling artesian wells is ancient."

   HINT Look for the sentence that expresses a personal view.

2. Read this sentence from the passage.

   The water remains there, held in place by great pressure on all sides.

   This sentence is a fact because

   A. it is based on a reasoned judgment.

   B. it can be verified through science.

   C. it expresses a strong belief.

   D. authors only write facts.

   HINT Review the definition of a fact.

Lesson Practice

Use the Reading Guide to help you understand the passage.

Reading Guide

Choose a sentence from paragraph 2 that is a fact.

The sentences in the section "Early Libraries" are mostly what type of statements?

A Brief History of Libraries

Books have always been at the center of learning. People have always felt the need to educate themselves and others; even ancient cave dwellers had messages they wished to write down for each other. People have turned to reading and writing, either of pictures or of words, to gather and share information. Sharing knowledge is a concept that evolved into centers of record-keeping and learning called libraries.

Today, people do not fully appreciate the usefulness of libraries. Many people hardly ever use them. Why should they? It is too easy to get information on the Internet or from television. People can buy books and magazines in bookstores or download them electronically. Books are cheap and accessible. This was not the case centuries ago, when there was no Internet or television. Back then, books were handwritten manuscripts that took a lot of effort and time to produce. Books were expensive and hard to come by. So, for most people, libraries were the main or only way to have access to books.

Early Libraries

The first people to establish libraries for general or scholarly use were the ancient Egyptians, Greeks, and Romans. The earliest library we know of was in Babylonia in the twenty-first century BCE. It housed a collection of clay tablets. A similar collection of clay tablets was found in the ruins of a library in Egypt. Many works in the Greek libraries were printed on papyrus or parchment. The first public library in Rome was established around 40 BCE. (It had been planned previously by the great ruler Julius Caesar.) The Chinese also had significant early libraries. They were among the first to use classification systems. Many of the people who used the libraries in ancient China were studying to take exams that would allow them to work for the government. The libraries gave all citizens access to the same textbooks. Typically, it was only the wealthy who actually owned books. This was not only because they could afford them but because, in societies in which many people were illiterate, they were among the few who could read.

Remembering that an opinion cannot be proven true, what are some opinions in the passage?

Some of the finest libraries were found in the castles of nobles or in monasteries. However, these were private collections.

Islamic Libraries

The Muslims established some of the most important medieval libraries. They valued books highly and established public libraries in major cities, including Baghdad, Cairo, and Damascus. The Cairo library actually housed more than one million manuscripts, and at one point Baghdad had more than thirty-six libraries. These libraries grew, as well, as the Muslims conquered territories. After they learned how to make paper from Chinese prisoners, the number of volumes they were able to place in libraries increased, because paper was cheaper than papyrus. For many years, Islamic libraries were superior to libraries in Europe. Scholarship, sciences, and the arts flourished in Arab lands.

European Libraries

In early medieval Europe, libraries were usually established in monasteries and convents. Copying books by hand was an important activity of the residents. The preceptors, who managed the libraries, were among the world's earliest librarians. As formal education grew, university libraries were started, as well. Some of these, such as the library at Oxford University, were funded by wealthy patrons. They played a central role in the growth of learning in Europe.

Jewish Libraries

One of the central goals of Jewish libraries in the Middle Ages was to preserve Jewish religious and cultural heritage. The libraries were housed in synagogues and consisted primarily of scholarly and religious texts.

Libraries Today

Today, libraries are very different from early and medieval libraries. Library collections are more diverse and easier to access. However, with so many competing sources of information and entertainment, many people rarely frequent the library. Hopefully, people will rediscover the value of libraries.

Answer the following questions.

1. Which sentence from the passage is a fact?

    A. "Why should they?"

    B. "The first public library in Rome was established around 40 BCE."

    C. "Books have always been at the center of learning."

    D. "Hopefully, people will rediscover the value of libraries."

2. Which sentence from the passage is an opinion?

    A. "Typically, it was only the wealthy who actually owned books."

    B. "The earliest library we know of was in Babylonia in the twenty-first century BCE."

    C. "Today, people do not fully appreciate the usefulness of libraries."

    D. "In early medieval Europe, libraries were usually established in monasteries and convents."

3. Which sentence from the passage is a reasoned judgment?

    A. "The libraries were housed in synagogues and consisted primarily of scholarly and religious texts."

    B. "However, these were private collections."

    C. "It housed a collection of clay tablets."

    D. "It is too easy to get information on the Internet or from television."

4. Read this sentence from the passage.

    For many years, Islamic libraries were superior to libraries in Europe.

    This sentence is a reasoned judgment because

    A. the author seems like someone who is very reasonable.

    B. no one will ever agree that this is true.

    C. it is based on an evaluation of Islamic and European libraries.

    D. it can be proven with clear historical evidence.

5. Choose a sentence from the passage and explain why it is a fact, an opinion, or a reasoned judgment.

    _____

    _____

Use the Reading Guide to help you understand the passage.

Reading Guide

Remember that a fact can be verified independently and objectively. How might you verify information within the second sentence of paragraph 1?

To identify an opinion, look for clue words that suggest judgment, such as *easy/difficult* or *dependent/independent,* and words that leave no room for exception, such as *must* or *will.*

Energy Independence

On your way to soccer practice, your mom pulls into a gas station to fill the tank of the family SUV. At $3.56 per gallon, this twenty-gallon fill-up will cost your family $71.20. Your mom fills the tank two times per week for a total of $142.40. That's $569.60 per month for your family to power this one vehicle, assuming that the price per gallon of gas remains the same. If it goes up, which often happens, these numbers will rise. While transportation is essential for the American family, so are items such as food, shelter, and clothing. Rising prices in all areas of American life create pressures on families to survive. To help relieve these burdens, the United States must achieve energy independence from oil through the development and use of alternative domestic energy sources.

This task will not be easy. The U.S. is the world's largest consumer of oil. In 2012, the U.S. used about nineteen million barrels of oil each day to power its transportation, construction, industrial, heating, and military needs. In short, the American standard of living and economy is dependent on an energy source that will one day run out.

Today, the U.S. imports nearly two times more oil than it produces. Much of this imported oil comes from countries that have unstable political environments or that maintain troubled relationships with the U.S. In some cases, the money the U.S. spends to import oil supports violent and dictatorial foreign governments. Countries in the Persian Gulf, such as Saudi Arabia, Kuwait, and Oman, supply the U.S. with about 13 percent of its oil. The U.S. gets another 19 percent of its oil from countries in Africa. Western sources such as Venezuela, Canada, and Mexico supply the U.S. with almost 50 percent of its oil. Due to this dependence on foreign oil, U.S. citizens are often subject to oil shortages and rising oil prices.

To identify a reasoned judgment, ask the following questions: Is this opinion logical and reasonable? On what standard is it based?

What reasoned judgment is made in paragraph 1?

As you read, remember to look for ways that the author supports opinions and reasoned judgments with facts and evidence.

In contrast to nonrenewable energy sources such as oil, natural gas, and coal, there are renewable energy sources available for American consumers. However, by 2009 only just over 10 percent of U.S. energy came from renewable sources. If the U.S. commits to the development and use of renewable energy sources, it can control costs, protect the environment from the pollution associated with burning fossil fuels such as oil, and reduce a dangerous dependence on imported oil.

There are two powerful and natural heat sources that can be used to create electricity. First, radiation from the sun can be converted into electricity using solar thermal plants. The sun heats water and creates steam that powers generators, or solar cells, which convert the sun's light into electricity. Secondly, geothermal energy comes from heat below the Earth's surface that transforms water into steam, which in turn powers generators that create electricity. Two additional natural sources of energy are wind and flowing water. Both are able to power generators and create electricity.

Finally, biomass is a form of energy that comes from plants. Plants store chemical energy from the sun that can be released through heat. Today, some cars run on ethanol—a fuel made from the sugars found in corn. Ethanol can also be made from sugar cane, potato skins, wheat, and rice.

Ultimately, the truth is simple. The world's oil supply will run out. The U.S. must invest in research and create legislation that will end its dependence on foreign oil and shift the country to alternative energy sources. Such steps are morally and economically sound and will protect your family the next time your car needs fuel.

Answer the following questions.

6. Read this paragraph from the passage.

> **This task will not be easy. The U.S. is the world's largest consumer of oil. In 2012, the U.S. used about nineteen million barrels of oil each day to power its transportation, construction, industrial, heating, and military needs. In short, the American standard of living and economy is dependent on an energy source that will one day run out.**

Place a box around two facts. Circle one opinion. Underline one reasoned judgment.

---

7. **Use your answer to Part A to answer Part B.**

Read the statements the author makes about nonrenewable energy sources.

"Much of this imported oil comes from countries that have unstable political environments or that maintain troubled relationships with the U.S."
"The U.S. gets another 19 percent of its oil from countries in Africa."
"Due to this dependence on foreign oil, U.S. citizens are often subject to oil shortages and rising oil prices."

Part A

Circle the statement that is BEST supported by the following text evidence:

In some cases, the money the U.S. spends to import oil supports violent and dictatorial foreign governments.

Part B

Is the statement you circled a fact, an opinion, or a reasoned judgment? Write your answer on the line.

---

8. Read each sentence from the passage on the left. Identify it as a fact, an opinion, or a reasoned judgment by drawing a line to the correct box on the right.

A. "In short, the American standard of living and economy is dependent on an energy source that will one day run out."

B. ". . . the U.S. imports nearly two times more oil than it produces."

C. "To help relieve these burdens, the United States must achieve energy independence from oil through the development and use of alternative domestic energy sources."

1. fact

2. opinion

3. reasoned judgment

9. **Use your answer to Part A to answer Part B.**

Part A

Choose opinions from the excerpts below. More than one correct choice is listed.

A. "Finally, biomass is a form of energy that comes from plants."

B. "Today, some cars run on ethanol—a fuel made from the sugars found in corn."

C. "[Wind and flowing water] are able to power generators and create electricity."

D. "Ultimately, the truth is simple."

E. ". . . by 2009 only just over 10 percent of U.S. energy came from renewable sources."

F. "The U.S. must invest in research and create legislation that will end its dependence on foreign oil and shift the country to alternative energy sources."

Part B

Choose an opinion you identified in Part A. Underline one piece of text evidence in the passage that is used to support the opinion.

16 Domain-Specific Vocabulary

RI.8.4, RH.8.4, RST.8.4, L.8.6

Getting the Idea

We all use words to communicate with others. Some words, such as *pattern, power,* or *contain,* are used frequently to discuss a variety of topics. Most of us are familiar with general words like these and use them often in speaking, reading, and writing. Other words are specific to academic or formal settings, such as school or the workplace. For example, students are frequently asked to *explain, analyze,* or *synthesize* information. Over time, students become familiar with these academic words.

Domain-specific vocabulary consists of words used in specific domains, or areas of knowledge, such as social studies, science, or technology. Experts in a domain come to understand and use words that are specific to their domain, while those who do not specialize in that domain may not understand such domain-specific vocabulary. You may be familiar with the word *concentrated,* meaning "thought about without distraction." However, this word takes on different meanings in different domains. Consider the following use of the word *concentrated:*

> During the sugar refining process, liquid or juice is removed
> from sugar cane by crushing, shredding, and rolling the cane.
> Next, the juice is purified and strained through the use of heat,
> chemicals, and filters. Then, the juice is *concentrated* into syrup
> form through a boiling and evaporation procedure.

The word *concentrated* has a meaning specific to the domain of manufacturing: "distilled to a stronger solution, usually by removing liquid." However, this word also has meanings specific to other domains. Consider the following use of the word *concentrated:*

> Conifers are a division of trees that display the following
> characteristics: long, pointed leaves that stay green all year
> round and cones that contain seeds. Conifers are *concentrated*
> in geographic areas that maintain cool temperatures.

In this example from the domain of science, the word *concentrated* means "grouped closely together."

As a student, you may encounter unfamiliar domain-specific vocabulary as you tackle new areas of study. Use context clues such as synonyms, antonyms, definitions, and examples within a sentence and within surrounding sentences to determine meanings. Then, when possible, check the meanings in a print or digital dictionary. As you become more proficient within a domain, its domain-specific terms will become a part of your working vocabulary.

Read the following sentence.

> The archaeology professor *concentrated* her field studies on the excavation of ancient Egyptian artifacts.

The context provides clues regarding the definition of *concentrated*. Archaeology, or the study of past human life and culture on the basis of artifacts or other objects, is a broad field. However, the professor studies Egyptian artifacts, narrowing a broad topic to a smaller subtopic. In the domain of social studies, *concentrated* means "focused." Identifying the domain and context clues will help you acquire domain-specific vocabulary.

Thinking It Through

Read the paragraph below and then answer the question that follows.

A carbohydrate is a type of organic molecule essential to the structure of living cells. Carbohydrates are found in starch and sugar food sources, such as potatoes and fruits. Carbohydrates provide the body with energy and control blood sugar. The body's first source of energy is glucose from carbohydrates. During digestion, the small intestine breaks down food particles from the stomach into simple molecules or nutrients, including carbohydrates. Then, carbohydrates are absorbed into the bloodstream through villi in the small intestine. The circulatory system delivers glucose to important organs, such as the brain and muscles. The liver helps the body maintain a constant blood glucose level.

Underline three domain-specific vocabulary words in the paragraph. Why would they be considered domain-specific?

_____

_____

_____

HINT   Which words would you expect to read only in a paragraph about a science topic?

 DISCUSS   In what other domains might you expect to find the word *energy*? Discuss your ideas with a partner.

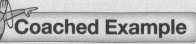

Read the passage and answer the questions.

Classification of Species

Taxonomic classification is the hierarchical system used for classifying living organisms, based on their similarities and differences. The seven main groupings in the hierarchy from largest to smallest are: kingdom, phylum, class, order, family, genus, and species. Carolus Linnaeus, a Swedish botanist, developed this system in the eighteenth century. He personally described and categorized more than 4,000 animal species and 7,000 plant species. Each specific type of plant or animal can be classified uniquely in the system. For example, modern humans are classified from kingdom down through species as Animalia, Chordata, Mammalia, Primates, Hominidae, *Homo*, *Homo sapiens*. Notice that the genus name, *Homo*, is repeated at the beginning of the species name. Therefore, each specific type of organism has a unique two-word name. This naming is referred to as binomial nomenclature. When a species name appears in print, both words should appear in italic type with the genus name beginning with a capital letter. Subsequent occurrences may appear with the genus name abbreviated, such as *H. sapiens*.

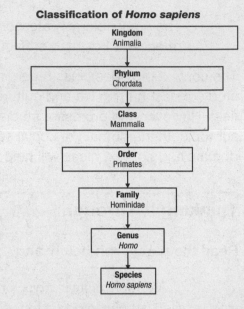

Classification of *Homo sapiens*

Kingdom
Animalia

Phylum
Chordata

Class
Mammalia

Order
Primates

Family
Hominidae

Genus
Homo

Species
Homo sapiens

---

1. Based on context clues, what do you think is the purpose of <u>taxonomic classification</u>?

   A. to categorize organisms by size

   B. to compare and contrast organisms

   C. to classify organisms by time period

   D. to identify and explain differences in organisms

   HINT Read the first sentence of the paragraph carefully.

2. In this passage, what is the meaning of the term <u>binomial nomenclature</u>?

   A. two names

   B. modern humans

   C. kingdom species

   D. genus name

   HINT Think about the makeup of the term *Homo sapiens*.

Lesson Practice

Use the Reading Guide to help you understand the passage.

Reading Guide

As you read, pay special attention to the underlined domain-specific vocabulary. Think about why it might be used in an article on sociology, or the study of human societies.

When you encounter multiple-meaning words, use context clues to determine the domain-specific meanings.

Which words are specific to the description of human societies?

Social Systems and Institutions

Oftentimes, when you see a story on the evening news about a woman who risks her life to save a puppy or read a story online about an outrageous stunt, you may ask, "Why did that person do that?" One way that sociologists try to understand individual human behavior is to study the social systems and institutions that affect human development as a whole. In a society, there are two powers at work. There are the systems and institutions that exist over long periods of time. These systems and institutions are interconnected and exert authority over a society and its individual citizens. Then, there are the forces that work to change these systems and institutions.

While the social systems and institutions that underlie society may vary slightly from culture to culture, there are general aspects that exist in all cultures. One such <u>system</u>, or method for organization, is time. People organize the events of their lives according to days, weeks, months, and years. Another such system is space. People assign specific activities to specific places. For example, people worship in churches, mosques, or synagogues. People are educated in schools. People eat in kitchens or dining rooms and sleep in bedrooms. In addition, people tend to assign work based on categories such as age, gender, ability, and training. Finally, people use language systems to communicate with one another.

To manage these social systems, people establish <u>institutions</u>, or organizations set up for specific purposes. For example, most societies have governments that make and enforce laws and restrict violence.

Remember that many words have both denotations, or dictionary definitions, and connotations, or shades of meaning that readers associate with them.

Remember that the suffix *–ologist* means "one who studies."

If you can't determine a word's meaning by using context clues within the text, look up the word's definition in a print or digital dictionary.

Many sociologists believe that a person's memberships in social systems and institutions, including personal relationships and societal positions, exert more influence over his or her choices and actions than individual freedom of choice. Some sociologists argue that the existence of such social systems and institutions ensures the <u>survival of a society</u> and, therefore, the survival of its individual members. Systems and institutions define the roles, values, rules, and behaviors that are appropriate for given situations. When people in a society or institution operate according to these criteria, it may ensure successful transactions among members. When transactions are unsuccessful, the result is often conflict or violence, which is a destructive force.

However, sociologists have noted that within the permanent systems and institutions in a society, unequal distributions of power, money, and property exist. These unequal situations tend to create layers or classes of people. It is possible that each class may develop its own roles, values, rules, and behaviors that differ from those of other classes. It is also possible that a powerful class may try to force its values and rules on another class. In fact, Karl Marx argued that "The ideas of the ruling class are, in every age, the ruling ideas." Such conflicting interests may cause people to work to change a permanent system or institution. Examples of this type of action can be seen in the South African anti-apartheid movement or the American civil rights movement.

So, what motivates a woman to risk her life to save a puppy? Does she take this action because society influences her to protect the weak? Or, does she take this action because she hopes for fame or a monetary reward that will change her status in society? Today, when <u>sociologists</u> work to answer such questions, they are not as concerned with explaining acts of heroism as they are with the rates of such acts. Who performs such acts where, when, and why? Nonetheless, the work of describing the organization and behavior patterns of human society must account for two forces: permanence and change.

Answer the following questions.

1. Read paragraph 2. Which words help reveal the meaning of <u>system</u>?

   A. underlie society

   B. exist in all cultures

   C. method for organization

   D. specific activities to specific places

2. Which of the words below is specific to the domain of sociology?

   A. culture

   B. heroism

   C. power

   D. property

3. Based on the passage's context, what does <u>institutions</u> mean?

   A. places of confinement

   B. social customs or conventions

   C. acts of establishing or setting in progress

   D. organizations set up for specific purposes

4. Based on paragraph 4, what does the author mean by the phrase <u>survival of a society</u>?

   A. Individuals continue to exist.

   B. A group continues to exist.

   C. Individuals cease to exist.

   D. A group ceases to exist.

5. Based on the passage, what does a <u>sociologist</u> do? Compare and contrast your response with a dictionary definition.

   _____

   _____

   _____

   _____

   _____

Use the Reading Guide to help you understand the passage.

Reading Guide

As you read, pay special attention to the underlined domain-specific vocabulary.

Why might a scientist need to exercise "tight controls" over the aspects of an experiment that vary or change?

Is an "expected outcome" a known or an unknown event or condition?

The Scientific Method

The scientific method is the proper way to conduct scientific research through experimentation. It is practiced in <u>disciplines</u> of science such as biology, chemistry, physics, and geology. As you will see by the simple example in italics that follows each step below, this method is also practiced to some degree in people's daily lives. However, note that while the example presented here demonstrates the reasoning that is part of the scientific method, the actual use of the scientific method in this situation would require tight controls on a number of <u>variables</u>.

Following the steps of the scientific method allows scientists to make accurate determinations and predictions about the natural environment and/or living organisms.

Step 1: Make observations. A scientist makes observations that are objective and <u>verifiable</u> by other researchers. These observations are not based on opinions, and they are about events that occurred in the past or occur under present conditions. *My car will not start.*

Step 2: Form a hypothesis. Based on observations of past occurrences or present conditions, a scientist uses reasoning to relate the observations to explanations. Knowledge of the past and present allows a scientist to form a general principle called a <u>hypothesis</u>. A hypothesis is a general idea that conforms to the observations and requires testing to determine its accuracy. *The car's battery is dead.*

Step 3: Make a prediction. Using a tentative hypothesis, a scientist finds a way to clarify whether the hypothesis can be supported. To accomplish this task, the scientist makes a <u>prediction</u> regarding the expected <u>outcome</u> of an action or a condition that can be imposed through experimentation. *If I replace the car's battery with a new one, then my car will start.*

As you read, notice instances in which the author provides the definition of an unfamiliar word within the context of a section.

What is the purpose of an experiment?

Step 4: Perform an experiment. Based on the prediction, the scientist performs an experiment in an attempt to confirm whether or not the prediction is correct. *I'll replace my car's battery with a new one and try to start the car.*

Step 5: Analyze the results of the experiment. A scientist evaluates the findings of the experiment to check whether the prediction is correct. *After I install the new battery, my car still will not start.*

Step 6: Draw a conclusion. There are two possible outcomes of an experiment: Either the prediction is correct or it is incorrect. If the prediction is correct, the results of the experiment support the original hypothesis. If the prediction is incorrect, the hypothesis on which it is based should be rejected and further research may be necessary. *Since the new battery doesn't make my car start, my new hypothesis is that the battery cables are faulty.*

Note that a prediction that is shown to be correct does not prove the original hypothesis, but rather, only supports it. There may be other explanations for a positive result. If the car in the example starts with the new battery, this does not necessarily prove that the original battery is dead. Perhaps the cable connections to the original battery are loose. The original battery may be operational, and the connections may be tightened when the new battery is installed. Hypotheses can be shown to be false, but they can never be proven true. However, they can be supported through repeated experimentations that produce the same results.

Answer the following questions.

6. Read this modified excerpt of paragraph 1 of the passage.

> However, note that while the example presented here demonstrates the reasoning that is part of the scientific method, the actual use of the scientific method in this situation would require tight controls on a number of <u>variables</u>, or factors that might _____ during an experiment.

Which phrase BEST completes the sentence?

A. disprove the hypothesis

B. invalidate the prediction

C. change, respond, or remain constant

D. be performed, analyzed, and evaluated

---

7. **Use your answer to Part A to answer Part B.**

Part A

Read this excerpt from the passage.

> To accomplish this task, the scientist makes a prediction regarding the expected <u>outcome</u> of an action or a condition that can be imposed through experimentation.

Circle the steps on page 197 that describe an *outcome*. Then write the step numbers on the line below.

Part B

Which is true of an outcome? There is more than one correct choice listed below.

A. can be correctly predicted

B. can be incorrectly predicted

C. proves a hypothesis

D. can cause revision to a hypothesis

E. is determined through experimentation

F. can support a hypothesis

G. can fail

8. Read this excerpt from the passage.

> **Knowledge of the past and present allows a scientist to form a general principle**
>
> **called a <u>hypothesis</u>. A hypothesis is a general idea that conforms to the**
>
> **observations and requires testing to determine its accuracy.**

Underline the phrases that define the two criteria of a *hypothesis*.

---

9. Read the sentence in each choice on the left. Then match the underlined word in the sentence to its closest definition on the right.

A. "It is practiced in <u>disciplines</u> of science such as biology, chemistry, physics, and geology.	**1.** punishments
	2. a guess based on study and observation
B. ". . . the scientist makes a <u>prediction</u> regarding the expected outcome of an action or a condition that can be imposed through experimentation."	**3.** an opinion or claim
	4. can be believed
C. "A scientist makes observations that are objective and <u>verifiable</u> by other researchers."	**5.** able to be shown as accurate
	6. categories of study or interest

Cumulative Assessment

Read the passage and answer the questions that follow.

Get Involved!

Imagine the following situations. You're at the hospital and you see a teenager playing checkers with a young child in another room. The child is a long-term patient, but for the moment she is happy and enjoying the game. You go camping with your family. During a hike, you pass a group of people clearing the path of fallen tree branches. They wave hello as you pass by. You're at the library. You see a woman tutoring children. You're on a busy street. You see a man walk four dogs out of an animal shelter and head for the park. If you assumed any of these people are paid employees, you were wrong. They are volunteers, providing a service to others free of charge. There are countless organizations, large and small, that need help beyond what their budgets allow. This is where volunteers come in, donating their time for a variety of worthy causes. Have you ever thought of volunteering? If you have even five hours a week to spare, you could make a difference in someone's life.

Why Volunteer?

People have their own reasons for donating their time and energy. It can be for purely selfless reasons—they want to help others in any way they can. Others have additional motivation, such as earning school credit, enhancing their college applications, or building up their résumés for future employers. Whatever the reason, the spirit of volunteerism is alive and well. The rewards are measured not in money or material gains but in the feeling of having done something worthwhile. You can become one of the millions of people around the country who take the time to volunteer.

Getting Started

Having a successful and rewarding volunteer experience is largely up to you. Avoid common mistakes like choosing a job that does not truly interest you or committing to more time than you actually have. If you are a student, be careful not to let volunteer work interfere with your studies. The majority of volunteer jobs have hiring requirements similar to those of a paying job. You have to complete an application, submit references, and schedule an interview. You often receive specialized training, depending on your responsibilities. The Internet is a great place to start looking for volunteer work. You may even be able to submit your application online. With many people applying for a limited number of openings, volunteer work can be highly competitive.

Start your search early and approach it with a professional attitude. Below are a few suggestions for places that are always looking for new volunteers.

Volunteer at a Hospital

A large hospital can hire thousands of volunteers a year. Many hospitals have special youth volunteer opportunities that include a summer program. They work around students' school schedules and give them special training. High school and college students interested in health careers gain valuable experience. It can be especially rewarding to volunteer at a children's hospital. Hospital stays, especially extended ones, can be extremely difficult for children. Not only do they suffer physical pain resulting from their illness or injury, but their time at the hospital can also be lonely. Many children are afraid and need comfort beyond what their family and regular hospital staff can provide.

Hospitals welcome adult and junior volunteers—sometimes as young as thirteen. By giving just a few hours a week of their time, volunteers can bring a little light into the lives of these children. They play with the children, comfort them, read to them, or just have a conversation with them. Many experts believe in the healing power of laughter. If you have a natural ability to make people laugh, this could be the perfect job for you. There is also office work available, like answering phones and scheduling patients.

Volunteer at an Animal Shelter

Often, it may seem like you can't walk down any street without encountering a stray dog or cat. These animals are often brought to animal shelters, where thousands of them are put to sleep as they wait in vain to be adopted. Due to lack of space and funds, animal shelters can hold only a limited number of strays and abandoned pets. These organizations are always looking for volunteers to help them carry on their great work. Whether it's cleaning cages, feeding and grooming the animals, or walking the dogs, volunteers provide invaluable assistance. There are also general office duties to be done, such as filing and stocking shelves.

Volunteer at a State Park

Do you like the outdoors? There are numerous volunteer opportunities for people who love nature. State parks throughout the country have year-round need for volunteers to help in a variety of ways. There is, for example, the Adopt-a-Trail program. It allows people to adopt a trail or part of a trail to help keep it safe and clean. This includes reporting any hazards on the trail and picking up litter. Volunteers can also become campground hosts, living for a period of time at a free campsite and aiding other campers. Volunteer conservationists help build and maintain cabins and other park structures and help create new signs and shelters. Visitor services volunteers perform various jobs, including selling trail passes, handing out brochures, answering phones, and working in the gift shop.

Why wait? Get involved now! There is a volunteer job out there for everyone. Join the ranks! And if you have a friend or family member with some time to spare, pass the word. Maybe, like you, they'll discover the rewards of volunteering.

1. What graphic could be used with this passage?
   A. a table of important hospitals
   B. a map of a public library
   C. a photograph of a volunteer with children
   D. a photograph of animals

2. Which sentence from the passage is a fact?

   A. "Maybe, like you, they'll discover the rewards of volunteering."

   B. "Start your search early and approach it with a professional attitude."

   C. "It can be especially rewarding to volunteer at a children's hospital."

   D. "It allows people to adopt a trail or part of a trail to help keep it safe and clean."

3. In the section "Volunteer at a Hospital," the author tries to persuade readers mainly by

   A. appealing to their emotions.

   B. providing logical reasons.

   C. relating a personal experience.

   D. quoting hospital volunteers.

4. Summarize the benefits of volunteering, according to the passage.

_____

_____

_____

_____

Read the passage and answer the questions that follow.

To Save the Forests

There have been many famous conservationists—President Theodore Roosevelt, Rachel Carson, Wangari Maathai, John Muir, and Ansel Adams, to name a few. All of them, in one way or another, brought attention not only to the beauty of nature but to the need to preserve it. Some of them were pioneers, like Rachel Carson, whose ideas in her book *Silent Spring* generated global interest in the environment, and Wangari Maathai, who started a tree-planting movement in Africa and became the first African woman to win the Nobel Peace Prize. Some, like Ansel Adams, captured their natural surroundings in photographs that would enchant others long after they were gone.

Conservationists are usually inspired by their life experiences. William Goodrich Jones is a perfect example of this. He played a vital role in preserving Texas forests and wildlife and bringing the cause to national attention. Jones was born in New York on November 11, 1860. His father was from Texas. Jones lived in Houston for a while before his father moved the family back to New York after the Civil War. In 1873, Jones's family made a decision that would have an unexpected influence on the young boy. They traveled to Europe, where they spent two years. Jones attended school in Germany, and one summer his father took him on a tour of the Black Forest. Jones got the chance to speak with rangers and other forest workers. He learned what it took to maintain a forest—to keep it alive and beautiful. He also learned that when a person cuts down a tree, that person should plant another in its place.

When his family returned to the United States, Jones continued his studies. Eventually, he graduated from Princeton University with a degree in business and became the president of a bank in Temple, Texas. Jones was a natural leader. He made it his mission to educate the townspeople on the importance of planting trees. He also worked to have Texas adopt an official Arbor Day in order to promote tree planting throughout the state.

Jones's deep-rooted interest in forestry and his public activism caught the attention of B. E. Fernow. Fernow was the chief of the United States Bureau of Forestry. He asked Jones to conduct a study and write a report about the condition of forestry in Texas, in particular the Pineywoods. Jones was only too happy to oblige, but what he discovered appalled him. Having seen forestry at its best in the Black Forest, Jones knew exactly what the loggers in Texas were doing wrong.

In his report, Jones explained that the logging industry was cutting down too many trees and doing so in a particularly wasteful manner. For example, to cut down and bring out one tree, loggers would sometimes cut up to one hundred younger trees in the process. Obviously, this was not an effective way to cut down trees. Jones predicted that if loggers did not change their methods, the forest would be gone within twenty-five years. In order to save the Texas forest, Jones recommended a controlled program of planned cutting and reforestation.

In 1914, Jones founded the Texas Forestry Association. Jones became its president, and the association helped create the Texas Department of Forestry. For the rest of his life, Jones worked to preserve forests and instill in others the importance of conservation. He pushed to make every town in Texas a "green town" through the establishment of parks.

Jones died on August 1, 1950. Today, he is fondly regarded as "the father of Texas forestry." In tribute to his life's work, Texas named a state park after him. The W. Goodrich Jones State Forest is located in Conroe, Texas. Visitors can enjoy a variety of activities, including hiking, camping, and horseback riding. In addition, the park is home to the endangered red-cockaded woodpecker. It seems appropriate that an endangered bird would find refuge in a state park named for a man who dedicated so much of his life to protecting forests and the wildlife that lives in them.

Jones, like other conservationists, was able to step back and look at the big picture. He understood too well that the reckless actions of today can have dire consequences tomorrow. In a world that is often inclined to consume and destroy the natural environment, William Goodrich Jones was the voice of reason and an inspiration to those who would follow in his footsteps.

5. When did Jones found the Texas Forestry Association?

    A. before he attended Princeton

    B. after he wrote a report on the state of forestry in Texas

    C. right after his family traveled to Europe

    D. after the Texas Department of Forestry was created

6. According to the map, which is nearest to the W. Goodrich Jones Forest?

    A. Ruth Bowling Nichols Arboretum

    B. Olive Scott Petty Arboretum

    C. Masterson Forest

    D. E.O. Slecke Forest

7. Which sentence from the passage is an opinion?

    A. "Jones was born in New York on November 11, 1860."

    B. "They traveled to Europe, where they spent two years."

    C. "Jones was a natural leader."

    D. "His father was from Texas."

8. Which would be another good title for this passage?

    A. "The W. Goodrich Jones State Forest"

    B. "Saving Endangered Species"

    C. "The History of Forestry"

    D. "A Worthy Cause"

9. BOTH "Get Involved!" and "To Save the Forests"

    A. discuss ways individuals preserve state parks.

    B. discuss the positive effects of recycling.

    C. name several conservation activists.

    D. explain how we can help make the air cleaner.

10. How are the approaches of the two passages different? Use examples from the passages in your response.

_____

_____

_____

_____

_____

CHAPTER

Writing

Chapter 3: Diagnostic Assessment

Chapter 3: Cumulative Assessment

This passage contains mistakes. Read the passage and answer the questions that follow.

(1) Many people love the idea of growing their own garden but don't know how to get started. (2) They are under the impression that they need to have a "green thumb." (3) It's true that growing a garden ain't easy. (4) However, anyone can grow a garden if he or she has the right information, the patience, and the time. (5) So, if you're one of those people who envies your neighbors' garden and wishes you had one of your own, it's time to start working toward your dream. (6) There are many resources for beginning gardeners. (7) The Internet has literally millions of articles on gardening. (8) You can find magazines and books on gardening in the library. (9) Most towns have local garden clubs. (10) You can also get tips from family and friends. (11) So, what are you waiting for? (12) Here are some basic tips to get you started.

(13) To help you decide what to plant where, watch your yard for several days, noting where the sun and shade appear in the morning, afternoon, and late afternoon. (14) First, you will want to plan your garden. (15) To ensure a successful garden, purchase only those plants or seeds that will grow in your climate. (16) They should also grow in your lighting and soil. (17) You will need to find out recent predictions for rainfall and temperature for the upcoming year. (18) Prepare your soil by hoeing or raking it and working some compost into the soil. (19) Mulch your plants to help keep in moisture. (20) Wait until the last frost in your region before setting plants out into the garden. (21) Finally, don't have overly high expectations. (22) Your garden is not going to look like the ancient Hanging Gardens of Babylon. (23) But if you put in the time, you will be rewarded with a garden of your very own.

1. What is the BEST way to combine sentences 15 and 16?

   A. Plants and seeds will grow more successfully in your climate, lighting, and soil in your garden.

   B. Purchase only those plants or seeds that will grow in your climate, lighting, and soil for ensuring a successful garden.

   C. To ensure a successful garden, purchase only those plants or seeds that will grow in your climate, lighting, and soil.

   D. To ensure success, purchase only those plants, or seeds, that will grow in your climate, lighting, and soil in your garden.

2. Which would be the BEST source to find the information in sentence 17?

   A. a gardening book

   B. an encyclopedia

   C. a textbook

   D. an almanac

3. The purpose of this passage is to

   A. get readers to appreciate the joys of nature.

   B. explain how to mulch plants for gardening.

   C. give readers historical background on gardening.

   D. help readers get started on growing a garden.

4. Which two sentences in the paragraph should be switched?

   A. sentences 6 and 7

   B. sentences 13 and 14

   C. sentences 17 and 18

   D. sentences 22 and 23

5. Which sentence contains a word that is not appropriate for the audience?

   A. "It's true that growing a garden ain't easy."

   B. "Finally, don't have overly high expectations."

   C. "The Internet has literally millions of articles on gardening."

   D. "They are under the impression that they need to have a 'green thumb.'"

6. Which source would be the BEST place to look for information about the ancient Hanging Gardens of Babylon?

   A. a magazine article about the Middle East

   B. a history book on ancient Babylon

   C. the dictionary entry for "Babylon"

   D. a blog by the president of a gardening club

Narrative Prompt

Michael goes to sleep after many hours of working on his homework. When he wakes up the next morning, he is the president of the United States. Write a story about what happens to him. What does he do? Where does he go? Who does he talk to? Be sure to include characters, a setting, and a plot in your story, as well as specific details to make your story interesting.

Use the checklist below to help you do your best writing.

Does your story

- ❏ have a point of view?
- ❏ have a setting, plot, and characters?
- ❏ develop the setting, plot, and characters with well-chosen details?
- ❏ connect its different sections with effective methods?
- ❏ use word choice to develop a mood?
- ❏ have a satisfying ending?
- ❏ have good spelling, capitalization, and punctuation?
- ❏ follow the rules for good grammar?

Write your response in the space provided. You may use your own paper if you need more space.

17 Write an Argument

W.8.1.a–e, W.8.4, W.8.5, W.8.10, RH.8.1, RH.8.2, WHST.8.1.a–e, WHST.8.4, WHST.8.5, WHST.8.10

Getting the Idea

As you may already know, an **argument** is an attempt to persuade someone to think or act in a certain way. It is an opinion supported with facts. How well you structure and write an argument will determine how convincing it will be.

- Your first paragraph is the **introduction**. This is where you state your **claim**, or thesis. The claim is the central idea that you want to persuade your readers to agree with. For example, you might write an argument with this claim: *Parents should not search their children's rooms without their knowledge.*

- Support the claim with the reasons you are presenting the claim. These reasons should be supported with relevant evidence so that the reader is more inclined to agree with you or respect your opinion. Write at least two to three supporting paragraphs, each with its own **topic sentence**. To support the claim above, your topic sentences might be: 1) *Children have a right to privacy.* 2) *A good parent-child relationship is built on trust.* 3) *Kids will become even more secretive.* Develop each topic sentence with details and evidence, such as the reasons why trust is important and examples of kids who have been in this situation.

- Write a **conclusion**. This is the last paragraph in the composition. It restates the main ideas in the argument. Include a concluding statement, such as: *Parents who search their children's rooms do more harm than good.*

Including expert opinions that support your claims will make your argument even stronger. There have likely been scientific studies on trust between parents and children, so it would be a good idea to do some research. Just make sure you check the author's qualifications—you want the sources you cite to be credible.

A strong argument is also free of **bias**, which is the tendency to favor one point of view without fairly considering other sides of the argument. An intelligent reader is going to know when an author is ignoring or hiding certain information that would weaken the argument. Imagine how much more persuasive your argument will be if you are able to acknowledge an opposing argument and explain why it is wrong?

Word choice is an important part of writing. Use precise and descriptive words to convey your meaning to your reader. The word *bad,* for example, is vague. Don't say: *Kids feel **bad** when their parents go through their **things**.* Say: *Kids feel **betrayed** when their parents go through their **belongings**.*

Use transitional words and phrases to create a bridge between ideas. These include *for example, in contrast, furthermore, for instance, however, in addition,* and *in closing.* Without transitions, your essay may sound too choppy.

Although your argument will express your opinions and point of view, you should maintain an objective, formal style and tone. In other words, no matter how strongly you feel about the subject, do not let your style become too emotional. You won't convince the reader through angry words or unfair, biased statements.

Here is an example of an overly emotional sentence: *Parents are always sticking their noses where they don't belong.* You could certainly say this more objectively. For example, *Sometimes parents are too curious about their children's activities.*

After your first draft is finished, you'll need to take another look at it. Read what you have written critically, consider a new approach if necessary, and make revisions. Share your writing with your teacher and other students in the class. They can catch errors you missed and make suggestions for improvements. Below is a graphic organizer that shows how you could plan the argument.

Claim	Parents should respect their children's privacy.
Topic Sentence 1	Children have a right to privacy.
Topic Sentence 2	A good parent-child relationship is built on trust.
Topic Sentence 3	Kids will become more secretive if they feel their privacy isn't respected.
Concluding Statement	Without enough respect for their children's privacy, parents may damage their family life.

Coached Example

Read the topic sentences below. Then write a supporting paragraph for each one, developing it with reasons and examples. You can also take the <u>opposite</u> point of view for either topic.

1. Students should be taught more geography in school.

_____

_____

_____

_____

_____

_____

HINT Think about why learning geography is important.

2. The voting age should be lowered from eighteen to sixteen.

_____

_____

_____

_____

_____

_____

HINT Explain why this would be a good (or bad) idea.

Lesson Practice

Use the Writing Guide to help you understand the passage.

<table>
<tr><td>

Writing **Guide**

Which sentence in the introduction is the author's central claim?

How could the author organize paragraph 2 more effectively?

</td><td>

Cloning Dolly

Many years ago, the idea of cloning sounded like something out of a science fiction movie. However, when Dolly the sheep was cloned from the nucleus of an adult cell in 1996, science fiction collided with reality. Dolly's birth proved that just because scientists *can* do something does not mean they *should*. Cloning should be banned throughout the world.

Dolly was the first mammal to be cloned from an adult cell. Before Dolly, scientists had created clones from embryonic cells. Dolly's birth came as a shock to the scientific community and the world. Some people were excited at this scientific breakthrough, but others were horrified. Their horror is understandable. Anyone who has read *Frankenstein* knows that things didn't turn out too well. Cloning is just as unnatural and unethical.

The scariest thing about cloning animals is that it may lead to the cloning of humans. Is that a power we really want anyone to have? It could be abused in so many ways. People could choose to clone others based on skin or eye color. If all it takes is a cell, people could be cloned without their knowledge or permission.

</td></tr>
</table>

Write the conclusion to this argument.

_____

_____

_____

_____

_____

Duplicating any part of this book is prohibited by law.

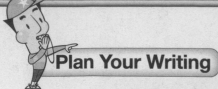

Plan Your Writing

Read the writing prompt, and then plan your response below.

The Constitution requires that in order to be president of the United States a person must be born a U.S. citizen. Someone who is born a citizen of another country can never run for U.S. president, even if he or she becomes a U.S. citizen through the process of naturalization. What do you think? Should a person who was not born a U.S. citizen have the right to become president? Be sure to support your argument with reasons, examples, and details.

Claim	
Topic Sentence 1	
Topic Sentence 2	
Topic Sentence 3	
Concluding Statement	

Write Your Response

Write your response on the pages provided.

Duplicating any part of this book is prohibited by law.

Duplicating any part of this book is prohibited by law.

Argument Writing Checklist

Use the checklist below to help you do your best writing.

Does your essay

❏ have a clear topic?

❏ show a point of view about that topic?

❏ have a logical structure?

❏ support reasons with details?

❏ connect reasons and details with the right words or phrases?

❏ use a style and vocabulary that is correct for the audience and purpose?

❏ have a solid conclusion?

❏ have good spelling, capitalization, and punctuation?

❏ follow the rules for good grammar?

Lesson Practice

Use the Writing Guide to help you understand the passage.

Writing **Guide**

What argument does the author present?

What reason in paragraph 2 supports the claim?

An opposing claim is an idea that disagrees with the author's claim. How does the author respond to the opposing claim in paragraph 3?

The Great Recession

From 2007 until 2009, the United States endured the Great Recession. A recession is a decline in economic activity. People stopped spending money, while businesses halted hiring and lowered the production of goods and services. Economists, politicians, and citizens have all debated the causes of the recession. However, one clear cause cannot be argued: Investing in housing in the United States led to poor decisions by banks and resulted in the fall of the economy.

In the early 2000s, many viewed owning a home as an investment. Demand was high, and home prices rose at a rate of almost 10% each year. Buying and selling homes seemed like a good way to make money. The problems began when buyers were given mortgages—loans from banks used to buy homes—that they could not afford. Mortgages are paid back with interest, the money charged by banks for the loan. Banks offered buyers huge loans for huge houses. Many banks offered adjustable rate mortgages with low interest rates. However, these low interest rates only lasted a few years, resetting to much higher rates. This was fine if buyers sold the house before the interest rates increased. In contrast, some homeowners couldn't afford mortgages with the higher rates. In addition, these buyers also didn't qualify for new loans; it became clear that many homeowners were approved for loans that they could not pay back.

In contrast, some blame the recession on buyers seeking bigger and better homes. But many argue that banks approved the loans. Furthermore, many buyers didn't understand the terms of the loans or how adjustable rate mortgages work. More evidence that banks caused the recession can be found in mortgage-backed securities. These are investments that included the "bad" mortgages that banks sold to other companies. The investments were worthless. By approving questionable loans in the first place and then selling them as investments, banks made unfortunate decisions that led to the housing market crisis and the Great Recession.

Plan Your Writing

Read the writing prompt, and then plan your response below.

Although the United States is made up of people from various countries, some argue that Americans do not have enough knowledge of different cultures. It has been proposed that college students should be required to travel to foreign countries in order to encounter new perspectives and learn more about different cultures. Write an argument for or against this proposal. Be sure to include your claim in the introduction and at least two paragraphs with topic sentences that support your claim. Remember to support your claim with facts and reliable sources and to restate your claim in the conclusion.

Claim	
Topic Sentence 1	
Topic Sentence 2	
Topic Sentence 3	
Concluding Statement	

Write Your Response

Write your response on the pages provided.

Argument Writing Checklist

Use the checklist below to help you do your best writing.

Does your essay

❑ have a clear topic?

❑ show a point of view about that topic?

❑ have a logical structure?

❑ support reasons with details?

❑ connect reasons and details with the right words or phrases?

❑ use a style and vocabulary that is correct for the audience and purpose?

❑ have a solid conclusion?

❑ have good spelling, capitalization, and punctuation?

❑ follow the rules for good grammar?

18 Write an Informative Text

W.8.2.a–f, W.8.4, W.8.5, W.8.10, WHST.8.2.a–f, WHST.8.4, WHST.8.5, WHST.8.10

Getting the Idea

An **informative text** gives the reader information about a topic, using facts, examples, and specific details. Biographies, history books, and newspapers are examples of informative texts. Texts that explain something are also informative. A science article that explains why earthquakes happen is informative. Additionally, an essay you write about yourself or your life is informative.

When you write an informative text, start by announcing the topic in the **introduction**. Let's say you decide to write about the Lewis and Clark expedition. After you introduce this topic, you need to develop it. There are certain key elements writers use to develop informative topics.

- **facts:** *Meriwether Lewis and William Clark were commissioned by President Thomas Jefferson to explore the northwest region of the United States and find a land route to the Pacific.*

- **examples:** *Sacagawea, their Shoshone Indian interpreter and guide, was a great help to them. One day, Sacagawea helped the explorers obtain the horses they desperately needed.*

- **details:** *In the summer of 1885, Lewis and Clark traveled across the Bitterroot Mountains in Montana and Idaho.*

- **quotations:** Lewis, who kept a journal during the exploration, wrote, *"The land is not fertile, at least far less so, than the plains of the Columbia or those lower down this river."*

Make connections between these elements by using transitional words and phrases, such as *for example, furthermore, in contrast, however, in addition, then,* and *likewise.* Transitions will help readers move from one thought to another, and they will also help the overall effect of your essay.

Maintain an objective style and tone in your writing. Your purpose is to inform— it is not to entertain or to persuade. So, you should not say, "Lewis and Clark were awesome explorers!" First, the word *awesome* is too informal. Second, the sentence shows a little too much enthusiasm for an informative essay. It distracts the reader from the facts of the essay and focuses too much attention on your point of view.

Be sure to write a **conclusion** at the end of your composition. It should restate the main ideas of the composition and include a concluding statement. For example, *Lewis and Clark made many important discoveries along their historic journey.* The conclusion should also follow logically from the statements that come before it.

Often, you need to use sources to support and develop your topic. How much information about Lewis and Clark do you have stored in your head? You probably don't know enough to write a composition about them without research. Use primary sources, such as the explorers' journals, or secondary sources, like a biography, to get the information.

If you write an informative text on a scientific subject, support it with accurate information, data, and evidence. Also, use the terms most appropriate for your subject. You might develop a composition on why earthquakes happen with facts about faults, plates, and seismic waves.

Many scientific or historical subjects are complicated and difficult to explain to a reader, so it might be a good idea to organize your ideas into larger sections using headings. Perhaps your composition on Lewis and Clark could be ordered sequentially—in the order that the expedition occurred—using headings such as "Meeting Sacagawea" and "Traveling Across Biterroot." You might also use a cause-and-effect organizational structure and explain the effects of certain events that occurred on their expedition. Before you can begin structuring your text, however, you will want to organize your research and ideas. The graphic organizer below shows one way to organize information on the topic.

Main Idea
The journey of Lewis and Clark was a difficult but ultimately rewarding journey.

Facts
Lewis and Clark were commissioned by Thomas Jefferson to explore the northwest region of the U.S. and find a land route to the Pacific.

Examples
Sacagawea, their Shoshone Indian interpreter and guide, was a great help to them. One day, Sacagawea helped the explorers obtain the horses they desperately needed.

Details
In the summer of 1885, Lewis and Clark traveled across the Bitterroot Mountains in Montana and Idaho.

Quotations
Meriwether Lewis, who kept a journal during the exploration, wrote, "The land is not fertile, at least far less so, than the plains of the Columbia or those lower down this *river*."

Conclusion
Lewis and Clark made important discoveries during their historic journey.

After you write a draft, get feedback on your informative text from your teacher and classmates. Listen to their suggestions on ways to improve your composition.

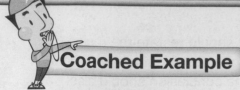

Coached Example

Read the topics below. Then use what you learned about informative texts to develop the topics.

1. Write an informative paragraph about an important person in your life. Use whatever facts, examples, and details you know about this person's life.

_____

_____

_____

_____

_____

_____

HINT You might write about a relative, a mentor, or a close friend.

2. Write an informative paragraph about a place you have been. Use whatever facts, examples, and details you can think of to describe this place.

_____

_____

_____

_____

_____

_____

HINT For example: You might write about a national park, an amusement park, or a museum.

Lesson Practice

Use the Writing Guide to help you understand the passage.

Writing Guide

How does the author support the main idea of the second paragraph?

What is the main idea of the third paragraph?

The Earth's Resources

A natural resource is something that is found in nature and is used by humans. There are two types of resources— renewable and nonrenewable. A renewable resource is something that is either always available or easy to remake. A nonrenewable resource is something that is in limited supply and will one day be exhausted. Both types of resources help to sustain life.

Renewable resources include anything that can be remade, reproduced, or regenerated easily. These resources include animals, plants, water, and certain forms of energy. Animals and plants reproduce, or make more offspring. Water is available because of the water cycle. Water, along with the sun and wind, can be used as energy. Since water, the sun, and the wind are always available, they are renewable resources.

Nonrenewable resources include fossil fuels. Examples of fossil fuels are oil, natural gas, and coal. They are made from fossilized remains of plants and animals. The fossilization process takes a long time, so fossils and fossil fuels are in limited supply.

For years, scientists and researchers have been figuring out ways to sustain our supply of natural resources. Recycling is the most common method so far, but new approaches will probably be developed in the future.

What is the author's main topic? List two examples the author uses to develop the topic.

_____

_____

_____

_____

_____

Duplicating any part of this book is prohibited by law.

Plan Your Writing

Read the writing prompt, and then plan your response below.

Think of an inventor whose accomplishments you respect. Write an essay that tells about the inventor's life. As you research, remember to choose resources carefully and create a bibliography. Be sure to develop your topic with specific facts, details, and examples.

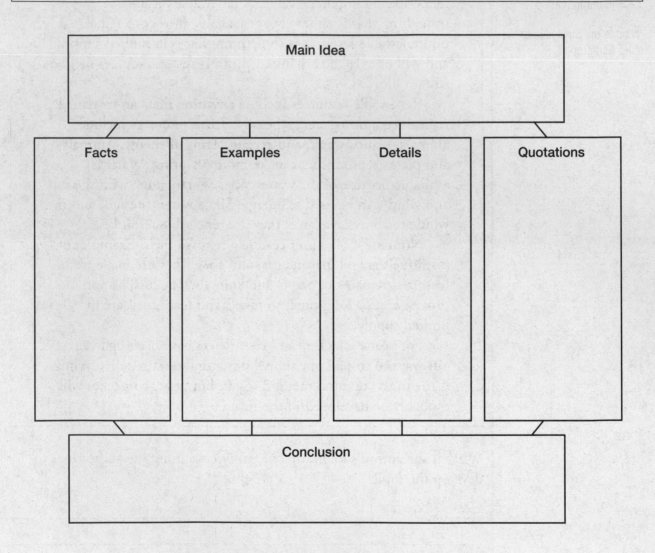

Main Idea

Facts

Examples

Details

Quotations

Conclusion

Write Your Response

Write your response on the pages provided.

Informative Writing Checklist

Use the checklist below to help you do your best writing.

Does your essay

❏ have a clear and focused subject?

❏ organize its information into logical categories?

❏ develop its topic with well-chosen facts, details, and other evidence?

❏ join ideas clearly with transitional words and phrases?

❏ use a style and vocabulary appropriate for the audience and purpose?

❏ build to a solid conclusion?

❏ have good spelling, capitalization, and punctuation?

❏ follow the rules for good grammar?

Lesson Practice

Use the Writing Guide to help you understand the passage.

Writing Guide

What is the topic of the passage? Where did you locate the topic or main idea?

What facts does the author include to support the main idea?

How does the conclusion reinforce the main idea of the passage?

Woman in the Industrial Revolution

The Industrial Revolution began in Europe and soon made its way to America, signaling a time of significant change. The economy shifted from handcrafted goods to machine-made, mass-produced goods. U.S. business owners took advantage of major advancements in machinery, building factories with machines that could mass-produce goods. With the sudden increase in demand for machine-made textiles came a new opportunity for women. As homemakers, women were traditionally responsible for crafting goods for their families. That allowed them to enter this new workforce and play a key role in the beginning of the Industrial Revolution.

The first textile mills were built in the 1790s in New England, producing cotton and providing work for entire families. Children often worked the machines, and women finished the work by weaving the yarn by hand into cloth. However, when the power loom was invented, taller workers were needed. Children were replaced by women who could run the looms to create cloth that was entirely machine-made. Young women flocked to factory towns because they could earn more working in factories than they could on family farms. Some viewed it as an escape from marrying farmers, and others viewed it as a path to independence. In contrast, some women worked in mills to help support their families and to save money for marriage.

Regardless of the reasons, working in factories was not glamorous or easy. The workdays were long, and the work was physically demanding. Women lived in boardinghouses near the factories and were often asked to pay high rents. When factory owners increased the work hours but not the pay, many women protested, arguing for ten-hour workdays. In 1836, the Lowell Mill Girls in Massachusetts fought against an increase in rents, stopping work until boardinghouse rents were lowered. Women were the first wave of workers who navigated the factory labor force, working hard and effecting change as key members of the Industrial Revolution.

Plan Your Writing

Read the writing prompt, and then plan your response below.

The Cold War was a conflict between the United States and the Soviet Union. The conflict was based on mistrust as well as on differences in ideas about the leadership of each country. The Cold War shaped the decisions of leaders for many years, and its impact is remembered even today. Do some research on this topic. Then write an informative essay that describes how the Cold War began and what led to its conclusion. Be sure to introduce your topic, support your main idea by including facts, examples, details, or quotations, and restate your main idea in the conclusion.

Write Your Response

Write your response on the pages provided.

Informative Writing Checklist

Use the checklist below to help you do your best writing.

Does your essay

❏ have a clear and focused subject?

❏ organize its information into logical categories?

❏ develop its topic with well-chosen facts, details, and other evidence?

❏ join ideas clearly with transitional words and phrases?

❏ use a style and vocabulary appropriate for the audience and purpose?

❏ build to a solid conclusion?

❏ have good spelling, capitalization, and punctuation?

❏ follow the rules for good grammar?

19 Write a Narrative

W.8.3.a–e, W.8.4, W.8.5, W.8.10, WHST.8.4, WHST.8.10

Getting the Idea

A **narrative** is a piece of writing that tells a story. Novels and short stories are examples of narratives. However, narratives do not have to be fiction. If you write a funny story about what happened to you at the zoo last year, you are writing a narrative. Even historical and scientific texts may include narrative elements. Read the tips below.

- **Make sure your narrative has a plot.** This is the story line, or sequence of events. When you plan your narrative, choose the events and details you want to include and describe them in order. A narrative is not simply a series of events, however. A narrative should contain a conflict, or a problem the characters need to solve. A plot may also involve a lesson that a character learns. The key thing to remember is that the events in the narrative should engage the reader—or be interesting enough to keep him or her turning the pages.

- **Include a setting in your narrative.** Tell when the events happen and where. The setting can be an important part of your story. Are you writing an adventure? Set the narrative in a wild jungle or on a fictional planet. Think about the time period carefully. It should be appropriate for the plot and setting of your story.

- **Write interesting characters.** These are the people or animals in your story. Include details about the characters that help readers understand them and care about what happens to them. Describe what the characters look like, how they act, what they wear, how they talk, and how they interact with other characters.

- **Paint a picture for the reader.** Use descriptive, colorful language to help the reader "see" what you are describing. Also, use precise language when it's possible. Instead of "run," say "dash" or "sprint." Your word choice will also establish the mood, or the feeling your reader gets from the story. For example: "Dark shadows moved eerily behind the trees as Kay crossed the lonely road." The words *dark, shadows, eerily,* and *lonely* create a scary mood.

- **Develop the story with dialogue, pacing, description, and reflection.** The **dialogue**, or the words characters say to each other, can really keep a story moving. Try to make your dialogue energetic and meaningful. In other words, don't just have characters say "hi" to each other—have them argue, or joke, or interact in another entertaining way. This pushes the story forward at a good rate. Pausing to describe a scene or show characters' thoughts, however, can add depth and meaning to a story if well done.

- **Establish the context and point of view.** For example, you write a narrative about Gia and Jen, who are hostile to each other every time they meet. Establish the context by telling the reader why: Jen had accused Gia of stealing her ring. Also, choose the point of view—the perspective from which the story is told. Maybe the narrator in this story is Jen. The reader sees what happens through her eyes.

- **Establish connections between events, time frames, and characters.** Narratives often have multiple story lines, characters, and changes in time and setting. Include transitions in your narrative so that the reader does not get confused. For example: *Back at Trevor's house…* or *Meanwhile* or *The next day…*

- **Write a satisfying conclusion, or ending, to your narrative.** For instance, "When Jen found her ring, she apologized to Gia, and the two friends hugged each other."

The graphic organizer below outlines a narrative.

Introduction	Event	Event	Event	Conclusion/ Ending
Gia and Jen are hostile to each other when they meet because Jen accused Gia of stealing her ring.	Gia tries to explain what really happened, but Jen doesn't believe her.	Jen checks with some friends to see if Gia's story is true.	Jen discovers that Gia's story is actually quite true, after all.	Gia and Jen make up, and they are good friends once again.

After you write a draft of your narrative, do not be shy to share your work with a peer or your teacher. Being able to write an effective narrative takes practice, and someone else might have valuable suggestions or ideas that you had not considered. Perhaps a character can be fleshed out more, or maybe some of the dialogue can be tweaked to sound more natural. Whatever the case, first drafts are never perfect.

Coached Example

Read the sentences below. Each sentence is the first line to a paragraph in a story. Complete each paragraph, using what you learned about writing narratives. Share your narratives with your teacher and class.

1. Aisha opened the door to the refrigerator and screamed.

_____

_____

_____

_____

_____

_____

_____

HINT What does Aisha see in the refrigerator? Is your story scary or funny? Is it realistic or fantasy?

2. Christopher swung at the baseball, and then he watched it crash through Mr. Bashir's window.

_____

_____

_____

_____

_____

_____

_____

HINT Christopher has a problem. How does he try to solve it?

Lesson Practice

Use the Writing Guide to help you understand the passage.

Writing Guide

The Nineteenth Amendment to the U.S. Constitution gave women the right to vote.

What does the tone of Susan's mother's dialogue tell you about her?

At Long Last

Suzanne fidgeted as her mother tried tying the bow on her hair for the third time. "Mother, really, I don't need this bow! I look fine without it," she said.

"Hush, child," her mother answered, pulling the ends of the red bow with her long fingers. "This is one of the most important days of our lives, and we must look presentable."

Suzanne crossed her arms and pouted. She didn't understand what the big deal was all about. An hour ago, her mother had rushed in the door, nearly tripping on her long skirts. Her eyes had been lit with a sort of wild happiness that had almost frightened Suzanne.

"We did it, Sue! We did it!" her mom had shouted. Then, she had hugged Suzanne so tightly that she had almost cut off her breath.

"Did what, Mother?" Suzanne had asked when her mother had finally released her.

"Why, won the right to vote, of course! That's only all I've talked about for the last year. It's finally done! The Nineteenth Amendment has been ratified. Mark this day, Suzanne! August 18, 1920. One day you will realize what this means."

Explain how the author's description and dialogue help you understand how Suzanne's mother is feeling.

_____

_____

_____

_____

_____

Plan Your Writing

Read the writing prompt, and then plan your response below.

When Ryan wakes up on Saturday morning, he is ten years older, but everyone else is the same age they were the day before. Write a story about what happens next. Be sure to include characters, a plot, and a setting. Your story must have a beginning, a middle, and an end. Use descriptive language.

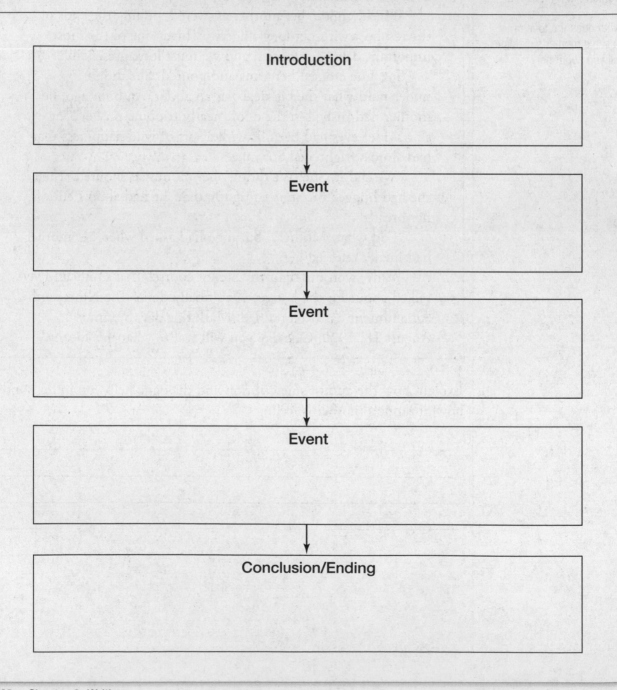

Introduction

Event

Event

Event

Conclusion/Ending

Write Your Response

Write your response on the pages provided.

Narrative Writing Checklist

Use the checklist below to help you do your best writing.

Does your story

- ❏ have a point of view?

- ❏ have a setting, plot, and characters?

- ❏ develop the setting, plot, and characters with well-chosen details?

- ❏ present events in a logical sequence?

- ❏ use descriptive, colorful language to develop a mood?

- ❏ have a satisfying ending?

- ❏ have good spelling, capitalization, and punctuation?

- ❏ follow the rules for good grammar?

Lesson Practice

Use the Writing Guide to help you understand the passage.

Writing Guide

How does the author introduce readers to the main characters?

What conflict does the writer introduce? How is the conflict set up?

Notice descriptive details in the text. How do they help the writer bring the characters and setting to life?

A Little Bit of Luck

Marcus practically skipped down the street on his way to Jia Li's house. The scorching summer sun, along with his excitement, made him glad to finally reach the shade of Jia Li's doorstep. Marcus couldn't wait to see her face when he told her what he had just discovered.

When Jia Li opened her front door, Marcus grabbed her hand and dragged her into the kitchen. "Jia, have you heard the news?"

"What news?" asked Jia Li with a perplexed look on her face.

"Our favorite band just announced that they are going to do a concert downtown in Piermont Park! I know how much you adore the lead singer," Marcus said, the words tumbling out as he tried to catch his breath.

"Wow!" Jia Li shouted. "I've always wanted to see the Sky Rockets play live! When is the concert?"

"August 30th—it's a Saturday afternoon," said Marcus, popping his cell phone out of his pocket to show his friend a photograph he had snapped of the poster he had encountered on the way over.

"Oh, no!" screeched Jia Li, her voice full of dismay. "August 30th is Grandfather's eightieth birthday party. All my relatives will be at our house that day for a dinner in his honor. I have to be there, too. My mom has already started making preparations, and I know she's counting on my assistance; it's all she talks about."

Not able to hide his disappointment, Marcus's face fell. "I can't believe we won't be able to go," he said sadly.

"There's no reason why you can't go," said Jia Li forlornly. "I suppose I'll have to wait for the next Sky Rockets appearance. But I really wanted to see them!"

That evening, Jia Li told her parents about her distressing news, although she knew there was no hope of any change in plans.

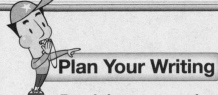

Plan Your Writing

Read the paragraph and the prompt that follows, and plan your response below.

The paragraph below is the conclusion of "A Little Bit of Luck."

Jia Li couldn't believe that she had gotten to sit in the front row and watch Simon Sky and the whole band perform almost every single song she loved. "And I got to be there for Grandfather's special day, too! I guess all you need," she thought, smiling, "is a little bit of luck."

Use the introduction and conclusion to write the middle part of the story. Sequence the events logically, making sure to connect the beginning and the ending. Add new characters, but consider the context, setting, characters, and point of view already introduced. Remember to include descriptive details and dialogue.

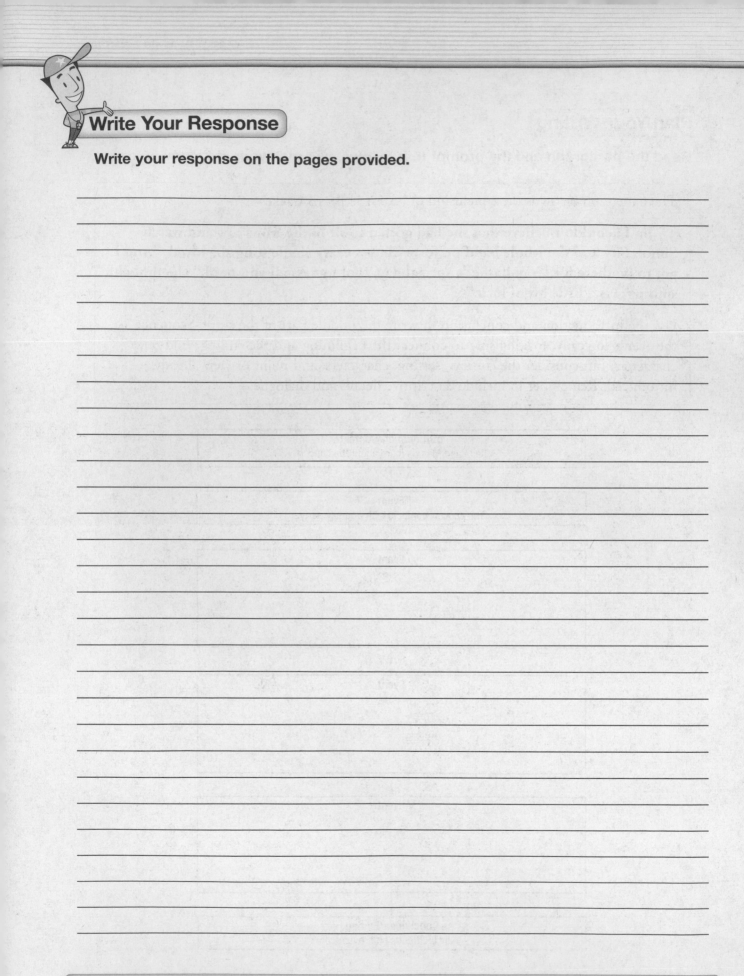

Write Your Response

Write your response on the pages provided.

Duplicating any part of this book is prohibited by law.

Duplicating any part of this book is prohibited by law.

Narrative Writing Checklist

Use the checklist below to help you do your best writing.

Does your story

- ❏ have a point of view?

- ❏ have a setting, plot, and characters?

- ❏ develop the setting, plot, and characters with well-chosen details?

- ❏ present events in a logical sequence?

- ❏ use descriptive, colorful language to develop a mood?

- ❏ use dialogue that is meaningful?

- ❏ work within the context established by the introduction and conclusion?

- ❏ have good spelling, capitalization, and punctuation?

- ❏ follow the rules for good grammar?

20 Considering Purpose and Audience

W.8.4, W.8.5, W.8.10, WHST.8.4, WHST.8.5, WHST.8.10

Getting the Idea

As you learned in previous lessons, there are different types of writing. When you create a text, you need to consider the **purpose**, or reason, for the writing. You also need to make the text appropriate for your **audience**, or the people for whom you have written the text. Your purpose and audience should guide your decisions on content, organization, and style.

For example, imagine you write a persuasive essay on teen curfews. Your claim is that teen curfews are unfair, so your position is clearly stated in the introduction. In the rest of your essay, you define what a teen curfew is and you summarize the curfew laws in several states. What you *don't* do is present any reasons or examples that support your claim. You forgot to argue. Since this is the purpose of a persuasive essay, your content does not match the purpose.

Perhaps your teacher asks you to write a narrative, or story. You decide to write about something that happened at your family's last Thanksgiving dinner. However, you think it would be a good idea to begin with a brief history of the Thanksgiving Day tradition. After a couple of paragraphs on the celebration between the pilgrims and the Native Americans, you finally begin writing about the events of the day. Now, a narrative can include facts and history, but this information must be included in the plot as part of the narrative. It cannot simply be attached to the beginning without a transition. Your composition is only *part* narrative.

The organization of your writing should also fit the purpose. Imagine you are writing an informative essay on the establishment of the Food and Drug Administration and its impact on food safety. A well-organized essay would explain why and when the FDA was founded and provide examples of the FDA's role in improving food safety. However, your essay jumps around between different unrelated examples and repeats ideas from earlier paragraphs. Now, this would be effective if your purpose was to *confuse*, but your purpose is to inform.

Your style is the way you express yourself, something you control through word choice. Consider your purpose and audience when you choose your words. Generally, your teachers are your audience when you write for school. Overly casual language and slang are not appropriate for this audience. So, don't write, "That dude Thomas Edison cooked up some awesome inventions!" Write, "Thomas Edison was a great inventor." Inappropriate style distracts your audience from the content.

Thinking It Through

Read the following paragraph, and then answer the questions that follow.

Everyone should follow a vegetarian lifestyle. If you make the right choices, you will find that you can have quite a bit of variety in the vegetables you eat. A vegetarian diet can be much healthier than one that involves the consumption of meat. Vegetables provide nutrients that meat often doesn't provide. Being a vegetarian also spares the lives of all those animals sacrificed for the dinner table.

What is the purpose of this writing? How do you know?

_____

_____

 Think about what the author asks her audience to do.

DISCUSS Do you think the author's word choice is appropriate for her purpose?

Coached Example

Read the passage and answer the questions.

Timir grabbed his mother's hand and took a deep breath. His mom smiled down at him and gave his hand a reassuring squeeze. Together, they walked into the plane, where a flight attendant was waiting to greet them. Timir could hear his heart pounding as he and his mom took their seats. He had a window seat, and he wasn't sure that was a good thing. Watching the ground get farther and farther away as they ascended was not exactly the best way to calm his nerves. The technical name for fear of flying is aviophobia. It can sometimes be cured through therapy or the use of certain computer software. Timir's fear of flying had kept him from traveling outside the country. But finally his mother had convinced him to face his fears. Timir pulled down the window blind. Then, he closed his peepers and tried to picture the sandy beaches and blue waters of their destination.

1. Which word from the passage is NOT appropriate for the audience?

   A. squeeze

   B. grabbed

   C. ascended

   D. peepers

   HINT The inappropriate word is slang.

2. Which sentence from the passage is NOT appropriate for the purpose?

   A. "The technical name for fear of flying is aviophobia."

   B. "Timir grabbed his mother's hand and took a deep breath."

   C. "His mom smiled down at him and gave his hand a reassuring squeeze."

   D. "Timir could hear his heart pounding as he and his mom took their seats."

   HINT The purpose of this passage is to tell a story.

Lesson Practice

Use the Reading Guide to help you understand the passage.

Reading Guide

Based on paragraph 1, what is the purpose of this passage?

Throughout the report, look for sentences that are out of place.

Which word in paragraph 3 is not appropriate for the purpose and audience?

Ways of Measuring: A Student Report

Today, we have standard systems of measurement for length, weight, and power. For example, a foot is equal to twelve inches; a pound is sixteen ounces. Most of the world uses the metric system. However, the United States uses the United States customary system. Hopefully, we will never switch to the metric system because it's pretty lame. Most people will have a hard time learning it. The modern system of measuring evolved over the centuries. It is an interesting history, and I am here to tell you all about it.

In early times, units of length were based on body parts. Historians believe that the earliest standard unit of measurement was the cubit. The cubit was equal to the length of a person's forearm from the elbow to the tip of the middle finger. Although this varied from person to person, it allowed the same person to measure lengths pretty consistently. The ancient Egyptians were among the first to use this system of measurement. They are also famous for building the pyramids.

The ancient Romans also used body parts as a measuring tool. They subdivided the human foot into twelve parts, or as we call them now, inches. The digit was also a unit of length measurement they used. Centuries ago, units of weight, volume, and power were based on commonly used containers: in other words, how much stuff a person or animal could move. For example, nowadays, the term *horsepower* is used to describe the power of a car's engine. The term originated in the 1700s, when a man named James Watt figured out how much power a horse could generate in a specific amount of time. So, originally the term literally applied to horses. By the way, the unit of power used for lightbulbs is named after Watt.

The ancient Chinese also developed systems of measurement. They had a pretty cool way to do it, too. Containers that they used to measure grain or liquids were defined according to weight and sound. Different containers for different weights made different notes when they were struck. As long as the containers had the same shape and weight, only containers that had the same volume made the same note. This reminds me of the time

Duplicating any part of this book is prohibited by law.

What improvements would you make to paragraph 4?

Overall, how does the student fail to consider his purpose and audience?

that my science teacher filled glasses with different levels of water and then played them like a xylophone. One unit of length measurement went from the place on your wrist where you take your pulse to the end of the thumb. Their measurement units changed, as well, from place to place in the country.

Trade among people increased the need to measure accurately and to have standards of measurement. This helped prevent people from giving someone less grain or corn than he was entitled to. European traders in the Middle Ages invented a system of measurement called "avoirdupois." This comes from an old French phrase meaning "weight of goods." Speaking of the French, the metric system was first proposed in France in the 1600s.

The United States customary system is also known as Imperial Units. It really is the easiest form of measurement. Some people believe that the United States should join every other industrialized nation and adopt the metric system. But it would really be difficult for people who are used to measuring in feet and gallons to start using meters and liters. OK, it's true that we already use liters for soda bottles, but that's not the same as changing the whole system. Let's keep our system of measurement exactly the way it is.

Duplicating any part of this book is prohibited by law.

Answer the following questions.

1. Which phrase in paragraph 1 should the student change to better suit his audience?

   A. "a hard time"

   B. "it's pretty lame"

   C. "modern system"

   D. "interesting history"

2. Which sentence in paragraph 2 should be removed to help the passage achieve its purpose?

   A. "The ancient Egyptians were among the first to use this system of measurement."

   B. "The cubit was equal to the length of a person's forearm from the elbow to the tip of the middle finger."

   C. "In early times, units of length were based on body parts."

   D. "They are also famous for building the pyramids."

3. The sentences about the Romans at the beginning of paragraph 3 would contribute better to

   A. paragraph 1.

   B. paragraph 2.

   C. paragraph 3.

   D. paragraph 4.

4. The student's statements about the metric system in the last paragraph do NOT belong in this passage because

   A. they give the impression that Americans are not capable of learning the metric system.

   B. his audience will not agree with his opinion.

   C. the purpose of the passage is to inform, not to persuade.

   D. the purpose of the passage is to persuade, not to inform.

5. Choose another part of the passage and explain why it is NOT appropriate. Use examples from the passage in your response.

   _____

   _____

   _____

   _____

The following questions do not relate to a passage.

6. **Use your answer to Part A to answer Part B.**

The following paragraph is from a student's research paper about the African savannah.

> The African government must pass stronger laws to protect elephants living in the savannah from poachers. The African savannah, located in wide bands across central Africa, is a tropical grassland with occasional trees that dot the rolling landscape. Natural and human-made fires regularly burn away old grass. This promotes the growth of new grass. Any poachers setting fires to trap elephants rather than to protect their habitat should be prosecuted harshly. In addition, temperatures are warm throughout the year. Due to Africa's tropical latitudes, the average seasonal temperature in the savannah is 26° C. African elephants often gather beneath the shade of acacia trees to find relief from the tropical heat.

Part A

Below are five purposes for writing. Based on the first sentence in the paragraph above, circle the one that BEST describes the student's purpose for writing.

Purposes for Writing	to describe
	to entertain
	to explain
	to inform
	to persuade

Part B

Does the content of the rest of the paragraph match the student's purpose you identified in Part A? Explain, using details from the paragraph.

_____

_____

_____

_____

_____

_____

_____

7. **Use your answer to Part A to answer Part B.**

The following topic sentence is from a student's research paper about nutrition. Read the sentence.

> **An understanding of carbohydrates, lipids, and proteins is important to any teen concerned with maintaining proper nutrition in his or her diet.**

Part A

The sentences below follow the topic sentence, but are not listed in a logical order. In each blank box, write the number 2, 3, 4, or 5 so that the sentences are well organized and support the writer's purpose to inform.

| 1 | In general, teen boys need about 3,000 calories per day. |

| | Fifty percent of these calories should come from carbohydrates. |

| | Teen girls need about 2,200 calories per day. |

| | Teen boys should consume about 208 calories of protein per day. |

| | Lipids should supply 25–35 percent of a teen's daily calories. |

| 6 | Teen girls should consume about 184 calories of protein per day. |

Part B

Explain your reasoning for the organization you chose in Part A.

_____

_____

_____

_____

8. The following paragraph is from a student's research paper about Madagascar. Read the paragraph. Then rewrite it, using a style that is appropriate for an audience of teachers.

Madagascar is an island that you can find by looking in the Indian Ocean. On a map, put your finger on Africa's southeastern coast and then slide it out into the ocean about 250 miles. Due to ridiculous winds, eastern Madagascar is soaking wet. It gets like 150 inches of rain per year! What's weird, though, is that western Madagascar is a baking hot desert. This happens because the soggy air dries out as it moves east to west across Madagascar. During the monsoon season, it rains like crazy! Western Madagascar gets something like 14 inches in the south and 80 inches in the north. Twisty tropical cyclones deliver heavy rain and floods to eastern Madagascar.

_____

_____

_____

_____

_____

_____

_____

_____

_____

_____

_____

_____

_____

_____

_____

_____

_____

_____

_____

_____

Duplicating any part of this book is prohibited by law.

9. **Use your answer to Part A to answer Part B.**

   A student is writing an essay to inform younger readers about lemurs. Four methods of organizing writing are listed below.

Organization	Chronological sequence of events
	Claim supported by reasons and evidence
	List of steps in a process
	Main idea followed by supporting details

   Part A

   Circle the organizational method that BEST supports the student's purpose for writing.

   Part B

   Choose the sentence below that BEST illustrates a style appropriate for the student's young audience.

   A. To the casual observer, a lemur is indistinguishable from a monkey.

   B. If you think that a lemur is a monkey, you might want to think again!

   C. Lemurs and monkeys are both common to the order of primates, but the two do not share a species.

   D. While lemurs and monkeys share a variety of traits, they are very different animals.

   _____

10. Which sentences are NOT appropriate for an informative paragraph about the diet of lemurs? There is more than one correct choice listed below.

    A. Lemurs are less intelligent than other primates, such as monkeys.

    B. During a drought, the lemur may ingest insects or lizards, as well.

    C. Lemurs have a life span of up to 18 years in the wild.

    D. Lemurs are unaffected by the cyanide they consume from bamboo trees.

    E. The bamboo lemur eats parts of a bamboo tree, including leaves and shoots.

    F. The lemur is among the world's most endangered primate species.

    G. Watching a lemur eat is one of the cutest things I've ever seen.

Duplicating any part of this book is prohibited by law.

21 Respond to Literature

W.8.9.a, W.8.10

Getting the Idea

Literature is written work derived from a writer's imagination and creativity. A work of literature can be a novel, a story, a drama, a poem, or even a graphic novel. Although each piece of literature is created uniquely, much of literature reflects patterns from long ago. Writers repeat themes (for example, the struggle between good and evil), character types (such as the hero or the villain), and events (such as a celebration or a journey) from traditional stories, such as myths and folktales. They do this because the themes, characters, and events that are important to traditional literature still speak to modern-day readers and apply to their lives. Recognizing these patterns is one way that a writer can respond to literature.

A **literary response** can take several forms. You might be asked to focus on the elements, or parts, of the work, such as the characters, setting, events, and theme, along with how they work together or relate to each other. This type of response is called a **literary analysis**. In a literary analysis, for example, you might respond to the way in which one character's traits affected the actions of the other characters.

If you are asked to focus on what you think or how you feel, you are writing a **literary reflection**. Literature is meant to evoke strong responses from readers, appealing to emotions and often sparking debate. For example, you might be asked to analyze the emotional impact of an event that led to a character making a poor decision. Writing about how that makes you feel will give you a better understanding of the story and help you learn more about yourself—both as a reader and as a person.

Whether your writing involves analyzing or reflecting on a piece of literature, you will need to use evidence from the text to support your ideas. For example, if you write that a character's need to be a hero led to others feeling inferior, you will need to cite details, events, actions, and dialogue from the text that reveal and support your claim. For each claim, you should typically seek to include two or three citations from the story to support your idea. Finally, although literature can often read as informal, your response is likely a formal assignment, so remember to keep the tone of your writing formal.

 Duplicating any part of this book is prohibited by law.

As you plan your writing for a response to literature, it's helpful to organize your ideas in a chart. The information you put in the chart should show that:

- you understand the theme, or the main message that the author is trying to convey.

- you have insight about the characters, setting, events, and ideas in the story. This includes identifying patterns from traditional stories that are repeated in the story.

- you can cite examples and evidence from the text that support your interpretation of the piece of literature.

Suppose you were asked to write an analysis of a story about Ricky, a student who bullies others until he is stopped by Gina and other members of their school's anti-bullying coalition. Your completed chart might look something like this.

	Supporting Detail	**Supporting Detail**	**Supporting Detail**
Theme: Understanding what causes a person's behavior can change that person's behavior.	Gina shares information about how bullies are often bullied themselves.	Ricky admits that he was bullied and that he bullied others to hide his own insecurity.	Ricky signs a pledge to break the bullying cycle.
Character Description: Ricky is actually quite shy; he bullies in order to appear outgoing and confident.	In the hallways, Ricky is loud, making his presence known. He slams the locker doors and yells at students.	When confronted one-on-one by one of the anti-bullying coalition members, Ricky speaks softly and looks down.	Ricky admits that he doesn't feel comfortable in large crowds and prefers listening instead of talking.
My Interpretation: Ricky doesn't consider the effects of his actions and just thinks that bullying helps him feel powerful.	Ricky feels invincible when walking in the halls and feels supported by his friends, who laugh at his behavior.	Ricky looks visibly upset when students who've been bullied share stories of how they feel.	Ricky is the first one to sign the pledge to stop bullying, saying, "I didn't know."

Coached Example

Read the passage and answer the question.

Honest Omar
based on the Cypriot folktale "Honesty and the Golden Axe"

As part of their school's service requirement, Omar and Justin both volunteered at the Overcrest senior center, riding their bikes there a few afternoons a week. They cleaned, did yard work, assisted with the cooking—whatever was needed. As Omar worked, he often listened to music through the earphones of his mp3 player, and the staff and senior citizens enjoyed watching him bob his head in time to the music.

One afternoon, Omar couldn't find his mp3 player. He looked everywhere, but the device was nowhere to be found. Everyone at the senior center knew that Omar adored music but probably couldn't afford a new player, so they pooled their funds and purchased one identical to his old player. "Here," Susannah, the center's manager, said, handing him the device, "look what we found! It's the player you lost."

But Omar shook his head, saying, "This one is new, so it doesn't belong to me."

Justin, who was nearby, walked over, took one look at the new player, and announced, "This is the player I lost!" He pulled another player from his pocket and said, "I found this old one yesterday."

"Uhh, thanks, Justin, for finding my player." Omar said, frowning. Justin handed the old device to Omar and reached for the new player.

"Not so fast," Susannah said. "This can't belong to you, because we bought it yesterday to replace Omar's lost one." Justin's face slowly turned beet red.

Susannah turned to Omar and smiled. "Take the new player as a reward for your hard work and enthusiasm, as well as for your honesty," she told Omar. "And Justin, please get to work; the bathroom floors need scrubbing."

---

1. Suppose you are asked to write a literary analysis that discusses how the traditional character types of hero and villain are reflected in this story. Describe an idea you might include. Remember to support your idea with evidence from the story.

_____

_____

_____

_____

HINT   Remember that a literary analysis discusses elements such as characters, setting, and theme. Your response should cite evidence directly from the text.

Lesson Practice

Use the Writing Guide to help you understand the passage.

Writing Guide

What details in the story help you better understand the character of Alice? What details tell you more about the Red Queen?

As you read, think about the fantastical elements the author includes. What effects do they have on the characters and the plot?

Where is this part of the story set? In what way does it reflect the characters Alice has met during her adventure?

excerpted and adapted from

Through the Looking Glass
by Lewis Carroll

At the beginning of the story, Alice steps through a mirror above the mantelpiece at home and into an imaginary world populated with strange characters, many of whom resemble chess pieces. After exploring the Looking Glass house, she finds herself in a beautiful garden, where she meets the Red Queen.

Alice curtseyed again, as she was afraid from the Queen's tone that she was a little offended; and they walked on in silence till they got to the top of the little hill. For some minutes, Alice stood without speaking, looking out in all directions over the country—and a most curious country it was. There were a number of tiny little brooks running straight across it from side to side, and the ground between was divided up into squares by a number of little green hedges, that reached from brook to brook.

"I declare it's marked out just like a large chessboard!" Alice said at last. "There ought to be some men moving about somewhere—and so there are!" she added in a tone of delight, and her heart began to beat quickly with excitement as she went on. "It's a great huge game of chess that's being played—all over the world—if this is the world at all, you know. Oh, what fun it is! How I wish I was one of them! I wouldn't mind being a Pawn, if only I might join—though of course I should like to be a Queen, best."

She glanced rather shyly at the real Queen as she said this, but her companion only smiled pleasantly, and said, "That's easily managed. You can be the White Queen's Pawn, if you like, as Lily's too young to play; and you're in the Second Square to begin with; when you get to the Eighth Square, you'll be a Queen—" Just at this moment, somehow or other, they began to run.

Duplicating any part of this book is prohibited by law.

In what ways do the characters seem real? In what ways are they fantastical?

In a fantasy story, characters' actions or events they experience often represent ideas that point to a message that the author is trying to communicate. What message might Alice's and the Red Queen's running reflect?

What descriptions help the author give the story a dreamlike quality?

The most curious part of the thing was that the trees and the other things around them never changed their places at all; however fast they went, they never seemed to pass anything. *I wonder if all the things move along with us*, thought poor Alice. And the Queen seemed to guess her thoughts, for she cried, "Faster! Don't try to talk!"

Not that Alice had any idea of doing that. She felt as if she would never be able to talk again since she was getting so much out of breath; and still the Queen cried, "Faster! Faster!" and dragged her along. "Are we nearly there?" Alice managed to pant out at last.

"Nearly there!" the Queen repeated. "Why, we passed it ten minutes ago! Faster!" And they ran on for a time in silence, with the wind whistling in Alice's ears, and almost blowing her hair off her head, she fancied.

"Now! Now!" cried the Queen. "Faster! Faster!" And they went so fast that at last they seemed to skim through the air, hardly touching the ground with their feet, till suddenly, just as Alice was getting quite exhausted, they stopped, and she found herself sitting on the ground, breathless and giddy.

The Queen propped her up against a tree, and said kindly, "You may rest a little now."

Alice looked around her in great surprise. "Why, I do believe we've been under this tree the whole time! Everything's just as it was!"

"Of course it is," said the Queen, "what would you have it?"

"Well, in our country," said Alice, still panting a little, "you'd generally get to somewhere else—if you ran very fast for a long time, as we've been doing."

"A slow sort of country!" said the Queen. "Now, here, you see, it takes all the running you can do, to keep in the same place. If you want to get somewhere else, you must run twice as fast as that."

Plan Your Writing

Read the writing prompt, and then plan your response below.

Think about the setting in *Through the Looking Glass*. How does it affect the actions of the characters in the story? How does it help the author get a message across to readers? Write a literary response that analyzes the setting, characters, and author's message. Be sure to organize your response and support your ideas with details from the passage.

	Supporting Detail	Supporting Detail	Supporting Detail
Setting:			
Character Description:			
Author's Message:			
My Interpretation:			

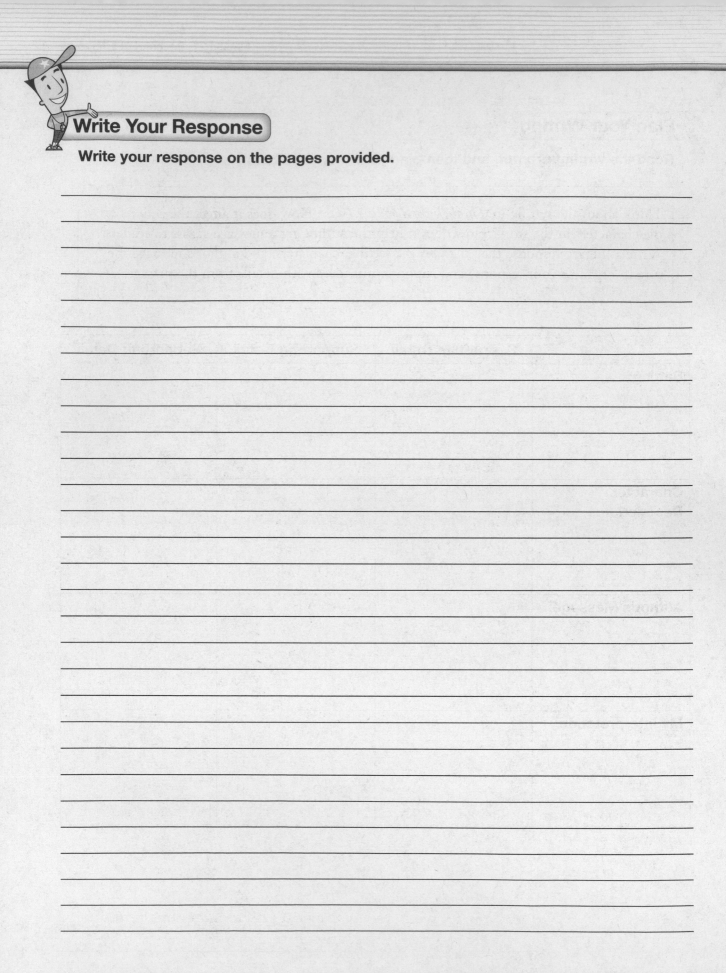

Write Your Response

Write your response on the pages provided.

Use the Writing Guides to help you understand the passages.

Writing **Guide**

How does the character of the truthful man affect the king's actions?

What theme, or message, is the author trying to convey?

What thoughts or feelings do you have after reading the folktale?

The Man Who Never Lied

adapted from an African folktale

Long ago, there lived a man who valued truth, having never told a lie, and his honesty was known throughout the land. Some admired the man's truthfulness, while others regarded the man with suspicion. One such man who feared this truth teller was the king, who was jealous of the attention that the man received. "Everyone calls this man wise, but we shall see about that."

The king summoned the truthful man to his palace, hoping to learn that he had told a lie at least once in his life, but the man replied, "King, I am sure that I have never once told a lie." The King became even more determined to catch the man in a lie, and spent the day concocting a plan.

The king brought the man to his palace again, saying, "Truth teller, you have earned a place in my court. For your first task, please travel to my summer home and tell the queen to prepare a feast for lunch. I am going hunting and will have a large appetite." After the man set off to deliver the message, the king laughed, telling his servants, "I am not hunting today; I hunt tomorrow. The truth teller will be caught telling a lie to the queen."

However the man who never lied was wise. When he arrived at the king's summer home, he told the queen, "I do not know when your husband will arrive. It could be today or tomorrow, so you may wish to prepare a feast on both days."

The queen prepared a feast that day, but the king did not come. The next day, she prepared another feast. The king arrived at midday and announced, "Queen, the truthful man told a lie, telling you I was to arrive yesterday. Surely your feast was wasted."

"King, the man did not lie," the queen said, leading him to the feast. "He told me you would arrive yesterday or today."

The king realized that the man who never lied deserved respect, for he spoke only the truth of what he saw with his own eyes.

The Captain's Party
based on the African folktale "The Man Who Never Lied"

Writing Guide

How would you describe each character? Choose three words that describe each.

How are Toby's actions affected by the actions that Caleb takes?

What message does the author want readers to receive? Do you agree or disagree with that message?

To the majority of Northwest High, Caleb was a great addition to the football team. He was an outstanding fullback who loved the game. Even more important, he was well liked by his teammates, who appreciated his kind and honest nature. But Toby, the team's captain, soon became jealous of the way that everyone followed Caleb, thinking to himself, *I'm the captain, so everyone should listen to me.* Toby didn't believe that anyone could be that good, and he set out to prove that Caleb was really a phony.

Toby was determined to hear Caleb say something unkind. But Caleb never slipped. After their teammate Ramón dropped the ball in practice, Toby goaded Caleb on, saying, "Did you catch Ramón's klutzy move?" But Caleb wouldn't take the bait, shaking his head and telling Toby that no, he must have missed that; he wouldn't say anything else.

Finally, Toby decided to trap Caleb in a lie. Catching up with Caleb after practice, Toby told him, "The team needs motivation before the next game, so let's throw a party in the gym to celebrate our last win. I'll plan the party, but you can let everyone know." Caleb agreed, and Toby was thrilled that his plan was working, thinking, *There won't be any party, and everyone will think that Caleb lied to them.* But Caleb had the ability to see a person's true nature, and he sensed Toby's insecurity and jealousy, so Caleb did more than just invite people to the party.

The night of the party, Toby waited outside the school gym, expecting that there'd be no decorations, no food, and no music. Everyone would be wondering why Caleb lied to them. Toby smiled as Ramón walked out of the gym. "So the party's pretty bad, huh?" he asked. "Too bad Caleb made everyone think it would be great."

"What are you talking about? The party's awesome!" Ramón said, dragging Toby into the gym, which was packed with people and decorated with banners thanking Toby for his great leadership. Everyone clapped for Toby, who looked at Caleb in awe.

"Sometimes the truth is hard to see," Caleb said quietly, and Toby knew that Caleb's honesty and kindness were not an act at all.

Plan Your Writing

Read the writing prompt, and then plan your response below.

Think about the characters in "The Man Who Never Lied" and "The Captain's Party." How would you describe the characters in each story? Which characters have similar traits? How do the characters' traits impact the events in each story and convey the theme? Write a literary response that expresses your thoughts. Remember to organize your response and support your insights with details from the passages.

	Supporting Detail	Supporting Detail	Supporting Detail
Character Description: "The Man Who Never Lied"			
Character Description: "The Captain's Party"			
Similarities in Traits and Actions:			
Impact on Events and Theme:			

Duplicating any part of this book is prohibited by law.

Write Your Response

Write your response on the pages provided.

Response To Literature Checklist

Use the checklist below to help you do your best writing.

Does your response

❏ answer the prompt completely?

❏ include a thoughtful, relevant analysis of setting, characters, plot, and/or theme?

❏ explain how those elements are connected?

❏ include text evidence that supports your response?

❏ have a concluding statement that sums up your response?

❏ use a formal and respectful tone?

❏ have good spelling, capitalization, and punctuation?

❏ follow the rules for good grammar?

22 Respond to Informational Texts

W.8.9.b, W.8.10, WHST.8.4, WHST.8.5, WHST.8.9, WHST.8.10

Getting the Idea

Informational text is text that provides information on a specific topic. Informational text can be found in encyclopedias, textbooks, newspapers, magazines, historical documents, and online sources such as those that end in .org (for organization) or .edu (for educational site). To create an informational text, an author conducts research to gather the information in the form of facts and possibly ideas and opinions from experts on the topic. For example, an author may write a scientific article about a new medication, gathering facts about the drug as well as ideas and opinions about how well it works from scientists who have tested the drug.

Informational texts are nonfiction, meaning they are factual, but that doesn't mean that authors include *only* facts. As authors share information, they may also include their own ideas and opinions in the form of an argument or a claim. Of course, an author should also include factual information to support his or her argument. Continuing with the example of the article on a new medication, the author may argue that the drug is the best choice to treat a disease, supporting the claim with facts that point to the medication's having fewer side effects than older drugs. Based on the information above, readers of informational text must identify and distinguish between information (facts) and opinions (claims).

When you are asked to write a response to informational text, the first step is to analyze and summarize the information. A summary requires you to identify the main idea and details of a text, restating them in your own words. As you analyze the text, consider the author's argument and the ways in which he or she supports it. If an author claims that a new medication is more effective, for example, that claim should be supported by facts, evidence, and reasons. As part of your analysis, you should think about how relevant and credible those reasons are. For example, data from a study that is several years old may no longer be valid. Perhaps an author of an article that is critical of the new drug included quotations from an expert who represents a competing drug company; the expert may not want the new drug to succeed, so the quote that he or she provides may not be credible.

As you summarize and analyze informational texts, you will encounter technical, historical, or scientific vocabulary that is unfamiliar. You can use context clues to determine the meaning of unfamiliar words, or you can use a glossary if one is available. Sometimes, footnotes are included to define terms or to explain historical events or scientific processes. Otherwise, unfamiliar words should be looked up in a dictionary.

When planning your response to informational text, you can organize an author's main idea and supporting details in a web, such as the one shown below. You can write the main idea of the text in the center circle, with supporting details in the circles around it. These details might include facts, expert opinions, or quotations from experts or other texts. You may also want to create a web for the author's claim and the evidence that supports it. This will help you determine if the author's reasoning is sound—in other words, part of your response should be an analysis of whether the author has done an adequate job arguing his or her point. As you take notes in your web, keep in mind that responses to informational texts require a formal tone. Organize your notes and ideas clearly and logically, keeping the tone formal.

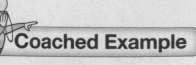

Coached Example

Read the passage and use it to answer the questions.

Fishing for Fishing Spots

Anglers—people who fish—are usually secretive about the locations of the best fishing spots, which are typically characterized as isolated areas with little noise and many fish. If you can't get an angler to help out, you can rely on technology to help you find a favorite spot. It may surprise you to learn how much technology is used in fishing. The sport requires only a pole, bait, and fish, but the Internet and tech gear are your friends. Search the Internet for a topographic map, which shows the surface of land, including natural features, such as rivers, and constructed features, such as highways and railroads. Study the map for a line that crosses bodies of water such as rivers, streams, or brooks. This line may represent a drop in ground level. These lower areas are where fish like to gather. Next, use an online mapping tool to identify the coordinates, and then plug them into your GPS, or global positioning system. The final step is to gather your fishing gear and go to your newly discovered fishing spot. There may be other anglers there, but they likely weren't going to tell you about the area anyway!

1. What is the main idea of this article? How does the author support the main idea?

_____

_____

_____

_____

_____

HINT Clues that point to the main idea of an article are often found within its title and first sentence or two.

2. Write a summary of how to find a fishing spot.

_____

_____

_____

_____

_____

HINT Supporting details are important in summaries. Think about each tool the author suggests using and how it might help the reader find a fishing spot.

Lesson Practice

Use the Writing Guide to help you understand the passage.

Writing Guide

What is the main idea of the first paragraph?

What claims does the author present in paragraph 3? How well do the details that the author includes support the claims?

As you read, think about whether or not the information that the author presents is credible. How can you tell?

Native American Relocation: A Grave Injustice

The discovery of the Americas by Christopher Columbus eventually led to a European desire for more land and a need to conquer the "wilds" of North America. In the fifteenth and sixteenth centuries, settlers from England, Spain, France, the Netherlands, and Sweden were sent to North America. They were charged with various goals by their countries' leaders. Some were sent to expand their countries' land holdings, creating settlements in their home country's name. Others were asked to collect the natural resources that the Americas offered, such as wood, wool, and fur. These resources could be traded, increasing a country's wealth. Some settlers were not sent by their countries. They made the long journey from Europe to flee religious persecution, to escape wars raging in their homelands, or to seek adventure and build new lives. Regardless of the reasons, colonial settlement of North America forever changed the lives of the Native Americans who had always called the land home.

European settlers approached their new land and its people with little regard. Some European colonialists considered settlement to be a conquest, invading the land and attacking the Native Americans. For example, in the Southwest, Spanish colonialists approached the areas with a sense of "occupation," enslaving Native Americans. Some colonialists, such as those in the Northeast, tried to work with Native Americans. However, these friendly relations soon collapsed when the settlers wanted more and more land and natural resources.

The conflicts often led to battles that resulted in many lost lives. The presence of the settlers harmed the Native Americans in ways other than direct violence. The population of Native Americans decreased as European diseases spread, as the settlers hunted and gathered the food that Native Americans relied upon, and as the settlers forced their way into larger and larger areas. The settlements evolved into states, and the states transformed into the new country of the United States. The Native American way of life was seriously threatened. Not only were populations dwindling, but the land available to Native Americans became severely limited.

Notice how the author
includes clues in the
text that help the reader
understand technical
or historical vocabulary
specific to the topic, such
as *policies* or *injustices*.

What details support the
main idea of paragraph 5?

What claim does the
author make in the
concluding paragraph?
How does the author
support the claim with
facts?

By the eighteenth century, the country was more formalized with the creation of laws and court systems. Some American leaders attempted to put forth policies that considered the safety and well-being of the Native Americans. In 1787, the Northwest Ordinance was the first policy statement of the United States, asking for the "property, rights, and liberty" of Native Americans to be considered in "good faith." However, the courts sided with colonial power, declaring the Native Americans to be dependent on U.S. law.

The discovery of gold on Native American land marked the end of efforts by settlers to coexist with Native Americans. Congress passed the Indian Removal Act in 1830, which designated land west of the Mississippi River as Indian Territories. The U.S. government claimed the act was to protect Native Americans, as President Andrew Jackson explained in a message to Congress: "It puts an end to all possible danger of collision between the authorities of the general and state governments on account of the Indians . . . . It will separate the Indians from immediate contact with settlements of whites; free them from the power of the states; enable them to pursue happiness in their own way . . . under the protection of the government." However, it was evident that the government was seeking control of the land, ensuring its riches in gold and other resources. By 1840, Native Americans had relocated west on their own or had been forcibly escorted by the U.S. army.

Native Americans continued their lives on reservations—areas of land offered to them by the U.S. government. Policies and programs put in place did little to help Native Americans; rather, the U.S. government encouraged Native Americans to adopt an "American" way of life. But Native Americans had their own way of life, with a long history of agriculture, hunting, and community. The European colonialists' greed and lack of respect for Native Americans was a grave injustice that will never be fully resolved.

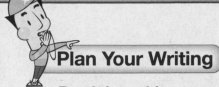

Plan Your Writing

Read the writing prompt, and then plan your response below.

In "Native American Relocation: A Grave Injustice," the author presents a claim and supports it with information about events that led Native Americans to relocate west of the Mississippi River. Identify the claim and analyze how the author supports it. Does the author present the information clearly and convincingly? Use details and facts from the article to support your answer. Use the web below to organize your ideas.

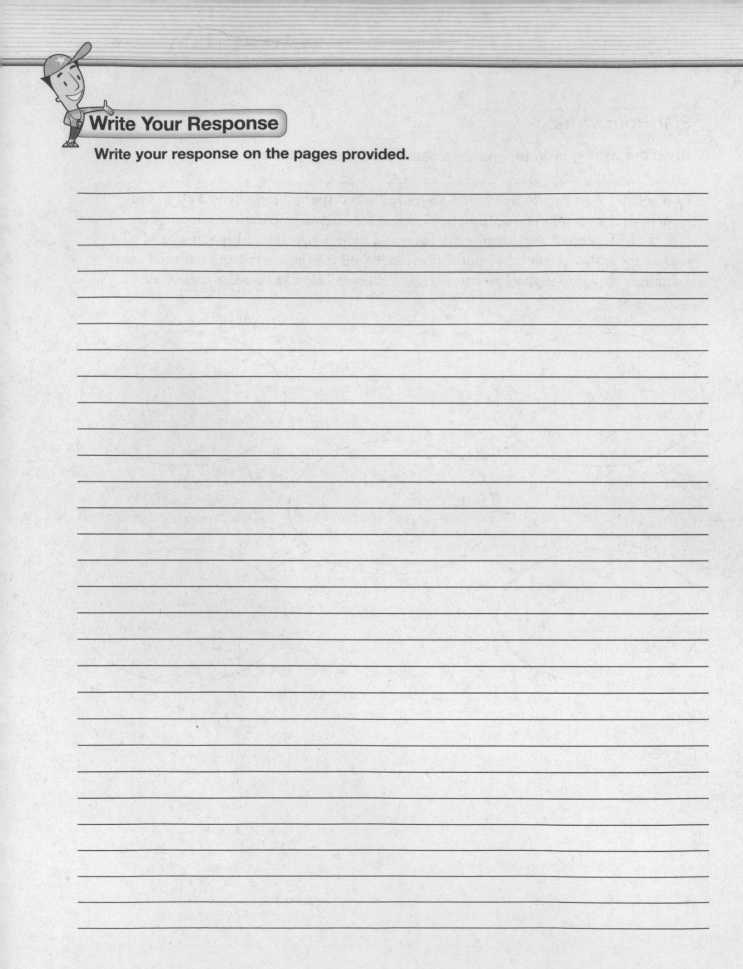

Write Your Response

Write your response on the pages provided.

Lesson Practice

Use the Writing Guides to help you understand the passages.

Writing Guide

As you read the article, think about the author's purpose for writing it.

What claim does the author make? Is the author's claim well supported? Why or why not?

Notice that the author mentions NASA several times throughout the article. Think about how that affects the credibility of the author's claim.

Why does the author mention Lagrange points in paragraph 3?

Keeping Up the Race to Space

On July 21, 2011, the shuttle *Atlantis* completed its final mission, signaling the end of the U.S. space shuttle program. The thirty-year space shuttle program led to the Hubble Space Telescope, the creation of the International Space Station, and international spaceflight collaboration. With the shuttle retired, many worry that the United States' interest in space exploration will eventually fade. In the several decades since U.S. astronauts landed on the moon, the popularity of and attention to space exploration has decreased. However, citizens can be excited about the future of space exploration again. NASA has many plans for the future.

The International Space Station is a key tool in the future of space exploration. Six full-time crew members conduct research in its laboratory. Research covers all areas of science, including physical science and space science. For example, researchers plan to conduct tests to determine how physical properties such as fire, particles, and proteins behave in space. The results of these studies will help researchers solve issues related to human exploration of space, develop new tools, and even gain understanding of human diseases.

Returning to the moon in order to learn more about Earth's history has always been on the space exploration agenda. By studying the geology of the moon, we may better understand Earth. NASA scientists are also studying other destinations in space, determining the best locations and methods of transportation. Many believe that we can better understand what will make life in space possible by researching new locations such as Lagrange points. In addition, sending humans to Mars will help us learn more about the planet and its potential for sustaining human life.

With new destinations planned, NASA is also working on technology that will allow humans to spend more time in space safely. Advances include improvements in spacesuits to protect human bodies from space environments and developing habitats where humans can live during long missions. The new era of space exploration is truly upon us.

Writing Guide

What is the purpose of the speech? How does its purpose differ from that of the article "Keeping Up the Race to Space" on the previous page?

Which ideas in the speech are supported by facts? Which are supported by opinions?

How relevant is the evidence the author includes? Think about how well the evidence helps the author make each point.

The last sentence of the speech contains a quotation taken from a poem. How does the quotation help the author support his claim?

from "Address to the Nation: Death of Space Shuttle *Challenger* Crew"
by Ronald Reagan

On January 28, 1986, Challenger *exploded after its launch from Cape Canaveral, Florida. Teacher Christa McAuliffe was a crew member, having won the opportunity to travel into space. President Ronald Reagan spoke to the nation immediately following the disaster.*

. . . We've never lost an astronaut in flight; we've never had a tragedy like this. And perhaps we've forgotten the courage it took for the crew of the shuttle; but they, the *Challenger* Seven, were aware of the dangers, but overcame them and did their jobs brilliantly. We mourn seven heroes: Michael Smith, Dick Scobee, Judith Resnik, Ronald McNair, Ellison Onizuka, Gregory Jarvis, and Christa McAuliffe. We mourn their loss as a nation together.

For the families of the seven, we cannot bear, as you do, the full impact of this tragedy. But we feel the loss, and we're thinking about you so very much. Your loved ones were daring and brave, and they had that special grace, that special spirit that says, "Give me a challenge and I'll meet it with joy." . . .

We've grown used to wonders in this century. It's hard to dazzle us. But for twenty-five years the United States space program has been doing just that. We've grown used to the idea of space, and perhaps we forget that we've only just begun. We're still pioneers. They, the members of the *Challenger* crew, were pioneers.

And I want to say something to the schoolchildren of America who were watching the live coverage of the shuttle's takeoff. I know it is hard to understand, but sometimes painful things like this happen. It's all part of the process of exploration and discovery. It's all part of taking a chance and expanding man's horizons. The future doesn't belong to the fainthearted; it belongs to the brave. The *Challenger* crew was pulling us into the future, and we'll continue to follow them . . .

The crew of the space shuttle *Challenger* honored us by the manner in which they lived their lives. We will never forget them, nor the last time we saw them, this morning, as they prepared for the journey and waved goodbye and "slipped the surly bonds of earth" to "touch the face of God."

Plan Your Writing

Read the writing prompt and then plan your response below.

Reread "Keeping Up the Race to Space" and President Reagan's speech about the *Challenger* disaster. The two passages make a similar argument about the idea of space exploration. What common argument do the passages make? In what ways does each passage use facts to support its claims? In what ways does each passage use the author's feelings or opinions? Support your claims with details from the passages. Use the web below to organize your ideas.

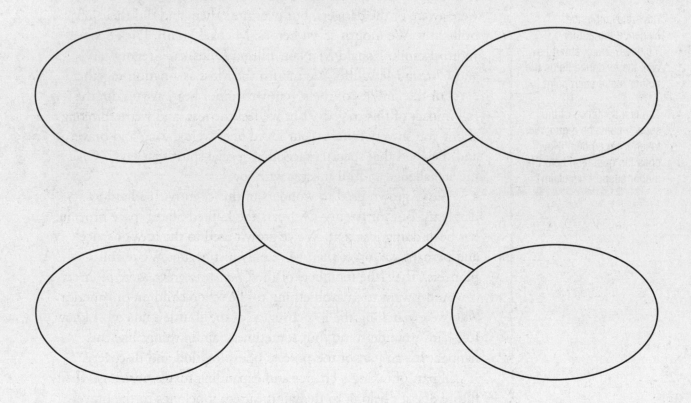

Write Your Response

Write your response on the pages provided.

Response To Informational Texts Checklist

Use the checklist below to help you do your best writing.

Does your response

- ❏ answer the prompt completely?

- ❏ clearly state the author's claim?

- ❏ analyze how the author supports the claim?

- ❏ determine the relevancy and credibility of the facts that the author includes?

- ❏ include facts and details that support your response?

- ❏ have a concluding statement that sums up your response?

- ❏ use a formal and respectful tone?

- ❏ have good spelling, capitalization, and punctuation?

- ❏ follow the rules for good grammar?

23 Revising, Editing, and Publishing

W.8.4, W.8.5, W.8.6, W.8.10, WHST.8.5, WHST.8.6, WHST.8.10

Getting the Idea

When you **revise**, you make structural changes to your writing. You rearrange paragraphs, rearrange sentences within paragraphs, clarify your main idea, or add missing information. When you **edit** your writing, you correct errors in sentence structure, grammar, punctuation, and spelling.

By revising and editing, you make your work suitable for publishing. You have essentially **published** your writing when others read what you write. You might write a story and hand out copies to your class. Perhaps you write for the school newspaper or publish your writings on the Internet—in either a personal blog or a social networking site. Publishing online has the advantage of being able to embed direct links to sources or related topics.

Think about organization. Sometimes an entire paragraph may need to be moved or cut. Every paragraph in an essay should support the essay's main idea. When you read over your draft, ask yourself: *Do my points follow logically from each other? Does the sequence of the information I'm presenting make sense?* If not, then you shouldn't be afraid to rearrange paragraphs to make your essay easier to read.

Write unified paragraphs. Just as every paragraph should build on an essay's main idea, every sentence in a paragraph should build on the topic sentence. If the topic sentence expresses an opinion, the sentences following it should support that opinion. If the topic sentence makes a broad statement about a factual subject, the sentences following it should provide facts that support that statement. Casual observations, jokes, and anecdotes, while amusing, may distract readers from your purpose.

Correct mistakes in sentence structure. As you read over your draft, you'll want to look at the way each sentence is built, as well. An essay with all short sentences could be dull for the reader. An essay with nothing but long sentences could be dull and hard to read as well. Vary your sentence structure, choosing sentence types appropriate for your purpose. Use a simple sentence to make a simple point. Use a longer sentence to give a list of items or to link two thoughts.

Avoid these sentence types:

- **fragments**

  Incorrect: <u>Although Lisa got up early.</u> She missed the school bus.
  Revised: Although Lisa got up <u>early, she</u> missed the school bus.

- **run-ons**

  Incorrect: Jim does not like vanilla ice <u>cream, he</u> thinks it's too bland.
  Revised: Jim does not like vanilla ice <u>cream. He</u> thinks it's too bland.

- **awkward sentences**

  Incorrect: Greta drove her friend to the hospital with the broken leg.
  Revised: Greta drove her friend with the broken leg to the hospital.

Correct mistakes in subject-verb agreement.

Incorrect: <u>One</u> of the books on the shelf <u>are</u> missing.
Revised: <u>One</u> of the books on the shelf <u>is</u> missing.

Use the comma between items in a series.

Incorrect: Ron excels in swimming tennis, and golf.
Revised: Ron excels in swimming, tennis, and golf.

Use apostrophes correctly to show possessions.

Incorrect: Tims' blog is about fantasy and science fiction.
Revised: Tim's blog is about fantasy and science fiction.

Correct spelling errors. Check a dictionary to confirm spelling and proper word usage.

Thinking It Through

Read the following sentence, and then answer the question that follows.

Warren like to go to the same part of the beach every Sunday.

Edit this sentence to correct the errors.

_____

HINT   Read the sentence out loud. What part sounds awkward and distracting? Why?

Coached Example

This passage contains mistakes. Read it and answer the questions that follow.

(1) Taking a trip to the town of Colonial Williamsburg in Virginia is like stepping back in time into our colonial American past. (2) The people there actually live, dress cook and travel just as they did nearly three hundred years ago. (3) There are no TV sets, cars, or tall apartment buildings—just small wooden or stone houses heated with wood stoves. (4) The people use horses and wagons for transportation. (5) Just as it was done, they prepare and serve supper in 1725. (6) The main meal of the day consists of "meats" and "sweets." (7) The meat dishes contain pork or chicken. (8) For sweets, there is an array of cakes, cookies, and fruit desserts. (9) After dinner, they play musical instruments, such as the harpsichord, the mandolin, or the harp.

---

1. How should sentence 2 be edited?

   A. The people there actually live, dress, cook, and travel, just as they did nearly three hundred years ago.

   B. The people there actually, live, dress, cook, and travel just as they did nearly three hundred years ago.

   C. The people there actually live, dress, cook, and travel just as they did nearly three hundred years ago.

   D. The people there actually live, dress cook, and travel just as they did nearly three hundred years ago.

   HINT Never put commas in a series before the first item or after the last item.

2. What is the BEST way to edit sentence 5 for clarity?

   A. In 1725, they prepare and serve supper just as it was done.

   B. They prepare and serve supper just as it was done in 1725.

   C. Just as it was done, they prepare in 1725 and serve supper.

   D. Just as they serve supper, they prepare and get it done in 1725.

   HINT Read each sentence aloud. Choose the one in which "in 1725" is placed most sensibly.

Lesson Practice

This passage contains mistakes. Use the Reading Guide to help you find the mistakes.

Reading Guide

Find the spelling errors in the passage.

Which sentence(s) in paragraph 2 contain errors?

Revise the sentence in paragraph 6 that has a comma error.

The Clever Thief
adapted from a Korean folktale

Long ago, there lived an old thief known for being extremely clever. In fact, he was so clever that he had never been captured. One day, however, he grew careless, and he was caught stealing spices from a shop.

Because the judge was delighted to finally have the old thief before him. He fined the man the highest amount the law allowed. The thief could not raise the sum and was sentenced to five years in jail. As he sat in his cell day after day, the thief devised a plan. One day, he called the prison guard over.

"Take me to the king!" the thief demanded.

"Now why would the king agree to see someone like you?" the guard asked.

"Tell the king I have in my <u>possession</u> an extraordinary gift and that I wish to present it to him."

The guard was intrigued by the thiefs request. The next day the thief was brought before the king at the royal court. The secretary of state the prime minister, and the army general were also present.

The thief bowed and spoke to the king. "Your Majesty, I have a most <u>valuable</u> gift for you." Then, he took a small box wrapped in gold paper out of his pocket and handed it to the king.

Eagerly, the king unwrapped the box and looked inside. The first expression on his face was shock, but this quickly turned to rage. The box was tied with a shiny silver ribbon. The king glowered at the thief and shouted, "What kind of insult is this? You dare to bring me an ordinary plum pit?"

"It is a plum pit, but I assure you it is not ordinary. The man who plants this pit will reap nothing but golden plums," the thief said.

The king laughed scornfully. "If that is true, why haven't you planted it yourself?"

Explain the error in paragraph 12. Remember that apostrophes are used to show possession.

Review the passage for spelling mistake.

The thief sighed. "It only works for those who has not cheated or stolen. For others, the tree will bear only ordinary plums. That is why I have brought it to you. I am sure that you have never stolen or cheated."

The king looked at the plum pit sadly he realized he could never grow golden plums. "I am afraid I cannot accept your gift," he told the thief. When he was a child he had stolen pennies from his mothers purse.

The thief pretended to be <u>suprised</u>. He turned to the secretary of state. "How about you, good sir? Surely, you will be able to reap golden plums."

But the secretary of state shook his head. He sometimes accepted bribes in return for favors.

"How about the prime minister then?" the thief asked. "He is neither a cheat nor a thief."

The prime minister lowered his eyes and said he would not plant the tree. Like the secretary of state, he accepted bribes.

The thief looked at the general. "And you, General? You're one of the most respected men in the country. Will you accept this plum pit?"

"I cannot," the general said gruffly. He had grown very wealthy by cheating his soldiers of part of their pay.

An <u>uncomfortable</u> silence filled the room as the thief stared at the men. Finally, he said, "So, all of you have cheated and stolen and maybe much worse, but you have never seen the inside of a prison cell. Meanwhile, I, who have stolen only a handful of spices, have been sentenced to five years in jail!"

The men looked at each other in shame. Then, the king spoke. "I suggest that the four of us pay this man's fine so that he will not go back to jail." They all quickly agreed. Later that day, the thief was a free man. He had won his freedom with nothing more than a plum pit.

Answer the following questions.

1. Which sentence from paragraph 2 is a fragment?

   A. "Because the judge was delighted to finally have the old thief before him."

   B. "The thief could not raise the sum and was sentenced to five years in jail."

   C. "He fined the man the highest amount the law allowed."

   D. "One day, he called the prison guard over."

2. Which word from the passage is spelled incorrectly?

   A. uncomfortable

   B. suprised

   C. possession

   D. valuable

3. Read this sentence from paragraph 6.

   The guard was intrigued by the thiefs request.

   How should this sentence be revised?

   A. The guard was intrigued by the thiefs' request.

   B. The guard was intrigued by the thief's request.

   C. The guard was intrigued by the thieve's request.

   D. The guard was intrigued by the thieves request.

4. Which sentence from the passage is written correctly?

   A. "The secretary of state the prime minister, and the army general were also present."

   B. "The king looked at the plum pit sadly he realized he could never grow golden plums."

   C. "'Meanwhile, I, who have stolen only a handful of spices, have been sentenced to five years in jail!'"

   D. "'It only works for those who has not cheated or stolen.'"

5. Which sentence from paragraph 8 belongs in a different paragraph? In which paragraph does the sentence belong?

   _____

   _____

The following questions do not relate to a passage.

6. The following paragraph is from a student's research paper about nutrition. Read the paragraph. Then rewrite it to correct errors in grammar.

> Dietary fiber is a special type of carbohydrate. Important for the bodys health. Fiber is found in foods such as fruits. Fiber is found in whole grains, beans, nuts, and vegetables. Fiber contributes to healthy intestines, which is essential in the digestive process. Fiber promotes low cholesterol levels, healthy blood pressure, and a lower risk of obesity. In addition, carbohydrates give food flavor supply nutrients for bacteria in the intestinal tract and help the body absorb calcium.

_____

_____

_____

_____

_____

_____

_____

_____

_____

_____

_____

_____

_____

_____

_____

_____

_____

_____

_____

_____

7. The following paragraph is from a student's research paper about trees. Read the paragraph. Then reorganize the sentences so their order is clear and logical. In each empty box, write the number 2, 3, 4, or 5 so that the sentences are in the correct order.

> **The acacia tree creates its own food through photosynthesis. The porous savannah soil does not hold water for long periods. In addition, the climate in which the tree grows is hot and dry. It produces sugar by using sunlight, carbon dioxide from other organisms, and water from the soil. Therefore, the acacia tree has adapted to feature waxy leaves that retain moisture. In turn, the tree produces food for herbivores, such as giraffes.**

| 1 | The acacia tree creates its own food through photosynthesis. |

| | The porous savannah soil does not hold water for long periods. |

| | In addition, the climate in which the tree grows is hot and dry. |

| | It produces sugar by using sunlight, carbon dioxide from other organisms, and water from the soil. |

| | Therefore, the acacia tree has adapted to feature waxy leaves that retain moisture. |

| 6 | In turn, the tree produces food for herbivores, such as giraffes. |

8. **Use your answer to Part A to answer Part B.**

The following paragraph is from a student's research paper about giraffes. Read the paragraph.

> The giraffe lives in the African savannah it lives in non-territorial groups of about twenty animals. It ranges in small areas during the wet season. Larger areas during the dry season. The giraffe is an herbivore it eats the shoots and leaves of acacia trees. It gets most of its water from its food. Beginning at four or five years old. A female giraffe may breed and give birth to a single offspring after fifteen months of development. Lions and hyenas prey on baby giraffes. Killing nearly half.

Part A

Underline all the fragments and run-on sentences in the paragraph.

Part B

Choose one run-on sentence you underlined in Part A. Rewrite the sentence correctly on the lines below.

_____

_____

---

9. Circle the sentences that are correct. There is more than one correct choice listed below.

A. My favorite TV shows' new season begins next week.

B. I can't go until I've finished my homework, walked the dog, and eaten dinner.

C. Christa and the others works at the movie theater.

D. Will the band perform here on their next tour?

E. Aisha wished she will be going to Spain next summer.

F. Our house, which is number 40, has green shutters.

G. Do the GPS give you the correct directions?

H. I hope enrolling in next semester's art course.

I. Donal and Bennett's houses are two doors away from each other.

J. It's important that the horse stay off its injured hoof.

10. **Use your answer to Part A to answer Part B.**

Part A

Read the paragraph from a student's research paper about heart disease. Underline the ideas in the box below that could be added logically to the paragraph.

> **A lipid, better known as a fat, is a type of organic molecule that is essential to the structure of living cells. Healthy lipids are found in many foods. Lipids are stored in the body and provide extra energy when the body needs it. However, if the body's store of lipids is too high, the result may be heart disease or diabetes.**

Extra carbohydrates also become lipids.

Cooking with olive oil has many health benefits.

If the body lacks carbohydrates, it may burn lipids for power.

Lipids store important nutrients, such as vitamins A, D, E, and K.

About 25% to 35% of a person's daily calories should come from lipids.

Avocadoes, eggs, olive oil, nuts, and fish all contain healthy lipids.

Part B

Revise the paragraph, incorporating the ideas you chose in Part A.

_____

_____

_____

_____

_____

_____

_____

_____

_____

_____

_____

_____

_____

_____

Duplicating any part of this book is prohibited by law.

24 Using Resources

W.8.7, W.8.8, W.8.9.a–b, RH.8.1, RST.8.9, WHST.8.7, WHST.8.8, WHST.8.10

Getting the Idea

A **resource** is something that you can use to help you write a research paper. It can give you new information, confirm what you already know, and support your statements. A **primary source** is source material that comes directly from the period or person you are researching. A **secondary source** discusses information originally presented elsewhere. A resource can be a printed text or in electronic form. Use the resources below to gather information for your research papers.

- **Books:** biographies, autobiographies, textbooks, and other nonfiction books on topics like history, science, and social issues.

- **Reference sources:** texts with factual information on many topics, such as encyclopedias, dictionaries, thesauruses, and almanacs.

- **Periodicals:** texts published at regular intervals, such as newspapers, magazines, or journals. These sources often provide up-to-date information, so they are helpful for topics that require recent information.

- **Web sites:** electronic pages of information. They are not always reliable, so you should confirm any information you find on a Web site against a print source. The more reliable Web sites end with *.org*, *.edu*, or *.gov*.

- **CD-ROMs:** compact discs containing electronic information. Encyclopedias and dictionaries are available on CD-ROMs.

- **Videos:** visual recordings, such as films and documentaries.

To help focus your research, it is a good idea to consider what you want to know about the subject. Write down research questions that might lead to an interesting research paper. If you are writing a paper about W. E. B. Du Bois, for instance, the question "Who was W. E. B. Du Bois?" is too broad because it does not give you any further direction in your research. A stronger question might be: "What actions did W. E. B. Du Bois take to help fight racism?"

Once you have decided what research question to investivate, it is important to choose the right resources. Primary sources are often more valuable because they present firsthand information and may be more reliable and accurate.

Duplicating any part of this book is prohibited by law.

Primary sources might include diaries, autobiographies, or letters. They may be more convincing to a reader than other sources. However, a good secondary source can be just as helpful as a primary source. For example, if you want to know what the Declaration of Independence says, you should read a copy of the document. If you want an *interpretation* of the document, you should look for a secondary source. Similarly, reading about an experiment might not always be as educational as performing an experiment.

You will have to select the best source for the topic you have chosen. If you are writing about current developments in space exploration, use the most recent source you can find, such as a scientific journal, magazine, or newspaper. A book from ten years ago will not tell you about current developments.

Always question the credibility and accuracy of your sources. If you don't trust the author of a source, don't use it. For instance, if you are writing about the history of jazz, a person's Web page on "really cool music" is probably not as good a source as an article from an encyclopedia. Also, use more than one source to support your facts.

Finally, be careful to avoid **plagiarism**. If you use someone else's words, you are responsible for quoting them and including an in-text citation. You also have to include an in-text citation if you paraphrase someone else's ideas in your own words. These citations are notes in parenthesis that tell the reader the source of the idea. A works-cited list/bibliography at the end of your paper should include all the sources you used in your paper.

Thinking It Through

Read the following sentence, and then answer the question that follows.

Marvin is writing a research paper about Abraham Lincoln.

Which type of source would MOST help Marvin find information on this topic, and why?

_____

_____

HINT   Think about a source that is most likely to give biographical information on historical figures.

Coached Example

Read the passage and answer the questions.

A cell is the smallest unit of life. There are two types of eukaryotic cells—a plant cell and an animal cell. A plant cell has more parts than an animal cell. Both kinds of cells take in nutrients and get rid of wastes.

A plant cell has a cell wall. This stiff wall protects the cell. The walls of plant cells stick to each other to give the plant its shape. Just inside the cell wall is the cell membrane, which allows water and nutrients to pass into the cell. It allows wastes, including oxygen, to pass out of the cell. The cell membrane also stops some materials from getting into the cell and harming it.

Near the center of the cell is the nucleus. The nucleus controls the cell's growth. The plant's genes are in the nucleus of its cells.

1. What type of source is this passage MOST LIKELY from?

   A. a textbook

   B. a newspaper

   C. a dictionary

   D. a video

   HINT Think about how each answer choice relates to the topic.

2. Which source would provide the MOST additional information on this topic?

   A. a scientific journal

   B. a Web site for gardeners

   C. an article about decorating with plants

   D. a biography about a famous scientist

   HINT Think about the focus of the passage, and choose the source that has a similar focus.

Lesson Practice

Use the Reading Guide to help you understand the passage.

Reading Guide

What do you learn about the passage from the title?

What source would you use to find San Salvador on a map?

excerpted and adapted from

Letter from Christopher Columbus to Luis de Sant Angel, 1493

As I know you will be overjoyed about the great success I have had in my voyage, I write this to tell you how, in thirty-three days, I sailed to the Indies with the fleet that the King and Queen, our Sovereigns, gave me. I discovered a great many islands, inhabited by huge numbers of people; and I have taken possession of all of them for our rulers by proclamation and display of the national flag. There has been no opposition. I named the first island I discovered San Salvador, in commemoration of His Divine Majesty. The Indians call it Guanaham. The second I named the Island of Santa Maria de Concepcion; the third, Fernandina; the fourth, Isabella; the fifth, Juana; and thus to each one I gave a new name. . . .

I heard from other Indians that this land was an island, and thus followed the eastern coast for one hundred and seven leagues, until I came to the end of it. From that point I saw another island to the east, eighteen leagues away, to which I gave the name of Hispaniola. I went there and followed its northern coast one hundred and seventy-eight leagues to the east, as I had done in Juana. This island, like all the others, is most extensive. It has many ports along the sea-coast excelling any I have ever seen—and many fine, large, flowing rivers.

The land there is elevated, with many mountains and peaks far higher than in the center island. They are most beautiful, of a thousand different forms, accessible, and full of many kinds of trees, so high that they seem to touch the sky. I have been told that they never lose their foliage. I saw them as green and lovely as trees are in Spain in the month of May. Some of them were covered with blossoms, some with fruit, and some had another appearance altogether. The nightingale and other small birds of a thousand kinds were singing in the month of November when I was there. There were palm trees of six or eight varieties, each one of them graceful and admirable in its own way, as are the other trees, fruits and grasses. There are wonderful pine woods, and very extensive ranges of meadow land. There is honey, and there are

What kind of textbook would contain the most information on Christopher Columbus?

What kind of source would supply the most information about early inhabitants of what we now call America?

many kinds of birds, and a great variety of fruits. Inland there are numerous mines of metals and innumerable people....

At every point where I landed, and succeeded in talking to them, I gave them cloth and many other things without receiving anything in return. Of course, they are a hopelessly timid people. It is true that since they have gained more confidence and are losing this fear, they have no suspicions and are so generous with what they possess that no one would believe it who had not seen it. They never refuse anything, when you ask for it. They even offer it themselves, and they show so much love that they would probably give their hearts if they could. Whether it be anything of great or small value, with any trifle of whatever kind, they are satisfied. I did not allow worthless things to be given to them, such as bits of broken bowls, pieces of glass, and old straps, although they were so pleased to get them, you would have thought they were the finest jewels in the world....

They firmly believed that I, with my ships and men, came from Heaven. People everywhere have received me this way, since they stopped being scared of me. They are, however, far from ignorant. They are most ingenious men, and they sail these seas in a wonderful way, and describe everything well. However, they never saw people wearing clothes before, or ships like ours....

Answer the following questions.

1. How can you tell this passage is a primary source?

   A. It is about Columbus's voyage to the Americas.

   B. It is a commonly studied subject in school.

   C. It uses very descriptive language.

   D. It was written by Columbus himself.

2. Which source would be the BEST place to look for information about Luis de Sant Angel?

   A. a magazine article about the history of Spain

   B. a journal article about Columbus's discoveries

   C. an encyclopedia entry called "The Americas"

   D. a book collection of maps tracing Columbus's journey

3. A documentary about Columbus's experiences in the Americas is a

   A. CD-ROM.

   B. periodical.

   C. Web site.

   D. video.

4. This passage would be MOST helpful to a student writing a research paper on

   A. Columbus's impact on future explorers.

   B. Columbus's life after he returned to Spain.

   C. the people Columbus found on the islands.

   D. the causes of Columbus's trip to the Americas.

5. What might be another primary source about this topic?

   _____

   _____

   _____

Duplicating any part of this book is prohibited by law.

The following questions do not relate to a passage.

6. **Use your answer to Part A to answer Part B.**

   Part A

   Choose the sources that would be MOST appropriate to use to research an essay about the importance of preserving national parks. There is more than one correct choice listed below.

   A. biography of George Catlin, an artist who originated the concept of national parks

   B. blog entry of a student who visited a national park on vacation

   C. almanac entry on the climate, including yearly rainfall and snowfall, of national parks

   D. photos on the U.S. National Park Service Web site of endangered wildlife that live in national parks

   E. encyclopedia entry, "History of the National Park System"

   F. novel about rock climbers in national parks

   G. article in a scientific magazine, "Conserving Animal Habitats"

   H. video about safety precautions at Grand Canyon National Park

   I. newspaper article about ranchers who claim that panthers eat their livestock

   J. interview of park rangers in the National Park Foundation newsletter

   Part B

   Which of the sources you chose are primary sources? Write the letter(s) on the line below.

   _____

Duplicating any part of this book is prohibited by law.

7.   **Use your answer to Part A to answer Part B.**

A student has been assigned to write a research paper on the topic of sports medicine. Below are four possible research questions that the student might consider.

Research Questions	How much money does someone who works in sports medicine make?
	Why is sports medicine important to athletes?
	How has technology affected the field of sports medicine?
	How is sports medicine different from other fields of medicine?

Part A

Circle the question that would MOST LIKELY lead to an interesting research paper.

Part B

Below, write three sources you might consult to find an answer to the question you chose in Part A.

_____

_____

_____

_____

_____

Duplicating any part of this book is prohibited by law.

8. **Use your answer to Part A to answer Part B.**

A student is writing a science research report on the impact of overfishing and has narrowed the focus to "Fishing Failure: How We Failed to Protect Fish Populations." The student has located several possible sources online.

Part A

Read the description of each online source. Circle the sources that are MOST LIKELY to be credible and accurate. There is more than one correct choice listed below.

A. www.fishery.gov: Statistics compiled by the U.S. Fish and Wildlife Service on fish populations in bodies of water

B. www.anglers.com: Official site of a local fishing club that is lobbying the state government in support of the rights of sport and hobby fishers

C. www.wildlifeprotection.org: Site of an international organization dedicated to protecting endangered species around the world

D. www.fishingforless.com: Sells fishing equipment at discount prices

E. www.palmeru.edu/research/fishingstock: Describes research on fishing and fish populations being conducted by scientists at Palmer University

F. www.fishingmadeeasy.com: Advice for beginning fishers from Captain Billy, a local boater and experienced fisherman from Florida

Part B

Choose one source you selected as credible and accurate. Write a question that might be answered using that source. Remember that the question should support the student's research report described above.

_____

_____

_____

Duplicating any part of this book is prohibited by law

9. For art class, a student has written a research paper on how artists utilize science, mathematics, and other content areas to create works. The student has included a section in the report about Leonardo da Vinci's use of science. Read the following paragraph from the report and the student's notes in the box below the paragraph.

> **Many people consider art to be only a creative endeavor. However, Leonardo da Vinci is proof that art crosses into many content areas, including science. Though he wore many hats, da Vinci was best known as a painter. He believed that an artist required a mind that embraced scientific theory, and he argued that visual observation was a science that could be applied to painting. Over his lifetime, da Vinci recorded his observations in journals that are still studied and valued even today.**

Research Notes: da Vinci and Applying Science to Art

- da Vinci: painter, sculptor, scholar, inventor, designer, musician, engineer

- Most famous works: *Mona Lisa*, *The Last Supper*, drawing of Vitruvian Man

- Scientific observation in nature: landscapes, plants, animals, astronomical bodies

- Codex Leicester: most famous of da Vinci's scientific journals; written between 1506 and 1513; documents his scientific observation of water gathered between 1506 and 1513; was purchased for $30 million in 1994

- Albert Einstein: "The greatest scientists are always artists as well." (1923)

Revise the student's paragraph, using the facts in the box to better support the key ideas. Make sure your paragraph is well organized and includes sentences that are clear and complete. Write your answer on the lines below.

_____

_____

_____

_____

_____

_____

_____

_____

Cumulative Assessment

This passage contains mistakes. Read the passage and answer the questions that follow.

(1) During the early 1900s, the United States had what is now called the Progressive movement. (2) This was a period in which people called progressives tried to fix the problems they saw in American society. (3) The party was started because of social and political unrest. (4) These problems developed because of the increase in immigration, the growth of urban areas, and the development of industry in the late nineteenth century. (5) Thus, progressivism began in cities, where there were lots of immigrant factory workers.

(6) Progressives were primarily white, upper-class and upper-middle-class people who wanted to put their wealth and social rank to use. (7) Some of them moved into slum areas and established houses for poor people called settlement houses. (8) One of the most famous settlement houses were Hull House. (9) It was founded in 1889 in Chicago by reformers Jane Addams and Ellen Gates Starr. (10) Starr traveled a lot and even went to Britain to learn bookbinding. (11) Hull House provided many badly needed services in the community. (12) It was a shelter for the homeless, a nursery, a boys' club, and even a theater. (13) Hull House also offered a bunch of classes, allowing people to improve their lives.

(14) The Progressive movement began in individual cities, but slowly began to change at the state and national levels. (15) Although progressives faced strong political resistance, they played a big part in the passage of acts and laws we take for granted today. (16) Worker's compensation, minimum wage, and child labor laws were among their accomplishments.

1. What is the correct way to revise sentence 8?

   A. One of the most, famous settlement houses, were Hull House.

   B. One of the most famous settlement houses was Hull House.

   C. One of the most famous settlement house's was Hull House.

   D. One of the most famous settlement houses' was Hull House.

2. Which source would give you the MOST insight into Jane Addams's motivations?

   A. a book about the Progressive Movement

   B. a newspaper article about Hull House

   C. a collection of Jane Addams's letters

   D. a biography of Ellen Gates Starr

3. The main purpose of this passage is to

   A. explain why Jane Addams founded Hull House.

   B. tell an interesting story about a famous reformer.

   C. persuade readers to become progressives.

   D. inform readers about a political movement.

4. Which sentence in paragraph 2 should be removed to improve organization?

   A. sentence 8

   B. sentence 9

   C. sentence 10

   D. sentence 11

Duplicating any part of this book is prohibited by law

5. Which phrase from the passage is NOT appropriate for the audience and purpose?

A. "a bunch of classes"

B. "slum areas"

C. "period in which"

D. "wealth and social rank"

6. What type of source is this passage MOST LIKELY from?

A. an online encyclopedia

B. a current newspaper

C. a scientific journal

D. a documentary

Duplicating any part of this book is prohibited by law.

Persuasive Prompt

Think about a change you would like to make in your school. It could be a change to classes, programs, school teams, policies—whatever you feel is most in need of adjustment. Write a letter to your school principal to convince him or her that this would be a good change. Be sure to include the reasons why the change is needed, as well as specific details to make your letter more persuasive.

Use the checklist below to help you do your best writing.

Does your letter

❏ have a clear topic?

❏ show a point of view about that topic?

❏ have a logical structure?

❏ support reasons with details?

❏ connect reasons and details with the right words or phrases?

❏ use a style and vocabulary that is correct for the audience and purpose?

❏ have a solid conclusion?

❏ have good spelling, capitalization, and punctuation?

❏ follow the rules for good grammar?

Write your response in the space provided. You may use your own paper if you need more space.

Speaking and Listening

Chapter 4: Diagnostic Assessment

Chapter 4: Cumulative Assessment

Diagnostic Assessment

Listen to the passage and take notes in the space on the next page. Then answer the questions that follow.

The Mystery of the Missing Bees

United States Honey-Producing Colonies

Duplicating any part of this book is prohibited by law.

Notes

Duplicating any part of this book is prohibited by law.

Answer the following questions.

1. What is the author's primary purpose in writing "The Mystery of the Missing Bees"?

   A. to inform readers that human activity is the cause of honeybee decline

   B. to inform readers that the well-being of honeybees and of humans is related

   C. to inform readers that honeybees are complex creatures in danger of becoming extinct

   D. to inform readers that honeybees have essential roles in human agriculture and economy

2. If colony collapse disorder continues, which of the following would MOST LIKELY occur?

   A. Farmers will discontinue using toxic pesticides.

   B. People will starve due to a lack of fresh vegetables.

   C. The price of honey will decrease due to increased production.

   D. The price of beef will increase due to the rising cost of feeding cattle.

3. Read the sentence from the passage.

   Sometimes, humans intentionally introduce species without realizing the devastating effects this may have; more often, species are introduced by mistake.

   In the context of the passage, what is the purpose of this sentence?

   A. It supports the definition of *invasive species*.

   B. It explains how chemical warfare affects honeybees.

   C. It provides background information on invasive species.

   D. It clarifies the dangers that invasive species pose to the honeybee population.

4. Based on the passage, which of the following is MOST LIKELY true about the author?

   A. The author is a scientist who studies the effects of agricultural chemicals on the life cycles of insects.

   B. The author is a biologist who is fascinated by the impact invasive species have on the environment.

   C. The author is a citizen who is concerned about environmental changes and their effects on honeybees and humans.

   D. The author is an economist concerned about the impact that honeybee populations have on food prices and the economy.

5. Who is MOST LIKELY the intended audience of "The Mystery of the Missing Bees"?

   A. students who are interested in ecosystems

   B. science teachers who are planning a bee unit

   C. politicians who decide on environmental laws

   D. scientists who are interested in the life cycle of honeybees

6. In what way does the graph support the author's claims?

   A. The author claims that the decline in the honeybee population is minimal.

   B. The author claims that colony collapse disorder is the main cause of the decline in the honeybee population.

   C. The author claims that parasitic mites were a relatively minor cause of honeybee population decline.

   D. The author claims that mites are a major cause of colony collapse disorder.

7. How has human activity affected honeybee populations? Use details from the passage to support your claim.

_____

_____

_____

_____

_____

_____

_____

_____

_____

_____

_____

_____

_____

_____

8. Think about how the author organized the passage. What is the central claim of the passage, and how does its organization help develop this claim?

_____

_____

_____

_____

_____

_____

_____

_____

_____

_____

_____

_____

_____

_____

Duplicating any part of this book is prohibited by law.

25 Discuss

SL.8.1.a–d

Getting the Idea

We communicate our opinions and ideas by having conversations with others. A **discussion** is a type of conversation in which two or more people talk about an article, a book, a topic, or an issue. During discussions, people use their various perspectives to explain their unique points of view. They respond to what they hear and build on it. Although discussions may be passionate, they also need to be polite and respectful so that everyone involved remains engaged and interested in participating. Sometimes, discussions need **leaders** to keep the discussion moving forward, evenly balanced, and on topic. A leader could be a teacher or an expert on the topic being discussed.

Here are some other characteristics of good discussions:

- The discussion is focused on a topic that everyone wants to understand better.

- Individuals listen and respond to one another, building on one another's ideas.

- Everyone is prepared to support their ideas and opinions with facts, details, and examples from the reading.

- A **moderator** makes sure that the rules of discussion are being followed and encourages participation.

- A **recorder** takes notes and creates an accurate summary.

- Individuals ask questions to clarify points and offer new insight. The goal should be to change other members' opinions and points of view on the issue.

- Participants track their progress toward goals and deadlines.

- Everyone steps back from time to time to summarize the ideas brought up so far and to raise questions.

- New information is acknowledged, and disagreements become questions to be debated respectfully.

Duplicating any part of this book is prohibited by law.

Take a moment to consider a conversation among three students about the article "The Mystery of the Missing Bees." Try to see how this conversation is not a productive discussion.

> Phil: This is pretty interesting stuff.
>
> Mia: Well, I don't see why the author wrote about bees. Who cares about bees?
>
> Phil: You say that because you weren't paying attention. I think we should do something about all of the bees disappearing.
>
> Allison: Mia's right. Who cares about bees?
>
> Mia: Why didn't the author write about bee stings? I got stung last summer. It hurt so much.
>
> Allison: I know! We should try to get rid of bee stings.
>
> Phil: My brother got stung last week.

Phil might have wanted to discuss bees, but he is unable to focus the conversation, and he then says something negative to Mia. Mia responds by changing the topic of the discussion, and it's downhill from there. No one discusses the specific content of the article or gets anything more out of it.

Now consider this discussion.

> Mia: I didn't realize that bees played such an important role on Earth.
>
> Allison: Yes, I can't imagine a world without honeybees.
>
> Phil: The author's argument is very convincing. At the end, the author suggests that we monitor all honeybee activity. Do you think that's even possible?
>
> Mia: It seems complicated. But the author indicates in the first two paragraphs that a lot of scientists are already doing it.
>
> Allison: I think it would be worth it. Especially considering all of the problems that honeybees are facing.
>
> Phil: Scientists can monitor the bees, but I don't know if they have the power to reverse the declining trend.

Here, the speakers work together—not by agreeing all the time, but by listening, thinking, and responding. Discussions should help us clarify, reconsider, or enrich our understanding. Hearing other points of view can help us rethink our own—and whether we wind up changing our minds or not, rethinking is always a worthwhile exercise.

Thinking It Through

Read this passage. Your teacher will lead a class discussion focusing on answering the question at the end of the passage. To prepare for this discussion, take notes while you read.

Most of the energy we use every day is from coal, gas, and oil. All have negative effects on the environment, and all are in limited supply. What if there were another source of energy that's always available and always clean? Well, such a source exists: wind! In towns and cities around the world, people are using clusters of windmills—called "wind farms"—to convert the energy of wind into electricity that people can use. Wind farms don't take up a lot of space and can even be built in the ocean. Unlike the smoke-spewing structures that produce energy from coal, gas, and oil, wind farms aren't at all ugly. Many years ago, ships used wind power to sail across oceans. Now, with wind farms increasing in number and size, we can use the wind to power our daily lives on land.

Are you convinced by the author's argument? Why or why not?

Notes

HINT   As you answer, be sure you look back at the paragraph for supporting evidence. Are there things you would need to know in order to be more fully convinced?

 DISCUSS   Discuss your answer with a partner.

Coached Example

Read the passage and answer the question. Then discuss your answers with a partner or in a small group.

Do you remember the last time you carried more than one textbook home from school? If so, you won't be surprised to learn that heavy backpacks are a major cause of lower-back pain in kids. Textbooks are not only heavy, but they are also expensive. Years go by before schools can afford to replace them; and during that time, they can become badly outdated. On top of all of this, textbooks get damaged or lost, too. How different things would be if every school used digital textbooks instead! With a small, lightweight e-reader, kids could download updated materials at the click of a button. E-readers can be used anywhere; and since materials are stored electronically, they don't get lost. It's time for schools to come into the twenty-first century and go digital!

1. Below are three claims that could be made, based on the passage.

Claim	Digital textbooks allow lots of flexibility.
	Print textbooks have more information.
	Digital textbooks are more interesting.

Part A

Circle the claim with the MOST relevant and sufficient evidence to support it.

> **HINT** The claim is the author's main argument.

Part B

Circle two facts in the article that BEST provide evidence to support the claim you selected in Part A. Write the two facts below.

_____

_____

_____

_____

> **HINT** Supporting facts are specific to the author's claim.

Lesson Practice

Read the passage and take notes on the following page. Use the Reading Guide to help you understand the passage.

Reading Guide

The author tells us an entertaining story. However, be sure to pay attention to the author's purpose for telling this story.

Mr. Hyde and Dr. Jekyll seem to be two very different people. Keep notes about how they relate to each other.

Dr. Jekyll's lawyer is Mr. Utterson. Pay close attention to Mr. Utterson's observations.

Dr. Jekyll and Mr. Hyde

Have you ever known someone who seems to be two completely different people at two different times? Most of the time, this person seems nice, responsible, and perfectly normal. However, this person has another side, too. In certain situations, this friendly person can be downright nasty. Maybe you've heard such people referred to as Jekyll-and-Hyde types. This expression comes from a famous novel by the British writer Robert Louis Stevenson. First published in 1886, it was titled *The Strange Case of Dr. Jekyll and Mr. Hyde.* It tells a strange tale, indeed!

As the story begins, we meet a lawyer named Mr. Utterson, who's telling a friend a horrible story about someone named Mr. Hyde committing a murder and running away, but then reappearing moments later to give the victim's relatives a check from a mysterious stranger who, we discover, is well respected by others.

Then things turn even stranger. Mr. Utterson has a client named Dr. Jekyll, who has just done a very odd thing: He has decided to leave all of his money to the murderous Mr. Hyde. Mr. Utterson is so troubled by all this that he begins to search for Mr. Hyde. When he spots him, he is shocked by Mr. Hyde's ugliness. Mr. Hyde explains that he is a friend of Dr. Jekyll's, and then unexpectedly gives Mr. Utterson his address. Later, Mr. Utterson goes to see Dr. Jekyll to ask what's going on. Dr. Jekyll assures Mr. Utterson that there's nothing to worry about.

About a year later, Mr. Hyde commits another murder. This time, the victim is an elderly man who was Mr. Utterson's client. Mr. Utterson tells the police Mr. Hyde's address, but Mr. Hyde has vanished without a trace.

When Mr. Utterson asks Dr. Jekyll about Mr. Hyde's disappearance, Dr. Jekyll seems just as puzzled as everyone else. Then, Dr. Jekyll shows Mr. Utterson a handwritten note he has received from Mr. Hyde. In it, Mr. Hyde apologizes to Dr. Jekyll for any trouble he has caused him and also states that he won't be seeing Dr. Jekyll again.

This could be the end of the story, except for one thing. "Isn't it strange," Mr. Utterson thinks to himself, "that Mr. Hyde's handwriting looks *exactly* like Dr. Jekyll's?" Here's what Utterson discovers: Feeling ashamed of his violent urges, Dr. Jekyll had developed a potion that temporarily turned him into the evil Mr. Hyde. After committing his crimes, Mr. Hyde just turned himself back into the normal-seeming Dr. Jekyll.

What was Stevenson trying to say something about human nature? Many think Stevenson created an exaggerated character to suggest that people have both good and bad in them. Is everyone capable of doing great good *and* great evil?

Take notes on the questions below. Then discuss the passage in groups, using your notes for guidance.

1. What deeper meaning about human nature does the author of this passage want to convey?

2. Do you think people would act differently if they didn't have to uphold their reputation?

Notes

Duplicating any part of this book is prohibited by law.

26 Listen and Respond to a Presentation

SL.8.2, SL.8.3, SL.8.6

Getting the Idea

Some speeches can be exciting or even inspiring. Others can be tedious and cause our attention to drift. What makes a good presentation? In this lesson, you will learn how to keep listeners focused to the end. You'll also learn ways to be an effective listener and discover how to critique a presentation.

We are surrounded by presentations every day. One of the most common types of presentations is a **persuasive presentation**, in which the speaker makes a claim and supports it with evidence. We see and hear this type of presentation every day as advertising on television and radio, on public transportation, and at the movie theatre. Most businesses use some form of persuasion. For example, fast food companies might try to persuade you to buy their food so that they can make a profit.

A persuasive speech heard in person can be especially compelling. It is important to think about and digest the message that the speaker is sharing with you. Think about the elements of a persuasive speech in order to decide whether the speaker is effective. Take notes during a presentation and write down how well the speaker follows the basic elements of an effective persuasive speech.

Elements of an Effective Persuasive Speech

- Body language should be relaxed, calm, and connected to the audience. The speaker should attempt to make eye contact with the audience.

- The presenter should not speak too slowly or hastily. Is the speaker talking so fast that it's hard to follow him or her?

- The argument should be logical, focusing on facts or statistics.

- There should be sufficient evidence supporting the claim, and the evidence should be relevant to the argument.

- The motive behind the presentation should be clear.

- The argument presented should be valid. The conclusion should be logical, based on the evidence that has been shared both verbally and visually. This creates a sound, convincing argument.

Duplicating any part of this book is prohibited by law.

- The presenter should use formal English effectively. Does the speaker use transition words, phrases, and clauses?

- Opposing viewpoints and a counterargument should be introduced.

- The presentation should have a strong closing. Does the speaker invite the audience to ask questions? Is it obvious that the speech was ending, or does the end come as a surprise?

Listening to a Presentation

Taking notes during a presentation will make it easier to focus and to come up with questions to ask the speaker. Work on being a supportive listener. Everyone gets nervous when giving a speech, so remember to be kind and listen as best you can.

What main idea is the speaker trying to present to the audience? What is the speaker attempting to do? Is he or she trying to change your mind about something?

Again, focus on the facts that are being shared in the speech. How does the speaker introduce the facts? The speaker could use statistics in the form of graphs or charts. What visual aids does the speaker use? Visual aids, such as pictures, video, and PowerPoint slides, make presentations more interesting for everyone. For example, if the speaker is trying to persuade you to like a certain band, he or she might share one of the band's music videos with the class.

Responding to a Presentation

After you've focused on the elements of the presentation and taken notes, it's time to ask questions. As you think of questions to ask, consider the following points:

- Was the speech persuasive?

- Did you enjoy the speech? Was there anything about the speech that might be improved? Be careful to give constructive criticism. Remember to be respectful. It is important to give examples of how the speaker might do things differently next time in order for the speech to be more effective.

- Questions may address whether there was sufficient evidence to support the claim and whether the argument was valid.

- Questions should show the speaker that you were in fact listening intently and would like more information. Questions should stay on topic.

- Let the speaker know if the visual aids helped you follow the speech.

Remember, when you are listening to your classmates give a presentation, you should give them your full attention. You will want people to listen to your presentation, too. Take notes on the things you like about others' presentations. This can help you decide what might work when it's time for you to address your audience.

Thinking It Through

Listen as your teacher gives a presentation on safety conditions onboard cruise ships. Take notes as you listen. Use your notes to help you answer the questions that follow.

Notes

Consider the following questions.

What was the most effective part of the presentation about safety standards on cruise ships? How could the presentation have been more convincing?

 Is the argument logical and supported by evidence?

DISCUSS Discuss your answers with a partner. What constructive criticism can you give your teacher?

Coached Example

Listen as your teacher gives a persuasive presentation. The chart below supports the presentation. Take notes as you listen.

Benefits of Online Courses

Cost	Comfort	Freedom	Relaxation
Online courses are cheaper.	You can study in the comfort of your own home.	You can make your own schedule.	It is relaxing to work at your own pace with no pressure.

Notes

Answer the questions below, and then discuss your answers with a partner.

1. Did your teacher state a definite position on the topic, or is the argument ambiguous? Support your answer.

_____

_____

_____

HINT   What is your teacher's opinion about the topic? How do you know?

2. How did your teacher use evidence to support his or her position? Explain.

_____

_____

_____

HINT   Do online courses have any special advantages or disadvantages?

Lesson Practice

Listen as your teacher gives a persuasive presentation. The photograph below supports the presentation. Listen and take notes in the space below. Use the Listening Guide to help you understand the presentation.

Listening Guide

What is being argued in this presentation?

What is the viewpoint of the presenter?

Does the presentation include facts or only opinions?

Notes

Answer the following questions.

1. **Use your answer to Part A to answer Part B.**

   Part A

   Which of these describes a fact from the presentation that helped support the argument?

   A. People who drive on dunes should drive carefully.

   B. It is best to drive on the grass on the dunes in order to protect the beach ecosystem.

   C. Now that signs are posted, there is no longer an issue with people driving on beaches.

   D. An increase in recreational activities is linked to increased beach erosion.

   Part B

   Which detail from the presentation BEST supports your answer to part A?

   A. "People have driven on beaches with dune buggies, motorbikes, and even four-wheel-drive trucks and SUVs."

   B. "The study discussed in this article suggests that the only way to protect the ecosystem around the dunes is to prohibit driving on beaches."

   C. "It has long been traditional for people to drive vehicles on the beaches in some places."

   D. "Signs should be posted, and people should be fined if they do not follow the rules."

2. Below are three claims that could be made based on the presentation "Driving on Beaches."

Claim	We need to move the habitats of animals that rely on dunes.
	We need to make it illegal to drive on beaches.
	We need to reduce the number of tourists going to beaches.

   Part A

   Circle the claim that is BEST supported by the evidence in the presentation.

   Part B

   Write two facts you heard in the presentation that support the claim you circled in Part A.

   _____

   _____

Duplicating any part of this book is prohibited by law.

27 Make a Presentation

SL.8.3, SL.8.4, SL.8.5, SL.8.6

Getting the Idea

Arguments in Presentations

People sometimes give presentations that take a clear position on a topic. To better teach or persuade an audience about the topic of the presentation, presenters must support their arguments. **Support** includes descriptions, factual information, details, and examples that back up the argument. **Claims**, which are opinions that support or describe the presentation's argument in order to make it more understandable or believable, are also used to strengthen an argument.

Staying Focused

In order to keep the audience's attention and get a message across, presenters need to keep the focus, or emphasis, on the main argument. All of the supporting information should be coordinated to create a solid argument. Support needs to make sense and get straight to the point. Presenting information that is unrelated to the argument will only confuse listeners, and the reason for your presentation will be lost. As you do research, keep in mind your reasons for using each piece of information to support your argument, and make sure your support is relevant.

Presentation Techniques

Prepare well before you give a presentation. Practice what you will say and be very familiar with your argument. This will allow you to maintain good eye contact with your audience. It will also give you the confidence to speak loudly and clearly because you will be certain about what you are saying.

While a clear, well-prepared presentation will enable your audience to understand the information you are presenting, additional multimedia or audiovisual aids can be useful in making your argument easier for your audience to understand. Such aids can also be used to strengthen your claims and keep your listeners engaged, which will convey your argument more effectively.

Duplicating any part of this book is prohibited by law.

Giving a Presentation

When preparing and giving a presentation, remember to use appropriate language. The act of giving a presentation is a more formal situation than chatting with your friends; therefore, you should speak using formal English. Avoid slang or off-color speech that could detract from your audience's focus on your argument.

Your use of language should also reflect the topic of your presentation. Different subject matter requires different vocabulary specific to that topic. If your topic requires special vocabulary to make it understandable, remember to define terms to your audience so that they can understand them. Appropriate language is important in adequately conveying information to your audience.

Practice Makes Perfect

If you do things to distract your audience, your message might be lost. Distractions could be nervous behaviors such as scratching your shoulder or touching your face, but also mumbling or clearing your throat too often. We all have a tendency to do this. What's the best way to avoid these distractions? Practice. If you practice your speech, you will be able to recognize problematic areas of your presentation and identify any nervous mannerisms you have. To practice, perform your presentation in front of a mirror or record it on video. You can also ask family or friends to be your audience. Ask them to give you constructive feedback, and then revise your presentation accordingly. Sometimes giving a mock presentation will calm your nerves and give you more confidence for the real presentation. Remember, your audience wants to hear what you have to say. Make your voice heard!

Thinking It Through

Listen as your teacher makes a presentation about the problem of poverty. Take notes in the box below as you listen. Use your notes to help you answer the questions that follow.

Notes

What was the argument of this presentation? What support was presented to strengthen that argument? Was the support relevant and focused?

_____

_____

_____

_____

HINT Your teacher uses a sequence of logical points to make an argument about poverty. Briefly write down these points as you hear them, and you'll be able to answer the questions.

 DISCUSS With a partner, discuss whether or not your teacher made a logical, well-supported argument.

Coached Example

Give a one-minute presentation to a partner on the following prompt. First, read the prompt. Then take notes about the presentation you will make. Use a separate sheet of paper or index cards.

> Some people say that soft drinks are not healthy foods at any age, but selling them in schools could teach bad habits from the start. Others say it is not the role of school officials to be telling students what they should be eating or drinking. Should soft drinks be sold in school cafeterias? What kinds of problems might result from students drinking too many soft drinks? How might you react if soft drinks were either taken away from or introduced into your cafeteria?

Take turns giving your presentation with your partner. When you are done, answer the questions that follow.

1. What kind of multimedia or audiovisual aid could your partner have used in his or her presentation to support its argument? Why would it have been of value?

_____

_____

_____

_____

HINT Multimedia and audiovisual aids can change the focus of the presentation. Aids should support the argument.

2. Can you think of another claim or piece of evidence that could have benefited your partner's presentation? Why would you add it?

_____

_____

_____

_____

HINT Irrelevant claims and evidence can be just as confusing or misleading as irrelevant multimedia or audiovisual aids. Be certain that your additional support is focused on the argument of the presentation.

Lesson Practice

Read the prompt below. Use the Presentation Guide and what you have learned in this lesson to help you prepare a five-minute presentation on the topic. The rubric at the bottom of the page shows how your presentation will be scored.

Presentation Guide

Remember to use reliable resources to find supporting information for your argument.

Find pictures or video clips that support your argument.

Make certain that your support, both verbal and visual, is cohesive and focused on the argument to help your audience better understand your presentation.

Many people have commented on the benefits of social media. Others point to the damaging effect it can have. Give a well-researched presentation on how social media negatively affects society. Some things to consider:

- What is social media? How can social media be abused?
- Think of a bad situation that resulted from your use of social media. Research situations in which social media had a negative effect. How could those situations have been avoided? Were the problems resolved? If so, how?
- Find statistics reflecting the effects of abusing social media. What does this say about the kinds of things that can result from negative uses of social media? What does it say about how social media should be used?

Score	Guidelines
4	The presentation is well researched and organized. The argument is supported with facts written in the student's own words. The presentation makes good use of research and claims to support understanding of the topic. The student uses correct grammar and language that is appropriate to the audience.
3	Most of the presentation is well researched and organized. Most of the facts support the argument and are written in the student's own words. Most of the research and claims are appropriate for the presentation and support understanding of the topic. Most of the language is proper and easy to understand.
2	Most of the presentation is not well researched and organized. Most of the facts are inaccurate, do not support the argument, and/or are not written in the student's own words. Most of the research or claims are either not appropriate for the presentation or do not support the topic. Most of the language used is difficult to understand.
1	The presentation is not well researched or organized. The presentation includes few accurate facts and/or facts do not support the argument and/or facts are not written in the student's own words. Insufficient research and claims are used, and they do not support the topic. All of the language used is difficult to understand.

Duplicating any part of this book is prohibited by law.

Next, take notes as you prepare for your presentation. Use a separate sheet of paper or index cards for your notes.

Now you and your classmates will give your presentations to the class. As your classmates deliver their presentations, answer the following questions. Support your answers with examples.

1. Did your classmates' claims and evidence adequately support their arguments? Was their support relevant and focused? What piece of evidence did you find most convincing?

   _____

   _____

   _____

   _____

2. Choose a presentation in which a classmate used multimedia or audiovisual aids that did not support the argument of their presentation. What might have been a better aid?

   _____

   _____

   _____

   _____

3. Choose a presentation—either yours or a classmate's—that used terminology specific to its topic. Were those terms defined for the audience? How did the use of these terms affect the presentation?

   _____

   _____

   _____

   _____

Cumulative Assessment

Listen to the passage and take notes in the space on the next page. Then answer the questions that follow.

Save the Music!

Participation in Music, Dance, or Art Outside School, 10th Grade

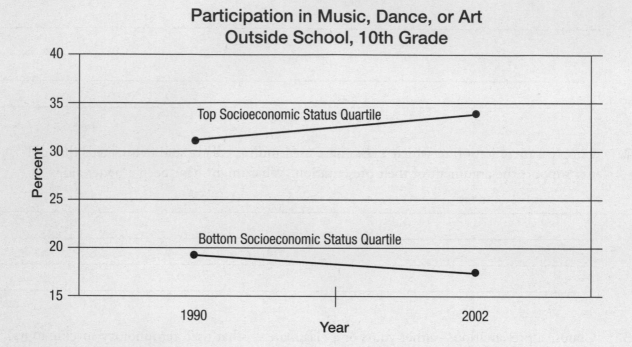

Notes

Answer the questions that follow.

1. Which statement BEST summarizes the author's position?

   A. All students need access to art classes.

   B. STEM classes are less important than art classes.

   C. All students should be required to take art classes.

   D. Art classes are more important than all other classes.

2. Who is MOST LIKELY the author's intended audience?

   A. students who are choosing whether to take art or music classes

   B. parents who vote for school board members and political leaders

   C. school board members who must win elections

   D. musicians who want the opportunity to perform in schools

3. If the passage were written in informal language, who would be the MOST LIKELY audience?

   A. parents who support the increase in STEM classes

   B. school board members who support mathematics and science

   C. parents who are trying to convince their child to take an art class

   D. students who want to help make a difference in their schools' budgets

4. How does the author acknowledge possible opposing views?

   A. by listing opposing views and letting the audience form their own opinion

   B. by listing opposing views and then disproving them

   C. by listing opposing views and dismissing them as unimportant

   D. by listing opposing views and then stating that both sides are equally valid

5. Read the following scenario.

> **The local school does not have enough money to hire a drama teacher, so the drama class is eliminated. A group of local actors offers to begin an after-school drama program. The program will run two days a week for eight weeks. Participating students will be charged a one-time fee of $150, which will cover costumes and props.**

Based on the passage, which reaction would the author MOST LIKELY have?

A. The author will support the program because some students will benefit.

B. The author will support the program because all students can participate.

C. The author will not completely support the program because it takes money from STEM.

D. The author will not completely support the program because it will exclude some students.

6. If the author had not discussed No Child Left Behind and declining funds, how would the argument change?

A. The argument would be less effective because the complexity of the issue would not be clear.

B. The argument would be less effective because it would have not had supporting evidence.

C. The argument would be more effective because irrelevant information would be eliminated.

D. The argument would be more effective because more time would be spent discussing the real issue of art and music cuts.

Duplicating any part of this book is prohibited by law.

7. Does the graph support or refute the central claim of the passage? Use relevant evidence from the passage and the graph to explain your answer.

_____

_____

_____

_____

_____

_____

_____

_____

_____

_____

_____

_____

_____

_____

8. Think about the author's argument and how the graph on page 340 supports it.

   What other visual aid would strengthen the passage's claim? Use relevant evidence from the passage to support your answer.

   _____

   _____

   _____

   _____

   _____

   _____

   _____

   _____

   _____

   _____

   _____

   _____

   _____

   _____

   _____

   _____

CHAPTER

5 Language

Chapter 5: Diagnostic Assessment

Chapter 5: Cumulative Assessment

5 Diagnostic Assessment

This passage contains mistakes. Read the passage and answer the questions that follow.

Mapping the World

(1) There are three basic kinds of maps: physical, political, and thematic. (2) Physical maps focus on physical features, such as mountains, rivers, and oceans. (3) These are used to identify the locations of landmasses and waterways, especially those that cross national borders. (4) Topographic maps are also physical maps, but they stand out in one important way. (5) Although like all physical maps they are two-dimensional, topographic maps use contour lines to indicate three-dimensional features. (6) For example, a topographic map will show hikers where there are mountains or rivers. (7) It will use different colors for different levels of height. (8) This lets anyone planning on crossing a mountain know exactly what they're in for!

(9) Political maps identify political borders, such as those finding around cities, countries, and states. (10) Because different countries produce their own maps, political maps can be subjective. (11) For instance, a home country might make other countries look smaller than they really are. (12) Many current U.S. textbooks use the map in which Greenland and Africa appear to be the same size. (13) In reality, Africa is more than ten times the size of Greenland.

(14) Thematic maps identify locations based on a theme, such as oil-producing nations, <u>unemployment</u> rates in different parts of the country, or population density. (15) These maps are found very useful by researchers and students. (16) They offer good, clear information at a glance.

(17) A globe is a spherical map of the world. (18) Globes offer a more accurate representation of Earth than projection maps can provide. (19) Even the best projection map will include some type of <u>distortion</u>. (20) After all, Earth is round, not flat.

(21) At first glance, maps might seem boring. (22) Maybe that's why many American students have an <u>aversion</u> to geography. (23) However, maps are not only useful—they speak to us about the world we live in.

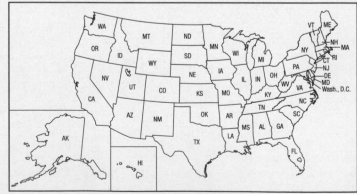

The United States

1. Which is the BEST way to revise sentence 15?

   A. These maps, found by researchers and students, are very useful.

   B. These maps by researchers and students are found very useful.

   C. Researchers and students these maps find very useful.

   D. Researchers and students find these maps very useful.

2. Why is a comma used in sentence 16?

   A. "They offer good" is an introductory phrase.

   B. There is a complete sentence on each side of the comma.

   C. The information that follows the comma is important.

   D. The words *good* and *clear* are coordinate adjectives.

3. What is the MOST LIKELY meaning of <u>aversion</u> in sentence 22?

   A. interest

   B. curiosity

   C. dislike

   D. purpose

4. In sentence 14, the root word of <u>unemployment</u> is

   A. employ.

   B. ploy.

   C. ment.

   D. un.

Duplicating any part of this book is prohibited by law.

5. In sentence 19, the word <u>distortion</u> suggests that projection maps

    A. have changed over time.

    B. have some inaccuracies.

    C. are completely wrong.

    D. are not like other maps.

6. On the lines below, rewrite sentence 9 correctly.

    _____

    _____

    _____

    _____

    _____

    _____

Duplicating any part of this book is prohibited by law.

This passage contains mistakes. Read the passage and answer the questions that follow.

October 3, 2010

Dear Mr. Gray:

(1) We are asking local businesses to donate services and merchandise for a public auction my school has organized. (2) Would you be interested in to donate? (3) The auction would benefit the homeless members off our community. (4) As you probably know, our city has seen a marked increase in homelessness in the last year. (5) Many of these homeless include children. (6) They are the <u>innocent</u> victims of a situation that is out of their control. (7) Their parents have <u>insufficient</u> funds to pay their rent or a light bill. (8) They cannot buy their children even the most basic things. (9) Your donation will make a difference in some of these children's lives.

(10) Your gift will be tax-deductible and provide you with free publicity. (11) The entire school will be reminded of your generosity since we will <u>record</u> your contribution. (12) The name of your business will be printed in the brochure for the auction. (13) We have done our part. (14) Now, the ball is in your court. (15) Please make a donation today.

(16) We look forward to hearing from you.

Sincerely,

Maya Kinnerley

7. Which of these sentences is imperative?

    A. "We look forward to hearing from you."

    B. "Now, the ball is in your court."

    C. "Please make a donation today."

    D. "We have done our part."

8. Which sentence from the passage contains a spelling error?

    A. "Your gift will be tax-deductible and provide you with free publicity."

    B. "The auction would benefit the homeless members off our community."

    C. "The name of your business will be printed in the brochure for the auction."

    D. "Your donation will make a difference in some of these children's lives."

9. Which of the following is the correct way to write sentence 2?

    A. Would you be interested to donate?

    B. Would you be interested in donating?

    C. Would you be interested in donated.

    D. Would you be interested in donate?

10. Read this sentence from the passage.

    Their parents have <u>insufficient</u> funds to pay their rent or a light bill.

    As used in the sentence, what does the word <u>insufficient</u> mean?

    A. more than enough

    B. having enough

    C. nearly enough

    D. not enough

Duplicating any part of this book is prohibited by law.

11. Read this sentence from the passage.

They are the <u>innocent</u> victims of a situation that is out of their control.

In this sentence, the word <u>innocent</u> emphasizes

A. the unfairness of the situation.

B. the young age of the children.

C. the guilt of the parents.

D. the harmlessness of children.

12. Which meaning of the word <u>record</u> is used in sentence 11, and how does context help you figure it out?

_____

_____

_____

_____

_____

_____

Duplicating any part of this book is prohibited by law.

28 Verbals

L.8.1.a

Getting the Idea

Verbals are words that are created from verbs; however, a verbal can serve the purpose of a noun, an adjective, or an adverb. Here are some examples of verbals: *learning, to read, relaxed.*

What do you notice about how these verbals are related to the verbs above? The word *learning* is created by adding *-ing* to the word *learn, to read* is created by adding the word *to* before the word *read,* and *relaxed* is created by adding *-ed* to the word *relax.*

There are three kinds of verbals: gerunds, infinitives, and participles. A **gerund** is usually the noun form of a verb, and it always ends in *-ing*. Keep in mind, though, that not every word that ends in *-ing* is a gerund.

Notice that the gerunds in the following sentences each function as nouns:

> My best friend and I love <u>swimming</u> in the pool every day.

> <u>Writing</u> is my favorite activity in school.

Another kind of verbal is the infinitive. An **infinitive** is a verb in its basic form that usually functions as a noun. The word *to* before a verb forms its infinitive. Sometimes, another verb will come right before the infinitive form of a verb.

Here are some examples of infinitives: *to watch, to drive, to speak.*

Notice the infinitive forms of the verbs in the sentences below:

> My best friend and I love <u>to swim</u> in the pool every day.

> <u>To think</u> that way can lead to disaster!

Mixing up gerunds and infinitives can make a sentence difficult to understand. Here is one way to remember how they are different. Many sports and activities are gerunds, such as *swimming, reading,* and *biking*. Infinitives are complete forms of verbs and sometimes follow another verb.

Duplicating any part of this book is prohibited by l...

Thinking It Through 1

Read the following sentences. Write them correctly on the lines provided. If the sentence is correct, write "correct as is."

1. I want helping you, but I just don't have time today.

_____

> **HINT** A gerund is more often used as a noun than as a verb.

2. Fishing is Derek's favorite sport, and he's done it all his life.

_____

> **HINT** Double-check the subject of the first phrase. Is it correct?

3. Every night, Louise enjoys to read a book before she falls asleep.

_____

4. I need to be alone right now.

_____

5. After dinner, the cat wants going outside.

_____

6. It's really important sleeping at least seven to eight hours a night.

_____

7. Since they live so far away, Mike and Heather really miss seeing their parents.

_____

8. This science project has had me to work late every night!

_____

The third kind of verbal is the participle. A **participle** is a word that acts as a modifier in front of a noun.

Here are some examples of participles:

> The <u>laughing</u> girl was the only one we could hear.
> All around the yard were the tree's <u>fallen</u> branches.

In these examples, the participle *laughing* is describing the noun *girl*. It describes how the girl was behaving. The participle *fallen* modifies the noun *branches*. It describes what had happened to the branches on the ground.

A **participial phrase** is a group of words that modify a noun. Here are some examples of participial phrases:

> People <u>guided by good intentions</u> are often kind.
> <u>Having been a singer</u>, Jim was very comfortable on stage.

In the sentences above, *guided by good intentions* is a participial phrase modifying the noun *people*. The participial phrase *having been a singer* is a participial phrase modifying the noun *Jim*.

A common error in participle usage is the **misplaced modifier**. When a participle is not modifying a specific noun in a sentence, it is considered misplaced.

Here are some examples of misplaced modifiers:

> While walking down the road, the ball bounced in my hands.
> Jen called our band a practice meeting.

In the first sentence, it seems as if the ball was walking down the road. In the second sentence, it seems as if Jen called the band a practice meeting, instead of a band.

Here are some correct ways to rewrite these sentences:

> While walking down the road, I bounced the ball in my hands.
> Jen called a practice meeting for our band.

Duplicating any part of this book is prohibited by law.

Thinking It Through 2

Read the following sentences. Write them correctly on the lines provided. If the sentence is correct, write "correct as is."

1. Speaking softly, the secrets were told by Louis.

    _____

    HINT This sentence sounds like the *secrets* were *speaking softly*. Move the phrase *speaking softly* closer to *Louis*.

2. A book was on the table that the famous author had written.

    _____

    HINT Move the phrase *that the famous author had written* closer to the noun *book*.

3. An insect bit Mrs. Jones while she was gardening.

    _____

4. Sitting by the fire, the rain was seen by us.

    _____

5. Aidan had given the old uniform to the school team not needed anymore.

    _____

6. The girl wearing glasses walked into the room.

    _____

7. While swimming, the fisherman caught the fish.

    _____

8. While napping, the pillow fell off my bed.

    _____

Duplicating any part of this book is prohibited by law

This passage contains mistakes. Use the Reading Guide to help you find the mistakes.

Reading Guide

As you read the passage, remember that gerunds end in *-ing*.

What is the infinitive in sentence 17?

What is the gerund in sentence 24?

Amsterdam: A Very Bike-Friendly City

(1) There are many different modes of transportation in the world. (2) Thousands of planes and helicopters fly along regular routes every day. (3) In many cities, trains and subways ride on land or underground. (4) In some parts of the world, horses or oxen are the way to get around, and people carry their goods in large carts. (5) For much of the world, cars and buses are the usual mode of transport. (6) And in some places, biking is the preferred way to travel.

(7) Some people may think that being interested in riding a bike stops at childhood. (8) However, in Amsterdam, both children and adults of all ages ride their bikes everywhere. (9) Amsterdam is located in Europe, in The Netherlands. (10) There are specially designed bike paths throughout this city. (11) The bike paths are small roads right beside the main street that only bikes are allowed to use. (12) This is safer for cyclists because they are separate from the cars on the main road.

(13) In Amsterdam, there are bike racks in front of many stores and restaurants. (14) This way, when people want to stop to shop or eat, they can simply park their bikes right outside. (15) Most cyclists use a bike lock; some bike locks are heavy chains, while others are made of thick cable. (16) This is one way protecting the bikes from theft. (17) In Europe, many bikes have baskets in the front to hold groceries or other items.

(18) Safety is important to consider when biking. (19) While biking, cars pass by cyclists. (20) But people on bikes must also look both ways before entering traffic. (21) Since biking is such a big part of the culture of the city of Amsterdam, much of the time, cyclists and motorists work together to make sure everyone stays safe. (22) All cyclists should travel around the city wearing helmets. (23) It's a critical safety measure.

(24) All in all, biking is a great way to get around. (25) It's cheap, environmentally friendly, and fun.

Duplicating any part of this book is prohibited by law.

Answer the following questions.

1. In sentence 6, the infinitive is

    A. in some

    B. biking

    C. preferred

    D. to travel

2. Which is the BEST way to replace the verb <u>protecting</u> in sentence 16?

    A. protect

    B. to protect

    C. protected

    D. have protected

3. Read this sentence from the passage.

    **While biking, cars pass
    by cyclists.**

    Which is the BEST way to revise
    this sentence?

    A. Cars pass by cyclists while they
        are biking.

    B. While biking, passed by cars
        are cyclists.

    C. While biking, cars are passed
        by cyclists.

    D. Cars, while biking, pass by cyclists.

4. Which is the BEST way to revise
    sentence 22?

    A. All wearing helmets cyclists should
        travel around the city.

    B. When wearing helmets, traveling
        around the city, all cyclists.

    C. All cyclists should wear helmets
        when traveling around the city.

    D. When wearing helmets all cyclists,
        travel around the city.

Duplicating any part of this book is prohibited by law.

The following questions do not relate to a passage.

5. Read the following sentences.

    She thoroughly enjoyed jogging, but not in this boiling humidity. She felt as if she were a lobster scrambling to climb out of a cooking pot.

    Underline the participles that function as adjectives.

    _____

6. Read the following sentence.

    Working diligently, the cast made this year's musical enjoyable to watch, even though the show lost money.

    Circle the participial phrase in the sentence that modifies a noun.

    _____

7. Read the following sentences. Fill in the blank with a phrase from the box that makes the sentence grammatically correct.

    Kaylie was taking care of her baby brother Lucas. While carrying him into the kitchen, _____.

    | the rattle dropped |
    | dropping his rattle |
    | he dropped his rattle |
    | she dropped his rattle |

Duplicating any part of this book is prohibited by law.

8. Draw a line from the first part of the sentence on the left to the part that BEST completes it on the right.

A. | Having studied art for years,

1. | Riley knew that the painting was a fake.

B. | She gave brownies to the children

2. | people asked if Ann knew about Picasso.

C. | One of three sisters,

3. | wrapped in foil.

4. | gathered in the kitchen.

5. | Sally's father was a teacher.

6. | Ella was the oldest.

9. Circle the correct sentences. There is more than one correct choice listed below.

A. Gathering in the air, the seagulls swooped together and cut like an arrow through the sky.

B. The seagulls swooping together, hovering in the air, and cut like an arrow through the sky.

C. The seagulls, swooping together, hovered in the air and cut like an arrow through the sky.

D. The seagulls swooped together, hovered in the air, and cutting like an arrow through the sky.

E. The seagulls swooping together, to hover in the air and to cut like an arrow through the sky.

F. Hovered in the air, the seagulls swooping together and cut like an arrow through the sky.

Duplicating any part of this book is prohibited by law.

29 Verb Voices and Moods

L.8.1.b–d, L.8.3.a

Getting the Idea

A **verb** is a word that shows action or occurrence or describes a state of being. For example, the verb is underlined in the sentences below.

> Vivian <u>laughed</u> during the entire movie.

> Ibrahim <u>is</u> unhappy about moving away.

> My grandfather <u>walks</u> to town every day.

Verbs are easy to spot in a sentence because they tell what the subject is doing. In the sentences above, Vivian, Ibrahim, and the grandfather are the subjects. A verb may either be used in the **active voice** or in the **passive voice**. In the active voice, a subject performs the action. In the passive voice, the subject is acted upon by someone or something else. Look at the chart below.

Verb	Voices	
throw	**active:**	Nestor throws the ball across the field. We threw the Frisbee all afternoon.
	passive:	The ball is thrown by Nestor across the field. The Frisbee was thrown all afternoon.
make	**active:**	Mrs. Tucci makes delicious muffins. My mother made a very good soup.
	passive:	Some delicious muffins are made by Mrs. Tucci. A very good soup was made by my mother.

Generally, you should use the active voice when you write. Your sentences will be more concise, or straight to the point. They will also probably be more entertaining or interesting. You may notice that the passive sentences above sound very awkward. Sentences in the passive voice can also be very wordy. However, at times you can use the passive voice for effect, when you want to emphasize the person or thing that is acted upon. For example, the sentence "Mr. Jones was inspired by his travels" draws attention to Mr. Jones, not to his travels.

Thinking It Through 1

Read the following sentences. Write them correctly on the lines provided. If the sentence is correct, write "correct as is."

1. At his mother's request, the cat was taken by Bill into the house.

_____

> **HINT** Remember that in the active voice, the subject performs an action.

2. A slice of pizza is being eaten by Ari before he goes to the movies.

_____

> **HINT** Which verb is in the passive voice in this sentence?

3. Fire nearly destroyed the White House in 1814.

_____

4. Deshawn is being driven to football practice by his mother.

_____

5. A museum employee stole the *Mona Lisa* and kept it for two years.

_____

6. The dead leaves and trash were swept up by a small crew of workers.

_____

7. Two turkeys were eaten by the extended family during their first Thanksgiving all together.

_____

8. The great white whale was hunted by the sea captain for a long time but never caught.

_____

Mood is the attitude a verb conveys in a sentence. If you change a verb's mood, the tone of the sentence containing it will change as well. The mood also depends on the sentence's purpose.

- The **indicative mood** is used to make a statement.
- The **imperative mood** is used for commands or direct requests.
- The **subjunctive mood** is used to speculate or express a wish.
- The **conditional mood** expresses an action or idea that is dependent on a condition.
- The **interrogative mood** is used to ask a question.

The chart below contains examples of mood in sentences.

Mood	Example
indicative	Al needs to clean his room today.
imperative	Al, clean your room today!
subjunctive	Al wishes he were finished cleaning his room.
conditional	If Al had cleaned his room, he could have played.
interrogative	Have you cleaned your room yet, Al?

- The indicative is the most commonly used mood. It may be used for many purposes.

- Imperative sentences do not need to end in exclamation points, but they often do. Writers use the imperative mood when they are trying to create a dramatic effect or when they are trying to be persuasive.

- Notice in the subjunctive example that the sentence uses the plural verb *were*, even though it refers to a singular subject, Al. Another example is, "She insists he wash his hands before dinner." Notice the verb is *wash*, not *washes*.

- The conditional sometimes expresses hypothetical statements. For example, "If you ate fruit, you'd be healthier." The past-tense verb *ate* is correct even though the sentence is about something that has not happened.

- You should always end interrogative sentences with question marks.

Thinking It Through 2

Read the following sentences. Write them correctly on the lines provided. If the sentence is correct, write "correct as is."

1. The water pipes froze during the winter storm?

_____

HINT Remember that a sentence in the indicative mood does not end with a question mark.

2. Bake the loaf for twenty minutes before you are taking it out.

_____

HINT Imperative voice sentences do not use gerunds often.

3. Myrna spends money as if she was the richest woman in town.

_____

4. If Brett makes the team, he will be very happy.

_____

5. Is it true that Mischa is moving to Hawaii for good!

_____

6. I'm begging you, turn loose of that statue?

_____

7. The rain continued for most of the afternoon.

_____

8. Where do you think you're going, wearing that ridiculous hat.

_____

Duplicating any part of this book is prohibited by la

Lesson Practice

This passage contains mistakes. Use the Reading Guide to help you find the mistakes.

Reading Guide

How would you rewrite sentence 6 to correct the error in mood?

How should sentence 9 be revised?

Is sentence 19 active or passive? How would you revise it to put it in a different voice?

Your Grandma Can't Cook

(1) Colin winced when his grandmother said she had fresh cookies baking in the oven. (2) His friend Bridget looked at him strangely. (3) She was visiting Colin for the first time. (4) She waited until Colin's grandmother stepped out of the kitchen.

(5) "What's the matter with you," she asked. (6) "If your grandma makes cookies, it would be a good thing!"

(7) Colin shook his head. (8) "It would be a good thing if she was a good cook. (9) I'm telling you, she can burn water."

(10) "Stop that, Colin. (11) That's really mean. (12) What if she hears you?"

(13) Colin stared at the door of his grandmother's refrigerator. (14) It was covered with crayon drawings. (15) The pictures had been drawn by him when he was five years old. (16) Even though every paper was stained and curling at the edges, his grandmother had continued to display them proudly on the door. (17) If Colin had felt any smaller at that moment, he will disappear.

(18) Just then, his grandmother returned. (19) She slipped on two oven mitts, and the tray was pulled out of the oven. (20) They were irregularly shaped and burned.

(21) His grandmother smiled and said, "Just a tad overdone."

(22) Colin smiled, too. "They're perfect," he said.

Answer the following questions.

1. How should sentence 5 be revised?

   A. "What's the matter with you."
      she asked

   B. "What's the matter with you!"
      she asked.

   C. "What's the matter with you?"
      she asked.

   D. "What's the matter with you"
      she asked.

2. Which sentence from the passage
   is imperative?

   A. She was visiting Colin for the
      first time.

   B. It was covered with crayon
      drawings.

   C. "That's really mean."

   D. "Stop that, Colin."

3. Which is the BEST way to revise
   sentence 15?

   A. He had drawn when he was
      five years old the pictures.

   B. He had drawn the pictures when
      he was five years old.

   C. The pictures were drawn by him
      when he was five years old.

   D. When he was five years old, the
      pictures had been drawn by him.

4. Read this sentence from the passage.

   **If Colin had felt any smaller at
   that moment, he will disappear.**

   Choose the correct way to revise
   this sentence.

   A. If Colin felt any smaller at that
      moment, he would be disappearing.

   B. If Colin had felt any smaller at
      that moment, he would have
      disappeared.

   C. If Colin was feeling any smaller
      at that moment, he would have
      disappeared.

   D. If Colin were feeling any smaller at
      that moment, he will disappear.

The following questions do not relate to a passage.

5. Read the following incomplete sentence.

If Mrs. Caron had read the letter, she _____ responded to it.

Which verb completes the sentence correctly?

A. had

B. will have

C. would have

D. won't have

---

6. **Use your answer to Part A to answer Part B.**

Part A

Which of the following sentences is correct?

A. The trash had been taken out by John before he were going to bed.

B. Why do you have to leave the party before we serve the cake?

C. Walk the dog for at least half an hour before you would return home.

D. Samira has to be practicing for her dance recital yesterday.

Part B

Which mood is used in the correct answer to Part A?

A. indicative

B. imperative

C. subjunctive

D. conditional

E. interrogative

---

7. Read the following paragraph.

The game was almost lost by our team. The score was tied when a touchdown was scored by Valley. At the last second, though, a field goal was kicked by Chad, and the game was won by us!

Rewrite the paragraph on the lines below so that it uses active voice appropriately.

_____

_____

_____

_____

_____

_____

8. **Use your answer to Part A to answer Part B.**

Read the sentences below.

Each day, I drop my little sister off at her bus stop before heading to school.
The cookies were stolen by someone in the kitchen.
The prime minister's goals were delayed by a vote in the House of Commons.
The plate broke when the dog jumped on the dining room table.

Part A

Circle the two sentences that are written in the passive voice.

Part B

Use the active voice to rewrite the sentences you circled in Part A.

_____

_____

_____

_____

_____

9. Which of the following sentences are written correctly in the subjunctive? There is more than one correct choice listed below.

A. If I were president, I would fund space exploration to Mars.

B. If he had only listened, he could have been a great student.

C. Julie plays piano as if she were the only person in the room.

D. Were you and Hayley going to the movies later?

E. This film was produced by James Cho.

F. Kento wished he were done with his math homework.

G. Prashant, do the dishes now.

H. What were you thinking when you decided to add salt to that dish!

30 Capitalization, Punctuation, and Spelling

L.8.2.a–c

Getting the Idea

Capitalization is the use of capital, or uppercase, letters in writing.

Rule	Examples
proper names	Amelia Earhart, Mr. Olsen, Mom, Uncle Tim
days of the week	Monday, Tuesday, Wednesday
names of months	January, August, December
major words in titles	"Casey at the Bat" (Do <u>not</u> capitalize words like "a/an," "the," "of," "and," "in," and "for.")
organizations	Fish and Wildlife Service, American Red Cross
names of places	Main Street, Harlem River, the Himalayas
languages	English, Spanish, German, Cantonese
names of holidays	Memorial Day, New Year's Day

Punctuation is the use of the correct marks to make sentences more readable. Use a **comma** to separate coordinate adjectives. For example: *Maria's blouse had **large, colorful** flowers.* The words *large* and *colorful* are coordinate adjectives that equally modify the noun *flowers.* Do not put a comma between noncoordinate adjectives. *He owned **several blue** jackets.* Adjectives are coordinate if you can insert the word *and* between them. They are also coordinate if you can switch the order of adjectives. *He owned blue several jackets* does not make sense. Commas also create a pause in a sentence. For example: *The puppy, after playing in the mud, was dirty.*

Both the **em-dash** and the **ellipsis** indicate a pause or break in a sentence. For example: *My computer—if anyone cares—is broken. I… uh… have no idea how it happened.*

An ellipsis also indicates an omission of content, as in a quotation from a book or other source. For example: "As Hodges states repeatedly in his essay, 'The people… will always defend their rights.'"

Thinking It Through 1

Read the following sentences. Write them correctly on the lines provided. If the sentence is correct, write "correct as is."

1. I'm going to my Aunt's house on the fourth of July.

_____

> **HINT** You should always capitalize the names of holidays.

2. We had a really, good time last tuesday, didn't we?

_____

> **HINT** Days of the week are also capitalized.

3. My letter—if you bothered to read it—told you what happened in Chicago.

_____

4. My friendly, new neighbor, mrs. Napoli, is teaching me to speak italian.

_____

5. My favorite book is… let's see… *Charlotte's Web* by E. B. White.

_____

6. Captain bly always had a kind word for the second Mate but never for the Cook.

_____

7. You'll need to eat earlier the lunchroom is only open until 1:30 today.

_____

8. The typhoon started far out in the pacific ocean and made its way toward hokkaido.

_____

Spelling is an important part of writing. Understanding spelling rules can help you spell correctly. Study the chart below.

Spelling Rules
To make regular verbs past tense, add the suffix *-d* to a verb that ends with a vowel. Example: *glue* ⟶ *glued*. Add the suffix *-ed* to a verb that ends with a consonant. Example: *wash* ⟶ *washed*.
To add a suffix to a word that ends in *-y*, look at the letter that comes just before the *y*. If it is a consonant, change the *y* to an *i*. Example: *cry* ⟶ *cried* (the letter *r* is a consonant). But, if the suffix begins with *i*, as in *-ing*, keep the *y*. Example: *cry* ⟶ *crying*.
In most cases, if a word ends in *-e*, drop the *e* to add a suffix that begins with a vowel. Example: *dance* ⟶ *dancing*. When the suffix begins with a consonant, keep the *e*. Example: *divine* ⟶ *divinely*.
In most cases, if a word ends in *-f*, change the *f* to a *v* and add *-es* to make it plural. Example: *knife* ⟶ *knives*. If a word ends in *-ff* or *-ffe*, add *-s* to make it plural. Examples: *cliff* ⟶ *cliffs*; *giraffe* ⟶ *giraffes*.
When a one-syllable word ends in a consonant after one vowel, double the final consonant before adding a suffix that begins with a vowel. Examples: *bat* ⟶ *batting*; *slip* ⟶ *slipped*.

Watch out for commonly confused words like *there, their*, and *they're*. These words sound similar, but they have very different meanings.

Thinking It Through 2

Read the following sentences. Write them correctly on the lines provided. If the sentence is correct, write "correct as is."

1. Ashley orderd custom shelfs for her prized book colection.

_____

HINT Remember the rules about the formation of plural nouns ending in *f*.

2. Sean was debateing weather he should attend the meeting or stay home.

_____

HINT Remember that some verbs change their spelling when they add suffixes or other special endings.

3. Bethenny was not satisfied with her swimming performance that day.

_____

4. Luke was quiete, but he apreciated the difficultie of the situation.

_____

5. I didn't recieve apologys from either of them, and I am not pleasd.

_____

6. After a few smal bumpes, the plane was roling along toward the gate.

_____

7. The officers knockd on the door two or three tims, but no one answerd.

_____

8. They had waited their entire lives for an opportunity like this.

_____

This passage contains mistakes. Use the Reading Guide to help you find the mistakes.

Reading Guide

Where should the other dash be inserted in sentence 5?

How should sentence 7 be revised?

What is the error in sentence 8?

Correct the error in sentence 12.

Forces of Nature

(1) There are some things not even the smartest strongest humans can prevent. (2) Often, those things arise from nature. (3) Earthquakes are, literally earth-shattering and sometimes life-changing natural events. (4) They're certainly events beyond human control, or even human anticipation in some cases.

(5) Though their effects are felt on Earth's surface, earthquakes actually originate far often several miles—below it. (6) Earthquakes occur when the giant plates of Earth, the plates that carry Earth's continents and oceans, move together. (7) Fortunately, the process is an extremely, slow one. (8) These plates move much more slowly then your fingernails grow. (9) It can take hundreds of years for these plates to press together with enough force to cause an earthquake.

(10) Most earthquakes occur where Earth's plates meet. (11) At these boundarys, the brittle outer layer of Earth—the crust breaks, causing faults. (12) There are, of course, diffrent kinds of faults. (13) "Strike-slip" faults occur when two plates slide past each other, much in the same way as cars pass each other on roads. (14) The famous San Andreas Fault, where the north american and pacific plates meet, is a fault of this type. (15) The second type of fault is a "dip-slip fault." (16) As its name suggests, this type of fault results when blocks of crust slide up or down a slope.

Answer the following questions.

1. Which revision corrects the error in sentence 1?

   A. There are some things not even the smartest, strongest humans can prevent.

   B. Their are some things not even the smartest strongest humans can prevent.

   C. There are some things not even the smartest, strongest Humans can prevent.

   D. There are some things not even the smartest, strongest, humans can prevent.

2. Which is the BEST way to revise sentence 3?

   A. Earthquakes are literally and earth-shattering sometimes life-changing natural events.

   B. Earthquakes are literally, earth-shattering and sometimes life-changing natural events.

   C. Earthquakes are literally earth-shattering and sometimes life-changing natural events.

   D. Earthquakes are literally earth-shattering, sometimes, and life-changing natural events.

3. Which sentence is the correct revision of sentence 11?

   A. At these boundarys, the brittle outer layer of Earth—the crust—breaks, causing faults.

   B. At these boundaries, the brittle outer layer of Earth the crust—breaks, causing faults.

   C. At these boundarys, the brittle outer layer of Earth the crust breaks, causing faults.

   D. At these boundaries, the brittle outer layer of Earth—the crust—breaks, causing faults.

4. Choose the correct way to revise sentence 14.

   A. The famous San Andreas Fault, where the north American and Pacific plates meet, is a fault of this type.

   B. The famous San Andreas Fault, where the North American and Pacific plates meet, is a fault of this type.

   C. The famous San Andreas Fault, where the North American and pacific plates meet, is a fault of this type.

   D. The famous San Andreas fault, where the North American and Pacific Plates meet, is a fault of this type.

The following questions do not relate to a passage.

5. **Use your answer to Part A to answer Part B.**

    Part A

    Which of the following sentences is punctuated correctly?

    A. Aunt Cate owned many, colorful, hand-knit sweaters.

    B. Substance—not style is vital when speaking the truth.

    C. That restaurant which just opened is serving a limited menu.

    D. As a child, I loved to sing "Mary Had a Little Lamb."

    Part B

    Rewrite the incorrect sentences in Part A so that they contain correct punctuation.

    _____

    _____

    _____

    _____

6. Read each sentence on the left. Then match the sentence to the word that correctly completes it on the right.

    A. We're going _____ on vacation.

    1. their

    B. I think _____ scheduled to perform soon.

    2. there

    C. How will they celebrate _____ birthdays?

    3. they're

7. Read the following sentences. Add commas to make the sentences clearer. If the sentence is clear as it is written, add nothing.

> **Jason eats slimy smelly green avocado sandwiches on rye bread every day.**

> **Herbivores such as elephants eat only vegetation.**

> **Steve went to the store bought two cartons of milk and left.**

---

8. The following paragraph contains spelling and punctuation errors. Circle the errors. Then rewrite the paragraph correctly on the lines below.

> **My best friend lives across the street and around the corner over there. His name is brayden and he pitchd for our baseball team. He has a really, nice older brother named Cole who is a sophomore in College. There coming over to our house for dinner tonight, but they're parents have other plans. Their's a chance my dad will grill hamburgers, which would be great. I already tryed to bake a peach pie for desert, but I burned the crust a bit.**

_____

_____

_____

_____

_____

_____

_____

_____

_____

_____

_____

_____

_____

31 Finding Word Meanings

RI.8.4, L.8.4.a, L.8.4.c–d, L.8.6, RH.8.4, RST.8.4

Getting the Idea

When you read, you often come across unfamiliar words. There are two main ways that you can figure out a word's meaning: through context and by looking it up in a reference book, such as a dictionary or thesaurus.

Context refers to the words, phrases, and sentences that appear before and after a particular word in a text. For example, read the following sentence.

> After he broke three <u>phalanges</u> in an accident, Andre could only type with one hand.

Suppose you don't know what *phalanges* means. The second phrase in the sentence, or the context, tells you that Andre could only type with one hand. Your logical conclusion is that Andre hurt his other hand. The first phrase tells you that he broke three phalanges. So, you can figure out that *phalanges* must refer to either fingers or hand bones, because he would be unable to use his hand only if he broke those bones. Indeed, phalanges are the bones in the fingers and toes.

Some words mean different things depending upon the way they are used. Context can help you determine how a multiple-meaning word is being used in a sentence. Look at the sentence below.

> Mrs. Dawson's health had <u>declined</u>, but her spirit was strong.

The word *declined* can mean "politely refused" or "deteriorated." If you remove the word *declined* from the sentence and replace it with each meaning in turn, only the word *deteriorated* makes sense in this sentence. By using context, you figure out that the author means that Mrs. Dawson's health had gotten worse.

Some words are only used to talk about certain subjects. Writers use the word *longitude*, for instance, when they are talking about geography. For example: *Judging by the longitude, the captain realized they had gotten way off course.* The context tells you that the captain was using longitude to figure something out. It also tells you the *longitude* made the captain think he was lost. So, *longitude* is a means of determining direction, according to the sentence.

If the context of a word doesn't tell you its meaning, you can always look it up in a dictionary or thesaurus. A **dictionary** is an alphabetical listing of words that provides their meanings, pronunciations, and origins. Read this dictionary entry.

> **spe•cious** \'spē-shəss\ *adj*. **1.** appearing to be true but actually false **2.** superficially attractive but actually of no real interest or value [14th C. From Latin *speciosus* "good looking," from *species* "appearance."]
>
> **-spe•cious•ly** *adv*. **-spe•cious•ness** *n*.

The stress mark, the long vowel *e*, and the upside-down letter tell you how to pronounce the word; *adj*. tells you that it is an adjective; the information in brackets is the word's origin, in this case Latin. The entry also lists other forms of the word.

A **thesaurus** is an alphabetical listing that gives numerous synonyms of words. Here is an entry from a thesaurus.

> **clever** *adj*. gifted, keen, cunning, smart, brilliant, inventive, astute, adept

Again, the abbreviation *adj*. in italics right after the entry tells you that the word is an adjective. Next, several words that mean the same thing as *clever* are supplied.

In some cases, you may look a word up in a glossary. A **glossary** is an alphabetized list of important words in a text, along with their definitions. Sometimes, a glossary will list the page on which a word appears.

Thinking It Through

Read the following sentence, and then answer the question that follows.

> For his paper on mollusks, Ian looked at pictures of snails, squid, and oysters.

What is a mollusk?

_____

_____

HINT   Another type of context clue is the use of examples.

Coached Example

Read the passage and answer the questions.

"Jonathan, you are a very <u>impertinent</u> young man! Do you have no respect for the classroom?"

Jonathan was awakened from his daydreams about the battle at Fort Sumter by Mrs. Kittredge, who was standing over him, with a deep, unmovable frown on her face. "Huh? Wha…?" was all he could say. It wasn't much of an answer, but it was all he could manage.

"I don't mean to <u>deprive</u> you of your rest, but we have studies to attend to here, serious subjects. Are you part of this class or not?"

"Yes, ma'am," Jonathan gulped.

By this point, the other students were chuckling at him. How could they be so cruel? Didn't they know that he had a vast knowledge of Civil War history? If the subject they were discussing was the Civil War, and not some poem by this guy Wordsworth, he would have been leading the class by now. Instead, he chose to rest his eyes. Could that be so wrong?

1. The word <u>impertinent</u> MOST LIKELY means

   A. curious.

   B. understanding.

   C. disrespectful.

   D. amusing.

   HINT Replace the unfamiliar word with each answer choice. Choose the one that makes the most sense in the sentence.

2. What is the MOST LIKELY definition of <u>deprive</u>?

   A. grant

   B. take part in

   C. allow to enjoy

   D. keep from possessing

   HINT Reread the surrounding sentences. Use the context to figure out the meaning.

Lesson Practice

Use the Reading Guide to help you understand the passage.

Reading Guide

Use context clues to figure out the meaning of the word *immense*.

What is a *guayavita*?

What does the word *obliged* mean in paragraph 3?

excerpted from
The Voyage of the *Beagle*
by Charles Darwin

October 8, 1835—I will first describe the habits of the tortoise (*Testudo nigra*, formerly called Indica), which I have referred to so often. These animals are found, I believe, on all the islands of the archipelago, certainly on most of them. They prefer to live in the high damp parts, but they also live in the lower, more <u>arid</u> districts. I have already shown, from the numbers which have been caught in a single day, how very numerous they must be. Some grow to an <u>immense</u> size: Mr. Lawson, an Englishman and vice-governor of the colony, told us that he had seen several so large that it required six or eight men to lift them from the ground; and that some had <u>afforded</u> as much as two hundred pounds of meat. The old males are the largest, the females rarely growing that large: the male can easily be distinguished from the female because his tail is longer.

The tortoises which live on those islands where there is no water, or in the lower, arid parts of the others, feed mainly on the <u>succulent</u> cactus. Those which frequent the higher, damp regions, eat the leaves of various trees, a kind of berry (called *guayavita*) which is sharp and dry in taste, and also a pale green lichen (*Usnera plicata*), that hangs from the boughs of the trees.

The tortoise likes to drink large quantities of water and wallow in the mud. Only the larger islands possess springs, and these are always near the central parts, fairly high up. The tortoises, therefore, who live in the lower areas are <u>obliged</u> to travel from a long distance away when thirsty. They leave broad and well-beaten paths, branching off in every direction from the wells down to the sea-coast; the Spaniards discovered the watering-places by following these paths.

When I landed at Chatham Island, I could not imagine what animal travelled so <u>methodically</u> along well-chosen tracks. Near the springs these huge creatures made a curious <u>spectacle</u>, one set eagerly travelling onwards with outstretched necks, and another set returning, after having drunk their fill. When the

Use a dictionary to confirm what you think *subsist* means.

Using context, figure out what *regardless* means in paragraph 4.

tortoise arrives at the spring, quite <u>regardless</u> of any spectator, he buries his head in the water above his eyes, and greedily swallows great mouthfuls, about ten in a minute. The inhabitants say each animal stays three or four days near the water, and then returns to the lower country; but their estimations of how often they visited were different. The animal probably visits more or less often depending on what food it can get. It is, however, certain, that tortoises can <u>subsist</u> even on these islands that have no other water than what falls during a few rainy days in the year.

Answer the following questions.

1. Read this sentence from the passage.

   They prefer to live in the high damp parts, but they also live in the lower, more <u>arid</u> districts.

   Based on the context, the word <u>arid</u> means

   A. stormy.

   B. chilly.

   C. moist.

   D. dry.

2. Which dictionary meaning of <u>afforded</u> does Darwin use in paragraph 1?

   A. provided

   B. could buy

   C. put up with

   D. managed to spare

3. Read this sentence from the passage.

   The tortoises which live on those islands where there is no water, or in the lower, arid parts of the others, feed mainly on the <u>succulent</u> cactus.

   The word <u>succulent</u> MOST LIKELY means

   A. dried out.

   B. chunky.

   C. moist.

   D. tough.

4. What does <u>methodically</u> mean in paragraph 4?

   A. with ordered precision

   B. full of mystery

   C. disorganized

   D. fearfully

5. What does the word <u>subsist</u> mean in paragraph 4? Explain how you know. Use examples from the passage in your response.

   _____

   _____

   _____

The following questions do not relate to a passage.

6. **Use your answer to Part A to answer Part B.**

   Read the following dictionary entry.

   > **ap·pli·ca·tion** \a-plə-'kā-shən\ n. **1.** a request or petition. **2.** a protective or medicated layer of material. **3.** an act of putting something to use. **4.** unflagging attention.

   ## Part A

   Which definition from the dictionary entry BEST describes the meaning of <u>application</u> as it is used in the following sentence from a historical biography?

   Nikola Tesla experimented with alternating current and its <u>application</u> in wireless communication.

   A. Definition 1   **C.** Definition 3

   B. Definition 2   **D.** Definition 4

   ## Part B

   Which words would BEST replace <u>application</u> as it is used in the sentence in Part A? There is more than one correct choice listed below.

   A. appeal   **E.** function

   B. balm   **F.** ointment

   C. diligence   **G.** relevance

   D. effort   **H.** implementation

7. **Use your answer to Part A to answer Part B.**

    Read this sentence from a science article.

    Stomach growling can result from the process of <u>peristalsis</u> as muscle contractions push food through the digestive system.

Part A

What is the meaning of the word <u>peristalsis</u> as it is used in the sentence?

A. stomach noises

B. contents of the digestive tract

C. contraction

D. movement of stomach muscles

Part B

Which word in the sentence BEST helps you understand the meaning of <u>peristalsis</u>?

A. growling

B. result

C. process

D. system

E. digestive

---

8. **Use your answer to Part A to answer Part B.**

    Read the following sentence.

    His job was full of <u>pedestrian</u> tasks such as making copies, getting coffee, and

    filing paperwork.

Part A

Circle words or phrases that help you determine the meaning of <u>pedestrian</u> as it is used in the sentence.

Part B

On the lines below, write the meaning of <u>pedestrian</u> as it is used in the sentence.

_____

_____

_____

32 Roots and Affixes

L.8.4.b , L.8.5.b, L.8.6

Getting the Idea

Words often have more than one part. The **root** is the main part of a word. An **affix** is a set of letters attached to the beginning or the end of a root word. A **prefix** is an affix added to the beginning of a root word that changes its meaning. A **suffix** is an affix added to the end, changing the meaning as well. Many of the roots and affixes we use to speak English come from Latin and Greek. Look at the charts below for some examples of roots and prefixes.

Root	Meaning	Example
aud	hear, listen	audition, auditory
cede	go	precede, secede
chron	time	chronicle, chronology
omni	all, every	omnipotent, omnivore
spect	look	inspect, spectacle
ject	throw	project, reject
sensus	thought, feeling	sentiment, sensitive

Prefix	Meaning	Example
dis-	not	disagree, disobey
en-	cause to be	enrage, enrich
il-, im-, in-	not	illegal, impossible, insecure
inter-	between	interlibrary, interstate
mis-	wrong	misinterpret, misdirect
pre-	before	prearrange, preregister
pro-	before, in favor of	proactive, pro-war
re-	again	redistribute, reclaim
sub-	under, below	submarine, subzero
super-	above	superhuman, superintendent
ultra-	more	ultraviolet, ultrasound
un-	not	unexpected, untrue

Duplicating any part of this book is prohibited by law.

Here are some common suffixes.

Suffix	Meaning	Example
-able, -ible	worthy or capable of	believable, sensible
-ful	having or being	tactful, beautiful
-ist	one who does something	activist, dentist
-ize	to make or act	mechanize, authorize
-less	lacking	thoughtless, ageless
-ly	attributes a quality	humorously, kindly
-ness	state of something	happiness, neatness
-ous	full of, characterized by	joyous, spacious
-ology	the study of something	zoology, biology

Use roots and affixes to figure out the meaning of words. First determine the meaning of the root. Then look at the way the root's meaning changes when an affix is added.

Thinking It Through

Read the following paragraph, and then answer the question that follows.

Erosion gradually wears away many natural landforms. Some of them have disappeared beneath the sea. Some volcanoes have become <u>submerged</u>, turning into, in essence, underwater mountains.

Explain the meaning of the word <u>submerged</u>.

_____

_____

HINT   The prefix *sub-* is attached to the root.

Coached Example

Read the passage and answer the questions.

Allison tried to calm her nerves as she waited for Mr. O'Brien to call her name. Most of the other kids had already auditioned for the school play. Allison had watched one student after another take the stage and read his or her lines perfectly. They were all so good that Allison began to reevaluate her decision to try out. What if she <u>misread</u> her lines? Suddenly, Mr. O'Brien called out Allison's name. Trying to keep her knees from shaking, Allison walked up the steps to the stage. Mr. O'Brien nodded his head, and Allison began to read the lines from the play she had worked all week to memorize. She had barely started when Mr. O'Brien raised his hand. "Allison, you're barely <u>audible</u>. Try again. And relax." Allison nodded. She took a deep breath and started over. When she finished, Mr. O'Brien smiled and told her he had the perfect part for her.

1. The word <u>misread</u> means

   A. read again.

   B. read quickly.

   C. read wrongly.

   D. read carefully.

   HINT Use your knowledge of the prefix *mis-* to figure out the meaning.

2. When Mr. O'Brien tells Allison that she is "barely <u>audible</u>," he means that he can hardly

   A. see her.

   B. believe her.

   C. trust her.

   D. hear her.

   HINT Think about the meaning of the root *aud*.

Lesson Practice

Use the Reading Guide to help you understand the passage.

Reading Guide

What is the suffix in the word *personal* in paragraph 1?

Which word in paragraph 2 describes someone who spreads propaganda?

Between 1933 and 1944, President Franklin Delano Roosevelt gave a series of radio broadcasts. These broadcasts were called the Fireside Chats. Their purpose was to educate the public about the economy, World War II, and other important issues of the time.

excerpted and adapted from

Franklin Delano Roosevelt's Fireside Chat, February 23, 1942

This generation of Americans has come to realize, with a present and <u>personal</u> realization, that there is something larger and more important than the life of any individual or of any individual group—something for which a man will sacrifice, and gladly sacrifice, not only his pleasures, not only his goods, not only his associations with those he loves, but his life itself. In time of crisis when the future is in the balance, we come to understand, with full recognition and devotion, what this nation is and what we owe to it.

The Axis propagandists have tried in various evil ways to destroy our determination and our morale. Failing in that, they are now trying to destroy our confidence in our own allies. They say that the British are finished—that the Russians and the Chinese are about to quit. Patriotic and <u>sensible</u> Americans will reject these absurdities. And instead of listening to any of this crude propaganda, they will recall some of the things that our enemies have said and are still saying about us. Ever since this nation became the arsenal of democracy—ever since <u>enactment</u> of Lend-Lease—there has been one persistent theme through all Axis propaganda.

From Berlin, Rome and Tokyo we have been described as a nation of weaklings—"playboys"—who would hire British soldiers, or Russian soldiers, or Chinese soldiers to do our fighting for us.

Let them repeat that now!

Let them tell that to General MacArthur and his men.

Let them tell that to the sailors who today are hitting hard in the far waters of the Pacific.

Let them tell that to the Marines!

How does the prefix *in-* change the meanings of the root words in paragraph 8?

Identify the prefix, root word, and suffix in the word *disarmament*.

The United Nations constitute an association of <u>independent</u> peoples of <u>equal</u> dignity and equal importance. The United Nations are dedicated to a common cause. We share equally and with equal zeal the anguish and the awful sacrifices of war. In the partnership of our common enterprise, we must share in a unified plan in which all of us must play our several parts, each of us being equally indispensable and dependent one on the other.

We of the United Nations are agreed on certain broad principles in the kind of peace we seek. The Atlantic Charter applies not only to the parts of the world that border the Atlantic but to the whole world; <u>disarmament</u> of aggressors, self-determination of nations and peoples, and the four freedoms— freedom of speech, freedom of religion, freedom from want, and freedom from fear.

The task that we Americans now face will test us to the uttermost. "These are the times that try men's souls."

Tom Paine wrote those words on a drumhead, by the light of a campfire. That was when Washington's little army of ragged, rugged men was retreating across New Jersey, having tasted (nothing) but defeat.

And General Washington ordered that these great words written by Tom Paine be read to the men of every regiment in the Continental Army, and this was the assurance given to the first American armed forces:

"The summer soldier and the sunshine patriot will, in this crisis, shrink from the service of their country; but he that stands it now, deserves the love and thanks of man and woman. Tyranny, like hell, is not easily conquered, yet we have this consolation with us, that the harder the sacrifice, the more <u>glorious</u> the triumph."

Duplicating any part of this book is prohibited by law

Answer the following questions.

1. What is the root of the word <u>sensible</u> in paragraph 2?

    A. sible

    B. sen

    C. sensi

    D. sensus

2. Based on the prefix <u>in-</u>, you know that <u>independent</u> describes something that

    A. depends on someone else.

    B. does not depend on someone else.

    C. changed before.

    D. is always changing.

3. What is the prefix in the word <u>disarmament</u>?

    A. dis

    B. ment

    C. disarm

    D. ament

4. What does the word <u>glorious</u> mean in the last paragraph?

    A. full of glory

    B. without glory

    C. act of giving glory

    D. because of glory

5. What are the root, prefix, and suffix in the word <u>enactment</u>? Explain what the word means.

    _____

    _____

    _____

    _____

Duplicating any part of this book is prohibited by law.

The following questions do not relate to a passage.

6. **Use your answer to Part A to answer Part B.**

   Read the following sentence.

   > **Years of dreaming, planning, and back-breaking effort led to the moment on May 10, 1869, when the Central Pacific and Union Pacific lines were joined to create one <u>transcontinental</u> railroad.**

   Part A

   Circle the affixes in the underlined word.

   Part B

   Which BEST describes the meaning of <u>transcontinental</u>?

   A. below a continent

   B. across a continent

   C. around a continent

   D. relating to a continent

   E. over a continent

---

7. **Use your answer to Part A to answer Part B.**

   Part A

   Read each word/affix pair below. Choose the pairs in which the word's part of speech changes when the affix is added. There is more than one correct choice listed below.

   A. irritate, -tion   D. conscious, -ness

   B. formal, in-   E. personal, inter-

   C. magnet, -ize   F. harmony, dis-

   Part B

   Choose one pair you selected in Part A. Explain what the word means before and after the affix is added.

   _____

   _____

Duplicating any part of this book is prohibited by law.

8. Read each sentence on the left. Then match the underlined word in the sentence to its closest definition on the right.

A.	There is no <u>justification</u> for the destructive choices that a bully makes.	**1.**	inadequacy
		2.	explain
B.	The worker's <u>incompetence</u> was evident when her supervisor found several errors in her report.	**3.**	reason
C.	The <u>subterranean</u> tunnels are difficult to navigate without a map.	**4.**	underground
		5.	beneath
		6.	unqualified

---

9. Read the following sentence.

    I liked the science fiction movie, but Kara thought the explanation of time travel was _____.

    Which word BEST completes the sentence?

    A. logicality

    B. logically

    C. illogical

    D. illogic

33 Denotation and Connotation

RL.8.4, L.8.5.b–c, L.8.6

Getting the Idea

Denotation is a word's dictionary definition, or what it literally means. **Connotation** is the emotional weight a word carries, or the set of associations implied by the word. Read the sentences below.

> Roxanne has always been <u>thrifty</u>. When she wants something, she holds out until it goes on sale.

Now suppose we substitute the word *cheap* in this sentence. Do you look at Roxanne a little differently now? Both words have the same denotation. They describe people who do not spend money easily. However, *thrifty* has the added meaning of someone who manages money wisely. The word *cheap* connotes stinginess. Describing Roxanne as cheap presents her in a negative light. In fact, words are said to have neutral, positive, and negative connotations. The words below all have the denotation of "large in size," but think about their associated meanings as you read these sentences.

- The **big** mansion had been turned into a museum.
- The **grand** mansion had been turned into a museum.
- The **oversized** mansion had been turned into a museum.

The word *big* is neutral. It has neither positive nor negative connotations. The word *grand* is positive. It connotes a sense of magnificence. The word *oversized* is negative. It connotes excess. Knowing words that have similar denotations but different connotations will give you a deeper understanding of each of those words. When you choose a word in your writing, be conscious of the emotional weight it carries. If you use the word *oversized*, for instance, make sure that you mean to convey something negative. Perhaps *grand* is a better choice for the context.

The chart below contains some more examples.

A word whose denotation is...	might be a word with a positive connotation, such as...	or it might be a word with a negative connotation, such as...
eager to succeed	ambitious, determined, motivated	pushy, ruthless
wanting to know	curious, inquisitive	nosy, prying, meddlesome
certain of success	self-assured, secure, confident	arrogant, cocky, smug

Authors choose their words carefully, and these words can influence your reaction to their texts and even your point of view. Think about the denotation and connotation of words when you read and write.

Thinking It Through

Read the following paragraph, and then answer the question that follows.

Beryl Markham (1902-1986) was a pioneer in the field of aviation. One of her most well-known feats was a flight, by herself, across the North Atlantic Sea; some might think, however, that this was a reckless stunt. Nevertheless, she was also an accomplished writer. She was the author of *West with the Night*, among other books.

Which words create BOTH a positive and a negative image of Markham?

_____

_____

HINT   Think about the meanings of the words and their associations.

Coached Example

Read the passage and answer the questions.

Carolyn opened her eyes and took a deep breath. Suddenly, she sat straight up in bed, her face <u>beaming</u>. There was no mistaking the <u>odor</u>. Her mother was baking her incredibly wonderful, ever-delectable, super-duperly scrumptious banana nut bread. Carolyn threw back the covers and slid her feet into her fluffy purple slippers. If she hurried, she could grab the first slice while it was still warm. She found her mom in the kitchen, reading a magazine. Carolyn ran up and wrapped her arms around her mother's shoulders. "Thank you!" Her mom smiled and took a sip of her coffee. "It's just a little treat to thank you for babysitting your brother this week."

1. Which of the following BEST describes the image created by the word <u>beaming</u>?

    A. Carolyn is satisfied.

    B. Carolyn is full of joy.

    C. Carolyn is surprised.

    D. Carolyn is very hungry.

    HINT The word *beaming* is associated with the brightness of the sun.

2. Which word should the author use in place of <u>odor</u> to create the MOST positive connotation?

    A. smell

    B. whiff

    C. stench

    D. aroma

    HINT Choose the word that best indicates that the odor of the banana bread is pleasant.

Lesson Practice

Use the Reading Guide to help you understand the passage.

Reading Guide

What is the effect of the word *abuse* in paragraph 4?

Remember that a word's denotation is its dictionary definition. Do you know the denotations of most of the words in this passage?

The Everglades—Are They Forever?

A kind of ecosystem found only in the United States, Florida's Everglades are <u>teeming</u> with life. Covering about four thousand square miles of freshwater marsh, rivers, and swamps, the Everglades stretch endlessly in tall, lush grass. Growing more than six feet tall and with razor-sharp edges, the grass camouflages much of the area's abundant wildlife.

In all, roughly 850 species of animals and over 900 kinds of plants call the Florida Everglades home. Alligators slide in a <u>leisurely</u> way through the swamps. Graceful birds soar through the air. Tiny frogs leap from lily pad to lily pad, croaking loudly in unified <u>harmony</u>.

"The Everglades is an area unique both for its location and for its diversity," says Sidney Goldstein, a scientist who's been studying the area. "From a scientific standpoint, it's one of the most amazing places I've ever been."

Sadly, that place is now in jeopardy. After years of <u>abuse</u>—like rampant pollution—the Everglades, and all its natural life, have begun, slowly, to die. The area's snake population illustrates this trend. Over recent years, both poisonous and nonpoisonous snake populations have declined drastically.

While people now <u>appreciate</u> the Everglades, early settlers thought the area was worthless. They certainly treated it that way. <u>Unaware</u> or <u>unconcerned</u> about the area's delicate balance, they immediately set out to dry some of the area's marshes. In the 1920s, engineers from the U.S. government forced much of the Everglades' water into one straight path. Then, they built dikes and canals to control flooding and direct the area's water to choice locations. Ironically, those efforts would have the opposite effect: they would deprive the Everglades of its water—in some places, entirely.

Without its natural water supply—in its natural swamps and marshes—the Everglades began to shrink. Without water to survive, the area's plant and animal populations have started to shrink as well. Certain kinds of alligators, sparrows, and wading birds—like pelicans—have already vanished. The question now is, "Can the Everglades be saved?"

Replace the word *prepared* in paragraph 7 with one that suggests Floridians will not give up.

Which words with positive connotations could replace the word *original* in paragraph 7?

According to the passage, what is the denotation of *phosphorus* in paragraph 7?

Think of a word that has the same denotation as the word *persuaded* in paragraph 8.

Most Floridians are <u>prepared</u> to fight to save their Everglades. And they've come up with all kinds of <u>original</u> solutions. Some have suggested raising roads and creating overpasses so water can flow, undisturbed, beneath them. Others have suggested removing the area's canals and cracking down on polluters. One group, the Everglades Foundation, has taken on one particularly big polluter: the sugarcane industry. The fertilizers sugarcane growers use contain <u>phosphorus</u>, a chemical that runs off into water and eventually kills native plants. The foundation is determined to get the sugar growers to cut back production so the plants in the Everglades can survive.

So far, the Everglades Foundation has succeeded. After collecting 2.5 million signatures, the foundation <u>persuaded</u> Florida voters to pass a law requiring polluters to pay for the damage they cause in the Everglades. Instead of paying, one sugar company sold back fifty thousand acres to the state so that the land could be restored to the Everglades.

Now, in that area, water runs naturally again. And the Everglades' plants and animals have reason to return. With luck, these efforts are just a start.

Duplicating any part of this book is prohibited by law.

Answer the following questions.

1. Which replacement for the word teeming in paragraph 1 carries a negative connotation?

   A. crowded

   B. abundant

   C. abounding

   D. full

2. The author uses the word leisurely in paragraph 2 to suggest that the alligators are

   A. lazy.

   B. deliberate.

   C. relaxed.

   D. sluggish.

3. What feeling do you get from the word harmony in paragraph 2?

   A. The croaking is a little annoying.

   B. The frogs croak day and night.

   C. The frogs make beautiful music.

   D. The croaking can barely be heard.

4. To create the MOST positive connotation, the author should replace the word appreciate in paragraph 5 with

   A. value.

   B. regard.

   C. respect.

   D. treasure.

5. Explain the difference between being unaware and unconcerned. Which one has the MORE negative connotation? Use examples from the passage in your response.

   _____

   _____

   _____

The following questions do not relate to a passage.

6. Read the following sentence.

   Cassie's mother <u>urged</u> her to try out for the cross-country team, the chess club, and the school play.

   The words below all have a similar denotation to <u>urged</u>. Choose the words with a negative connotation. There is more than one correct choice listed below.

   A. advised   F. forced

   B. commanded   G. influenced

   C. pressured   H. motivated

   D. coerced   I. moved

   E. desired   J. solicited

---

7. Read the following sentence.

   The cunning scoundrel devised a scheme.

   Rewrite the sentence to give it a positive connotation.

   _____

   _____

---

8. Read the sentence below.

   Khalil was surprised at how _____ the team looked after the first day of soccer practice.

   Which word would give the sentence the LEAST positive connotation?

   A. polished

   B. competent

   C. seasoned

   D. accomplished

Duplicating any part of this book is prohibited by law.

9. Use your answer to Part A to answer Part B.

    Read this sentence.

    Sofia was an <u>enthusiastic</u> member of the Kung Fu Club.

Part A

In this sentence, the denotation of the word <u>enthusiastic</u> is

A. passionate.

B. reluctant.

C. talented.

D. weary.

Part B

Which of the following words with a similar denotation to <u>enthusiastic</u> has a positive connotation?

A. anxious

B. ardent

C. fanatical

D. rabid

E. unwilling

10. Read the words in the word bank. Decide whether each word's connotation is positive or negative. Write each word from the word bank in the correct column below.

tranquil	lifeless
untroubled	mundane
lethargic	serene

Positive

_____

_____

_____

Negative

_____

_____

_____

Duplicating any part of this book is prohibited by law.

5 Cumulative Assessment

This passage contains mistakes. Read the passage and answer the questions that follow.

Life in the Mountains

(1) The Appalachian region of the United States stretches through several states, from the northeast to the central/southern region. (2) There are no exact boundaries, but the area covers approximately two hundred thousand square miles. (3) This beautiful area of land embodies a culture all its own, and it stands as a uniquely American entity. (4) The Appalachian mountains largely isolate people in some areas of the region from other parts of society. (5) They are also of great importance to the people and their way of life.

(6) Many of the people in the area trace their roots to the wave of European immigrants who settled in the mountains in the 1700s. (7) They were mostly from Scotland, Germany, and England. (8) In the centuries that followed, immigrants from other countries joined them. (9) They came to Appalachia looking for land, freedom, and opportunities. (10) They discovered a <u>lush</u> landscape rich in natural resources. (11) The area had an abundance of coal that provided jobs for many settlers. (12) Unfortunately, strip mining turned out being environmentally disastrous. (13) If they had only considered their prospects, they might not have worked for the mining companies.

(14) Many things about the region have changed. (15) But the people of Appalachia <u>retain</u> their own traditions, music, dialect, and foods. (16) For many, the Appalachian region is the <u>embodiment</u> of home, the American way of life, and an ideal for the way life should be.

Duplicating any part of this book is prohibited by law

1. Which of these sentences is conditional?

   A. "Many things about the region have changed."

   B. "If they had only considered their <u>prospects</u>, they might not have worked for the mining companies."

   C. "There are no exact boundaries, but the area covers approximately two hundred thousand square miles."

   D. "This beautiful area of land embodies a culture all its own, and it stands as a uniquely American entity."

2. Read this sentence from the passage.

   The Appalachian mountains largely isolate people in some areas of the region from other parts of society.

   Which word in this sentence needs to be capitalized?

   A. mountains

   B. people

   C. region

   D. society

3. What is the MOST LIKELY meaning of the word <u>retain</u> in sentence 15?

   A. preserve

   B. reject

   C. forget

   D. share

4. In sentence 16, the root word of <u>embodiment</u> is

   A. em

   B. ment

   C. body

   D. bod

5. The author uses the word <u>lush</u> in sentence 10 to help you visualize an area that is

   A. covered with fresh snow.

   B. surrounded by black cliffs.

   C. in the heart of the desert.

   D. filled with trees and flowers.

Duplicating any part of this book is prohibited by law.

6. On the lines below, write sentence 12 correctly.

_____

_____

_____

_____

_____

_____

Duplicating any part of this book is prohibited by law.

This passage contains mistakes. Read the passage and answer the questions that follow.

(1) Our school needs to offer more language classes. (2) Presently, students can only choose between French and Spanish. (3) While these are interesting and valuable languages, so are German, Chinese, Russian, Japanese, Hebrew, and other languages from around the world. (4) Our school has students that come from many different cultures and backgrounds. (5) Why should they not have the opportunity to learn languages other than French and Spanish? (6) Offering a wide variety of foreign language classes will encourage students to learn not only more about their own backgrounds, but also about others.

(7) Learned foreign languages is not only important to us as students now. (8) It can enhance the quality of our lives in the future. (9) Many jobs require that their employees speak more than one language. (10) Even if it's not a requirement, it is certainly an advantage. (11) Being <u>multilingual</u> may help one find a rewarding job. (12) In addition, travel is enjoyed by millions of people around the world. (13) We can get from the United States to Europe or Africa in hours. (14) If technology keeps developing the way it has there's a good chance that we'll be traveling even faster twenty years from now. (15) Think how much easier it will be to visit other countries if we speak their languages. (16) The people are likely to be more <u>receptive</u> to us when they see that we want to truly communicate with them. (17) Foreign languages <u>enrich</u> our lives if we are willing to embrace them.

7. Which is the BEST way to revise sentence 12?

    A. In addition, millions of people traveling around enjoy the world.

    B. In addition, travel is by millions of people enjoyed around the world.

    C. In addition, travel around the world is enjoyed by millions of people.

    D. In addition, millions of people around the world enjoy traveling.

8. Read this sentence from the passage.

    If technology keeps developing the way it has there's a good chance that we'll be traveling even faster twenty years from now.

    Which punctuation mark does this sentence need?

    A. an ellipsis mark after *developing*

    B. a dash after *technology*

    C. a comma after *has*

    D. a comma after *faster*

9. Which is the correct way to write sentence 7?

    A. Learn foreign languages is not only important to us as students now.

    B. Learning foreign languages is not only important to us as students now.

    C. To learn foreign languages is not only important to us as students now.

    D. Learns foreign languages is not only important to us as students now.

10. Read this sentence from the passage.

    Being <u>multilingual</u> may help one find a rewarding job.

    As used in the sentence, what does the word <u>multilingual</u> mean?

    A. speaking many languages

    B. speaking two languages

    C. speaking only one language

    D. bad at learning languages

Duplicating any part of this book is prohibited by law.

11. Read this sentence from the passage.

    Foreign languages <u>enrich</u> our lives if we are willing to embrace them.

    In this sentence, the word <u>enrich</u> suggests that foreign languages

    A. can make us rich in the future.

    B. add meaning to our lives.

    C. make our lives easier.

    D. make us smarter.

12. What is the meaning of the word <u>receptive</u> in sentence 16? How does context help you figure it out?

    _____

    _____

    _____

    _____

    _____

    _____

Duplicating any part of this book is prohibited by law.

English Language Arts, Grade 8

SUMMATIVE ASSESSMENT

Name: _____

Read the passage and answer the questions that follow.

The Song of Wandering Aengus

by *William Butler Yeats*

I went out to the hazel wood,
Because a fire was in my head,
And cut and peeled a hazel wand,
And hooked a berry to a thread;
5   And when white moths were on the <u>wing</u>,
And moth-like stars were flickering out,
I dropped the berry in a stream
And caught a little silver trout.

When I had laid it on the floor
10   I went to blow the fire a-flame,
But something rustled on the floor,
And someone called me by my name:
It had become a glimmering girl
With apple blossom in her hair
15   Who called me by my name and ran
And faded through the brightening air.

Though I am old with wandering
Through hollow lands and hilly lands,
I will find out where she has gone,
20   And kiss her lips and take her hands;
And walk among long dappled grass,
And pluck till time and times are done,
The silver apples of the moon,
The golden apples of the sun.

1. Which lines have a similar meter?

   A. 6 and 7

   B. 7 and 8

   C. 10 and 11

   D. 22 and 23

2. Read the following statement.

   The old man feels at home in the wilderness.

   Which lines from the poem best support this statement?

   A. "It had become a glimmering girl With apple blossom in her hair"

   B. "And cut and peeled a hazel wand, And hooked a berry to a thread"

   C. "But something rustled on the floor, And someone called me by my name"

   D. "Though I am old with wandering Through hollow lands and hilly lands"

3. What is the theme of the poem?

   A. doing something correctly

   B. surviving on one's own

   C. finding something of value

   D. wandering through nature

4. What happens to the girl in the poem?

   A. She disappears.

   B. She falls into the stream.

   C. She dies.

   D. She rises into the sky.

Duplicating any part of this book is prohibited by law.

5. Which dictionary definition of <u>wing</u> is used in the poem?

    A. an appendage used by a bird in flight

    B. a part of a building

    C. old-fashioned term for "act of flight"

    D. a section of an auditorium

6. Which phrase BEST describes the old man?

    A. friendly and good-hearted

    B. lost in thought

    C. tired and anxious

    D. sad and lonely

7. What are the different settings in the poem, and what is their effect on the work? Use examples from the poem in your response.

_____

_____

_____

_____

Duplicating any part of this book is prohibited by law.

Read the passage and answer the questions that follow.

excerpted and adapted from

Narrative of the Life of Frederick Douglass, an American Slave
by Frederick Douglass

The plan which I adopted, and the one by which I was most successful, was that of making friends of all the little white boys whom I met in the street. As many of these as I could, I converted into teachers. With their kindly aid, I obtained at different times and in different places, I finally succeeded in learning to read. When I was sent on errands, I always took my book with me, and by doing one part of my errand quickly, I found time to get a lesson before my return. I used also to carry bread with me, enough of which was always in the house, and to which I was always welcome; for I was much better off in this regard than many of the poor white children in our neighborhood. This bread I used to bestow upon the hungry little urchins, who, in return, would give me that more valuable bread of knowledge. I am strongly tempted to give the names of two or three of those little boys, as a testimonial of the gratitude and affection I bear them; but prudence forbids;— not that it would injure me, but it might embarrass them; for it is almost an unpardonable offence to teach slaves to read in this Christian country. It is enough to say of the dear little fellows, that they lived on Philpot Street, very near Durgin and Bailey's ship-yard. I used to talk this matter of slavery over with them. I would sometimes say to them, I wished I could be as free as they would be when they got to be men. "You will be free as soon as you are twenty-one, *but I am a slave for life!* Have not I as good a right to be free as you have?" These words used to trouble them; they would express for me the liveliest sympathy, and console me with the hope that something would occur by which I might be free.

I was now about twelve years old, and the thought of being *a slave for life* began to bear heavily upon my heart. Just about this time, I got hold of a book entitled "The Columbian Orator." Every opportunity I got, I used to read this book. Among much of other interesting matter, I found in it a dialogue between a master and his slave. The slave was represented as having run away from his master three times. The dialogue represented the conversation which took place between them, when the slave was retaken the third time. In this dialogue, the whole argument in behalf of slavery was brought forward by the master, all of which was disposed of by the slave. The slave was made to say some very smart as well as impressive things in reply to his master—things which had the desired though unexpected effect; for the conversation resulted in the voluntary emancipation of the slave on the part of the master.

In the same book, I met with one of Sheridan's mighty speeches on and in behalf of Catholic emancipation. These were choice documents to me. I read them over and over again with unabated interest. They gave tongue to interesting thoughts of my own soul, which had frequently flashed through my mind, and died away for want of utterance. The moral which I gained from the dialogue was the power of truth over the conscience of even a slaveholder. What I got from Sheridan was a bold <u>denunciation</u> of slavery, and a powerful vindication of human rights.

The reading of these documents enabled me to utter my thoughts, and to meet the arguments brought forward to sustain slavery; but while they relieved me of one difficulty, they brought on another even more painful than the one of which I was relieved. The more I read, the more I was led to abhor and detest my enslavers. I could regard them in no other light than a band of successful robbers, who had left their homes, and gone to Africa, and stolen us from our homes, and in a strange land reduced us to slavery. I loathed them as being the meanest as well as the most wicked of men. As I read and contemplated the subject, behold! that very <u>discontentment</u> which Master Hugh had predicted would follow my learning to read had already come, to torment and sting my soul to unutterable anguish. As I writhed under it, I would at times feel that learning to read had been a curse rather than a blessing. It had given me a view of my wretched condition, without the remedy. It opened my eyes to the horrible pit, but to no ladder upon which to get out. In moments of agony, I envied my fellow-slaves for their stupidity. I have often wished myself a beast. I preferred the condition of the meanest reptile to my own. Anything, no matter what, to get rid of thinking!

It was this everlasting thinking of my condition that tormented me. There was no getting rid of it. It was pressed upon me by every object within sight or hearing, animate or inanimate. The silver trump of freedom had roused my soul to eternal wakefulness. Freedom now appeared, to disappear no more forever. It was heard in every sound, and seen in every thing. It was ever present to torment me with a sense of my wretched condition. I saw nothing without seeing it, I heard nothing without hearing it, and felt nothing without feeling it. It looked from every star, it smiled in every calm, breathed in every wind, and moved in every storm.

8. The author uses the word <u>denunciation</u> to suggest that Sheridan

    A. is unclear about his opinion on slavery.

    B. has no opinion on slavery but believes nevertheless in human rights.

    C. is opposed to slavery but not passionate about it.

    D. feels very strongly that slavery is wrong.

9. Which statement from the passage is a fact?

    A. "In moments of agony, I envied my fellow-slaves for their stupidity."

    B. "It was this everlasting thinking of my condition that tormented me."

    C. "Every opportunity I got, I used to read this book."

    D. "'Have not I as good a right to be free as you have?'"

10. What happened before Douglass got the book "The Columbian Orator"?

    A. He read Sheridan's speeches.

    B. He became friends with the children in his neighborhood.

    C. He no longer wanted to read.

    D. He gave reading lessons to other slaves.

11. Which phrase in the passage BEST supports Douglass's argument against slave holders?

    A. "stolen us from our homes"

    B. "disposed of by the slave"

    C. "I saw nothing without seeing it"

    D. "the reading of these documents enabled me to utter my thoughts"

12. Based on the prefix <u>dis-</u> and the suffix <u>–ment</u>, you know that the word <u>discontentment</u> means

   A. creating satisfaction.

   B. expressing satisfaction.

   C. having satisfaction.

   D. lacking satisfaction.

13. Which of the following is the BEST summary of this passage?

   A. A young slave learns how to read, and from reading books about slavery comes to hate it even more than he did before.

   B. A slave grows up hating the fact that he will never be free.

   C. A slave learns to read, begins to read books about slavery, and encounters ideas that make him think he is better than other slaves.

   D. A young slave befriends local boys who teach him to read.

14. Contrast Douglass's feelings about reading before and after he reads "The Columbian Orator." Use examples from the passage in your response.

_____

_____

_____

_____

Read the passage and answer the questions that follow.

"A Merry Christmas"
by Louisa May Alcott
adapted from Little Women

Jo was the first to wake in the gray dawn of Christmas morning. She remembered her mother's promise and, slipping her hand under her pillow, drew out a little crimson-covered book. She woke Meg with a Merry Christmas, and bade her see what was under her pillow. A green-covered book appeared, with the same picture inside, and a few words written by their mother, which made their one present very precious in their eyes. Presently Beth and Amy woke to rummage and find their little books also, one dove-colored, the other blue, and all sat looking at and talking about them, while the east grew rosy with the coming day.

"Where is Mother?" asked Meg, as she and Jo ran down to thank her for their gifts, half an hour later.

"Goodness only knows. Some poor creature came a-beggin', and your ma went straight off to see what was needed," replied Hannah, who had lived with the family since Meg was born, and was considered by them all more as a friend than a servant. "She will be back soon, I think, so fry your cakes, and have everything ready."

A bang of the street door sent the girls to the table, eager for breakfast.

"Merry Christmas, Marmee! Many of them! Thank you for our books. We read some, and mean to every day," they all cried in chorus.

"Merry Christmas, little daughters! I'm glad you began at once, and hope you will keep on. But I want to say one word before we sit down. Not far away from here lies a poor woman with a little newborn baby. Six children are huddled into one bed to keep from freezing, for they have no fire. There is nothing to eat over there, and the oldest boy came to tell me they were suffering hunger and cold. My girls, will you give them your breakfast as a Christmas present?"

They were all unusually hungry, having waited nearly an hour, and for a minute no one spoke. Only a minute, for Jo exclaimed impetuously, "I'm so glad you came before we began!"

"May I go and help carry the things to the poor little children?" asked Beth eagerly.

"I shall take the cream and the muffins," added Amy, heroically giving up the article she most liked.

Meg was already covering the buckwheats, and piling the bread into one big plate.

"I thought you'd do it," said Mrs. March, smiling as if satisfied. "You shall all go and help me, and when we come back we will have bread and milk for breakfast, and make it up at dinnertime."

They were soon ready, and the procession set out. <u>Fortunately</u> it was early, and they went through back streets, so few people saw them, and no one laughed at the queer party.

A poor, bare, miserable room it was, with broken windows, no fire, ragged bedclothes, a sick mother, wailing baby, and a group of pale, hungry children cuddled under one old quilt, trying to keep warm.

How the big eyes stared and the blue lips smiled as the girls went in.

"Ach, mein Gott! It is good angels come to us!" said the poor woman, crying for joy.

"Funny angels in hoods and mittens," said Jo, and set them to laughing.

In a few minutes it really did seem as if kind spirits had been at work there. Hannah, who had carried wood, made a fire, and stopped up the broken panes with old hats and her own cloak. Mrs. March gave the mother tea and gruel, and comforted her with promises of help, while she dressed the little baby as tenderly as if it had been her own. The girls meantime spread the table, set the children round the fire, and fed them like so many hungry birds, laughing, talking, and trying to understand the funny broken English.

"Das ist gut!"

"Die Engel-kinder!" cried the poor things as they ate and warmed their purple hands at the comfortable blaze. The girls had never been called angel children before, and thought it very agreeable, especially Jo. That was a very happy breakfast, though they didn't get any of it.

And when they went away, leaving comfort behind, I think there were not in all the city four merrier people than the hungry little girls who gave away their breakfasts and contented themselves with bread and milk on Christmas morning.

"That's loving our neighbor better than ourselves, and I like it," said Meg, as they set out their presents while their mother was upstairs collecting clothes for the poor Hummels.

15. Which event in the passage is part of the rising action?

    A. The girls are asked to give their breakfast to a poor family.

    B. When the girls wake up, they find books under their pillows.

    C. The girls go through back streets on their way to visit the Hummels.

    D. When the girls go downstairs, they learn that their mother is not home.

16. None of the girls speaks immediately after their mother describes the poorer family because

    A. they are shocked and surprised.

    B. they did not entirely understand what their mother said.

    C. they are hungry, and they are not sure they want to go.

    D. they are upset with their mother.

17. What is the theme of this passage?

    A. Helping others is rewarding.

    B. You should be kind to others always.

    C. You should never be ashamed to ask for help.

    D. Obeying one's parents is very important.

18. What is the root of the word fortunately?

    A. tune

    B. fort

    C. fortunate

    D. fortune

19. Which part of this passage's structure makes it a story?

    A. It contains dialogue, clearly designated within the passage.

    B. It contains several well-defined characters.

    C. It is divided into several paragraphs, all part of a longer work.

    D. It is broken up into lines and stanzas.

20. What pattern from literature is followed in this passage?

    A. coming of age

    B. rags to riches

    C. growth and learning

    D. forbidden love

21. Read this sentence from the passage.

That was a very happy breakfast, though they didn't get any of it.

Explain the irony in this sentence. Use examples from the passage in your response.

_____

_____

_____

_____

The Farmer and His Hired Help

Once upon a time there lived two young brothers who had barely enough to eat. The older brother, Aamir, decided to go away and look for work elsewhere, while the younger brother, Ghaazi, stayed at home to look after the family affairs.

The next morning, Aamir came across a prosperous farm. In front was a large sign, asking for hired help. Delighted at his good fortune, Aamir knocked on the farmer's door. The farmer, noting that Aamir looked strong and fit, offered him the job.

"But first," the farmer added, "you must agree to the following conditions. You must work for me until springtime. If you do not do your duty or if you lose your temper at any time, you will have to pay me fifty pieces of gold. If I lose my temper at any time, I will pay you a one hundred pieces of gold. If you cannot pay the penalty, you will have to work for me for seven years without pay."

Although he did not like the terms at all, Aamir was truly desperate, so he agreed. He reasoned he could keep his temper until springtime. So, he signed the farmer's contract and moved into his room.

The next day, the farmer woke him up at dawn and took him to a wide meadow. "You must mow this meadow as long as there is light."

Aamir immediately got to work. He mowed the field until it was nighttime. When he arrived back at the house, he was ready to drop from exhaustion. The farmer stared coolly at Aamir and asked, "What are you doing back here?"

"I'm going to sleep. The sun set hours ago."

"Yes, it did, but look out the window. What do you see? A bright, shining moon that provides plenty of light. That was our agreement—you must work as long as there is light."

Aamir frowned. Did the farmer really expect him to work all day and all night?

"You are frowning. You are not angry, are you?" asked the farmer slyly.

"No," Aamir answered, <u>recovering</u> quickly. "But please allow me to rest for a few hours."

"Are you refusing to do your duty?" the farmer asked.

Aamir realized he would have to go back to the field or violate his contract. He mowed the grass until the sun rose in the sky. Then, his feet crying out in pain, he dropped to the ground and promptly fell asleep. A few minutes later, the farmer came upon the sleeping farmhand.

"Get up," he commanded. "Don't you see the light of day? You must continue mowing."

Aamir forced himself to his feet, no longer able to contain his anger. "You are a tyrant!" he yelled. "I wouldn't treat a dog this way!"

The farmer grinned. "You have lost your temper. I will take my fifty gold coins now."

Aamir, penniless and hopeless, began to weep at the thought of working for this evil man for seven years without pay. He convinced the farmer to let him pay the penalty in installments, while still receiving payment for his work. He signed the new contract and returned home, where he told Ghaazi of his awful experience.

"And now I must find a way to pay that villain fifty gold coins!" Aamir cried.

"Maybe not," Ghaazi said thoughtfully. An idea was developing in his head.

The next day Ghaazi went to the farm and asked the farmer for work. The farmer hired him under the same conditions as Aamir, to which Ghaazi readily agreed. But the following morning, Ghaazi slept late into the morning, forcing the farmer to come and knock on his door. "The meadow will not mow itself! Get up!" he exclaimed impatiently.

"You're not angry, are you?" Ghaazi asked.

The farmer lowered his voice. "Of course not," he said. "I just need you to start your work."

"Of course," Ghaazi said amiably and <u>proceeded</u> to get dressed. But he did it so slowly that the farmer began to feel his blood rise. "Come on out! It is almost noon!"

"Are you sure you're not angry?" Ghaazi asked.

The farmer took a deep breath. "Not at all," he said. Then he led Ghaazi to the meadow. When they arrived, the other farmhands were having their lunch, and Ghaazi pointed out that he and the farmer should eat lunch, too. The farmer reluctantly agreed. Ghaazi ate his lunch as slowly as possible. Finally, the farmer said, "You are taking all day! Stop eating!"

"Those sound like angry words," Ghaazi remarked.

"I am merely asking you to do your duty," the farmer responded in a strained voice.

At that moment, two good friends of the farmer stopped by unexpectedly. They all proceeded to the farmhouse, where the farmer ordered Ghaazi to kill a goat for dinner.

"Which one?" asked Ghaazi, aware that the farmer had many goats.

"Kill any goat you find along the path," the farmer said, doing his best to hide his frustration.

"I shall do my duty gladly," Ghaazi said and hurried outside.

A short while later, the farmer's neighbors came running into his house. "Come quickly! Your helper has killed every one of your goats. He has wiped out your entire flock!"

The farmer screamed and rushed outside. "What did you do, you imbecile?"

"My duty," Ghaazi said innocently. "You said to kill any goat along the path, and they were all on the path."

"No, no, no! Bad luck to you forever! Go away and never come back!"

"As you wish," Ghaazi replied. "But you have clearly lost your temper and owe me one hundred gold coins."

The farmer, eager to be rid of his destructive farmhand, hastily paid the penalty. Ghaazi paid off his brother's debt and returned home—fifty gold coins richer.

22. How does the structure of this passage support its third-person point of view?

   A. Reading dialogue in quotation marks is easier than reading a play.

   B. The story only gives you as much information as you need.

   C. It supplies only the dialogue spoken by characters.

   D. It allows you to find out characters' thoughts and emotions.

23. What is the conflict in the passage?

   A. Aamir and Ghaazi want more to eat.

   B. The farmer wants to cheat Aamir, but Aamir resists.

   C. The farmer and Aamir are seeing who can work faster.

   D. Aamir and Ghaazi both want to work for the farmer.

24. Read the following statement.

   The farmer's own strictness works against him.

   Which of the following BEST supports this statement?

   A. He earns fifty coins from Aamir by tricking him.

   B. He makes Aamir work night and day without payment.

   C. Ghaazi gets money from him without working.

   D. He laughs at Aamir's foolishness as he cheats him.

25. Read this sentence from the passage.

   "Of course," Ghaazi said amiably and <u>proceeded</u> to get dressed.

   As used in the sentence, what does the word <u>proceeded</u> mean?

   A. started and continued an action

   B. learned a new action

   C. repeated an action

   D. ended an action

26. How does the farmer's character affect the plot of the passage?

   A. The farmer's generosity prompts him to offer Aamir one hundred pieces of gold.

   B. The farmer's affection for Ghaazi allows Ghaazi to take advantage of him.

   C. The farmer's concern for his workers makes him treat Aamir well.

   D. The farmer's greed determines how he treats Aamir and how Ghaazi treats him.

27. The author uses the word <u>recovering</u> in paragraph 11 to suggest that Aamir

    A. has been hurt while working for the farmer.

    B. has realized he made a mistake by looking angry.

    C. is easily angered by the farmer.

    D. is getting ready to quit working for the farmer.

28. Which of the following familiar characters from literature does this passage contain?

    A. the young woman in distress

    B. the dangerous outlaw

    C. the cruel master

    D. the wise village elder

29. How are the themes of "A Merry Christmas" and "The Farmer and His Hired Help" similar? Use examples from the passages in your response.

_____

_____

_____

_____

Read the passage and answer the questions that follow.

Peter Cooper

Who He Was

For many reasons, inventor Peter Cooper was a giant among men. He was one of the few who believed wealth and education didn't belong just to the rich. Through hard work, generosity, and determination, he fulfilled the American dream, helping countless others to fulfill it as well.

The Start: 1791

Born in 1791 in New York City, Cooper was, by many accounts, a reckless child. Early on, he was scarred by many accidents. With virtually no opportunities for a formal education, he began working at his family's hat-making business when he was slightly more than a child. But while he worked tirelessly at several different jobs throughout his life—as a brewer, a cabinet maker, even a grocery-store owner—his lack of an education always plagued him.

Fortunately, Cooper was naturally intelligent and curious. In fact, he was a born inventor. Eventually, he took a job working for a carriage maker. It was there that Cooper devised his first creation: a machine for fastening the hubs of carriage wheels. Other inventions were soon to follow. Cooper's inventing career had begun.

It wasn't a career without challenge, however. While Cooper may have been good at inventing things, he was less adept at making them successful. So Cooper continued exploring business options, eventually buying and running a glue factory. This venture would earn him many millions and— in an unusual twist—bring the family its most famous invention. One day, while working in the factory, Cooper's wife accidentally created a now-famous by-product of glue: flavored gelatin. Today, it's a product known as Jell-O. Cooper obtained the very first American patent for it in 1845.

The Inventions

Cooper's wife may well deserve the credit for creating Jell-O, but Cooper had many inventions of his own. He invented a ferry powered by energy built up in the tides; he also patented a musical cradle and a process for making salt. Most notably, in 1825, he built the first steam train to run on an American railroad, the *Tom Thumb*. In 1827, the Baltimore & Ohio Railroad became the first railroad to transport passengers and freight. Like Robert Fulton before him with the first successful steam ship, Cooper had to put up with a lot of suspicion. Many doubted that a steam train could work along the railroad's steep, winding grades, but the *Tom Thumb* quickly put an end to their doubts. It was one of Cooper's greatest accomplishments to date.

Cooper's technology advancements did not stop there. In 1847, he organized the Trenton Iron Company, which produced the iron beams used to build the dome of the U.S. Capitol. Years later, he helped pay for a trans-Atlantic telegraph cable. He went on to head the North American Telegraph Company, which controlled over half of the telegraph lines in the United States.

Social Causes

Cooper was not just an inventor interested in making money. He had a strong sense of morality and justice. And he was not afraid to take an unpopular stance. He was active in the antislavery movement, even before the start of the Civil War. He also joined the Indian reform movement, which sought to protect and improve the conditions of Native Americans. Between the years 1870 and 1875, Cooper sponsored delegations to major cities, enhancing public awareness of the struggle for Indian rights. He also led the fight to establish a public school system. Cooper had strong opinions about how the government was run and did not hesitate to criticize policies and practices that he viewed as hurtful to the general public.

The School

Through all of his achievements, Cooper remained acutely aware of his lack of education. He had become one of America's richest, most successful men, and yet he still had not learned to spell. Always remembering his humble though hard-working roots, Cooper spent the last 30 years of his life creating and nurturing a school for the "boys and girls of [New York City], who had no better opportunity than [he]."

In 1859, The Cooper Union for the Advancement of Science and Art was born in New York City. Cooper said: "My hope is that the love and desire for scientific knowledge will cause unborn thousands to throng the hall of Cooper Union.… I trust the young will here catch the inspiration of truth in all its native power and beauty.…" As one of the first colleges to offer a free education to working-class children and to women, Cooper Union was a pioneer in education. Cooper's example inspired other education leaders, such as Andrew Carnegie, Ezra Cornell, and Matthew Vassar.

At first, Cooper Union held night classes for men and women in applied sciences and architecture. The college's Female School of Design, open during the day, offered women free art classes as well as training in the then new occupations of photography, telegraphy, "typewriting," and shorthand.

Cooper had founded far more than a ground-breaking school, however. He had established a place that fulfilled his greatest dream: to give some of his wealth back to society, to give talented young people the one privilege he had lacked—an education. In short, he had simply wanted to provide an education "equal to the best."

Since 1859, Cooper Union has educated thousands of artists, architects, and engineers, many of them leaders in one <u>field</u> or another. As one former student notes, "We owe a great debt to Peter Cooper." When Cooper founded his school, many of the other business leaders of the day scoffed. But Cooper had again done more than simply prove his naysayers wrong. He had left a lasting, valuable legacy. In 2006, a big part of that legacy was recognized when he was <u>inducted</u> into the National Inventors Hall of Fame.

1791	1825	1847	1859	1870-1875	1883
Born in New York City	Built the *Tom Thumb*	Organized the Trenton Iron company	Founded the Cooper Union	Tried to increase awareness of Indian rights	Died in New York City

30. According to the timeline, which of the following is true?

A. Cooper attended college between 1870 and 1875.

B. Cooper founded the Cooper Union in 1859.

C. Cooper started the Baltimore and Ohio Railroad in 1827.

D. Cooper was born in 1807.

31. What is the main idea of paragraph 7?

A. Morality and justice were extremely important to Cooper.

B. Cooper was against slavery.

C. Morality and justice were less important to Cooper than making money.

D. Cooper cared about Native Americans.

32. Read this sentence from the passage.

> **In 2006, a big part of that legacy was recognized when he was <u>inducted</u> into the National Inventors Hall of Fame.**

As used in the sentence, what does the word <u>inducted</u> mean?

A. urged to do something about

B. came to a conclusion about

C. made a member of

D. taken away from

33. Cooper sponsored delegations to enhance public awareness of the struggle for Indian rights

A. after Cooper Union was established.

B. before the invention of Jell-O.

C. before he organized the Trenton Iron Company.

D. before he became an accomplished inventor.

34. Which of the following resources would be MOST helpful to find further information about Cooper?

A. a CD with recordings of commercials for Jell-O

B. books about the period in which Cooper lived

C. a DVD about modern life on Native American reservations

D. a Web site on Cooper's inventions and achievements

35. Read this dictionary entry.

> **field** *n.* 1. an open area of grass 2. a profession or career 3. A playing area for football, baseball, soccer, or similar sport *v.* 4. to handle or answer

Which definition of <u>field</u> is used in this passage?

A. 1

B. 2

C. 3

D. 4

36. What role did cause and effect play in Cooper's life?

_____

_____

_____

_____

Products of the Imagination

We are lucky that over the centuries people have had the imagination to dream up some marvelous inventions. Two of these inventions are found throughout the world. One can be smaller than an inch and has a practical use. The other can be hundreds of feet long and its primary purpose is to generate great fun—or terror, depending on how you look at it. What are these inventions? The paper clip and the roller coaster.

Have you ever wondered who invented the paper clip? It's something found in most offices and homes. Most of us use paper clips again and again without thinking of where they came from—or what life would be like without them. Sure, you could staple your papers together, but perhaps you're disinclined to put holes in them. For that reason, the paper clip is a beautifully simple idea.

Hundreds of years ago brass clips were used to bind important documents, but these expensive clips were quite rare and likely did not resemble today's paper clips. Long before there were paper clips as we know them, people cut a small slit in the papers and then tied them together, sealing the tie with wax. Fastening papers with ties and wax instead of a paper clip is like using ten buttons to close a coat because you don't have a zipper. Straight pins were also used to pin papers together, but because they were handmade, they were quite expensive and in meager supply. Therefore, not many people used them. The pins also made holes in the paper, and these holes were made larger with each pinning and unpinning, wearing out the paper much as staples might. Clearly, a more efficient fastener was needed.

Norwegian Johan Vaaler is often credited as the inventor of the paper clip. He patented his device in Germany in 1899. He did not make use of his patent, however, perhaps because a more functional version of his clip was already in use. Vaaler may or may not have invented the clip, but he is honored for doing so in Norway. A giant paper clip was erected near Oslo to honor Vaaler.

Vaaler's clip received an American patent in 1901, but it is not the double-loop clip common today. Samuel B. Fay patented the first bent-wire clip in 1867 as a clip to hold tickets to fabric. Matthew Schooley, of Pennsylvania, patented a paper holder in 1896, and in 1900, a U.S. patent was issued for a paper clip called the Konaclip. Cornelius Brosnan of Springfield, Massachusetts, was the Konaclip patent holder. Brosnan's may have been the first successful clip.

From this period, many patented and unpatented clips began to appear on the market. As early as 1890, the British Gem Manufacturing Company was producing the double loop clip most common today. The Gem paper clip first appeared on a U.S. patent issued to William Middlebrook of Waterbury, Connecticut, in 1899 for a machine to produce paper clips. The Gem clip was marketed by Cushman & Denison Manufacturing of New York. This company trademarked the name "Gem" for use with paper clips in 1904. By 1908, the Gem clip was in wide use in the United States and abroad. Gem clip was the common name for paper clips in the early 1900s. In Swedish, the word for any type of paper clip is *gem*.

SUMMATIVE ASSESSMENT

Now what about the roller coaster? How did this popular ride come to be? The history of this amusement park staple began in seventeenth-century Russia, with the popular ice slides of the period. How the idea made the jump to the use of wheeled cars is a matter open to debate. The first wheeled cars were likely put into use in France in 1817. These were successful, and, in 1846, a looping coaster was tried in France. The loop had a diameter of thirteen feet and was part of a coaster with a forty-three-foot hill. The loop for this coaster was imported to France from England, where a loop with a 6.5-foot diameter had already been tried.

La Marcus Thompson popularized the first amusement roller coaster in the United States. Thompson was an inventor and businessman who probably used the ideas of Richard Knutson to create a track fifty feet high and six hundred feet long. He premiered his spectacular coaster in Coney Island, Brooklyn, in 1884. One rider predicted that the ride would be a great success, and he nailed it. The coaster was immensely popular. Later that year, Charles Alcoke created a coaster that ran on a circuit. In 1885, Phillip Hinkle came up with the idea of the "lift hill," the initial hill on a coaster that used cables to pull the cars up. This allowed for a greater initial ascent and descent.

Roller coasters became central to amusement parks, which were very popular by the 1920s. This period is known as the golden age of the roller coaster. In July 1955, Walt Disney opened Disneyland in California. The first tubular steel-tracked roller coaster was the Matterhorn Bobsled Ride, built for Disneyland in 1959.

So, next time you use a paper clip or ride a roller coaster, remember that like many inventions, they were the product of human imagination.

37. Which of the following phrases is not appropriate for the purpose or audience?

  A. "he nailed it"

  B. "a matter open to debate"

  C. "in meager supply"

  D. "a beautifully simple idea"

38. Which of the following MOST LIKELY motivated people to invent the paper clip?

  A. Brass clips did not resemble today's paper clips.

  B. People used to pin papers together, but the pins wore out the paper.

  C. Gem clip was not a popular name for paper clips.

  D. People used to tie papers together and seal the tie with wax.

39. Where did Johan Vaaler live?

  A. the United States

  B. France

  C. Norway

  D. California

40. Which source would give you the MOST information about Disneyland?

  A. a guide to the state of California

  B. a book about Walt Disney's movies

  C. a book about popular amusement park rides

  D. a book about Walt Disney's life

41. Which of the following is the BEST summary of paragraph 1?

A. The paper clip and the roller coaster are very different inventions.

B. Two very different inventions, the paper clip and the roller coaster, were products of inventors' imaginations.

C. The paper clip is more useful than the roller coaster, and it took more imagination to invent.

D. The inventors of the paper clip and the roller coaster had very complex, capable imaginations.

42. Which of the following MOST accurately describes how the authors' purposes in "Peter Cooper" and "Products of the Imagination" are similar?

A. Both passages were written to inform.

B. Both passages were written to persuade.

C. "Peter Cooper" was written to inform; "Products of the Imagination" was written to persuade.

D. "Peter Cooper" was written to persuade; "Products of the Imagination" was written to inform.

43. In "Peter Cooper" and "Products of the Imagination" both authors are writing about inventors and inventions. How are the authors' approaches different? Use examples from the passages in your response.

_____

_____

_____

_____

Read the passage and answer the questions that follow.

To the School Board:

I have been a music teacher at Pleasantville Middle School for twenty-two years, and it has been a wonderful and rewarding experience. I had looked forward to teaching there for another twenty years. Unfortunately, a recent turn of events has made this unlikely. You have voted to cut the budget for all music and arts programs by nearly 50 percent. This will result in fewer music and arts classes for students and fewer teaching opportunities for teachers.

Whenever the need arises to trim the budget, music and art programs are the first to be sacrificed. How could anyone think to spend even *less* on music and arts? It is time that people recognized an undeniable truth: these programs are just as important as other academic disciplines.

When I first began my teaching career, I had a student named Christopher. He was a good kid but came from a large family that had trouble making ends meet. His father worked two jobs, and his mother had her hands full taking care of the children and the home. Christopher struggled in school and had no one at home to help him improve his academic performance. He was a straight-C student by seventh grade. Then one day, he showed up at my office door. He wanted to learn how to play the clarinet.

By the end of the school year, Christopher had learned how to read music and played the clarinet well enough to join the school band. He had an aptitude for music that was simply amazing. He also made a few of his own compositions. This student, who couldn't wrap his brain around math or science, was rapidly becoming a virtual Mozart. And a terrific thing happened—Christopher's grades started to improve. He had a more positive attitude and greater confidence.

Mastering the clarinet had proved to him that he could learn new things and that he could practice and practice until he got it right. He never became an honor roll student, but he became a *better* student; and sometimes that is all we can ask.

Not everyone is an academic achiever. However, I believe that everyone is born with a gift. And this talent may have nothing to do with history, mathematics, science, or writing. For some, it's drawing, for others it's acting; some excel in music, and others shine in sports. This is not to say that the traditional subjects in academics are not important. However, music and arts programs give students of all academic abilities the chance to learn a skill that may be more suited to their natural talents.

Studies have indicated that there is a correlation between studying music and improved academic performance. Like Christopher, many students who take music classes see improvement in other subjects. This has played a role in lowering drop-out rates and reducing <u>disruptive</u> behavior. Students do better in class and are happier in school when they can participate in music and arts programs they truly enjoy. If a student has real difficulty with academic subjects and is constantly frustrated by his or her failure to achieve, the idea of cutting class is more likely to appeal to that student. But improved grades and the joy of going in to play an instrument or sing in the chorus makes school a place more students *want* to be, not a place they feel they *have* to be.

Some people point out that good grades are crucial to getting a good job in the future. Indeed, many employers will look at a <u>potential</u> employee's academic record. However, many jobs require specific skills and training that employees can only acquire while on the job. They learn through experience. Not every employer is looking for that academic superachiever.

Skills like creativity, discipline, and working cooperatively with others are also strongly desired. These skills are very much a component of music training.

Next Saturday, I am going to the Pleasantville Concert Hall, where one of the most respected orchestras in the country will be performing. I would not miss it for the world. I strongly encourage all of the members of the school board to attend. On stage will be one of my former students, Christopher. His talent on the clarinet took him to heights that he might never have reached without the music program at our middle school. Perhaps after you leave the concert hall, you will choose to increase the budget for music and arts, not reduce it.

Sincerely,

Ariana Fernandez

44. Which of the following statements from the passage is an opinion?

   A. "You have voted to cut the budget for all music and arts programs by nearly 50 percent."

   B. "It is time that people recognized an undeniable truth: these programs are just as important as other academic disciplines."

   C. "He also made a few of his own compositions."

   D. "On stage will be one of my former students, Christopher."

45. The author makes an allusion to Mozart in this passage to make a point about the student's

   A. prodigious talent.

   B. ability to write classical music.

   C. talent at math and science.

   D. improvement in math and science.

46. Which of the following graphics would BEST illustrate the ideas in this passage?

   A. a map showing schools that still have music and arts programs

   B. a flowchart showing the steps in applying for a job with an orchestra

   C. a timeline showing the history of music and arts programs in the United States

   D. a table showing academic performance in schools with music and arts programs

47. Which of the following would be MOST useful in supporting the writer's argument?

   A. an outline of the course of study for one of the writer's music classes

   B. the program for the concert at Pleasantville Concert Hall

   C. examples of some of Christopher's grades, showing improvement

   D. the names of some other star pupils from the teacher's class

48. Read this sentence from the passage.

> **Indeed, many employers will look at a <u>potential</u> employee's academic record**

As used in the sentence, what does the word <u>potential</u> mean?

A. might happen

B. promise

C. capable of

D. possible

49. What is the root of <u>disruptive</u>?

A. rupt

B. dis

C. disrupt

D. ive

50. Summarize the main idea of this passage.

_____

_____

_____

_____

The following passage contains mistakes. Read the passage and answer the questions that follow.

The Mysterious Silence

(1) It was Saturday, the day before Jo's sixteenth birthday. (2) Jo should have been happier. (3) But how can you be happy when you're losing your best friend? (4) Jo didn't know why, but for the past week Bev had been avoiding her.

(5) They'd always been constant steady inseparable companions. (6) Now, whenever Jo called Bev to do something together, Bev always had an excuse not to. (7) She had to go somewhere with her parents, or take her younger brother to band practice, or visit a cousin or something.

(8) "Don't worry about it," her mother said. (9) "I'm sure she's not deliberately avoiding you. (10) I'm sure nothing's wrong." (11) Easy for her mom to say, but Jo was the one who was being constantly rejected. (12) Jo and Bev had been friends since the first grade.

(13) It happened again just this morning. (14) Jo called Bev to see if she wanted to go to the mall. (15) And of course Bev said she couldn't. (16) This time she had to take her brother to the Dentist.

(17) Jo would have asked Bev what was going on if she weren't afraid it would ruin her birthday. (18) But she wasn't going to let Bev—her ex-best friend Bev—ruin her day.

(19) Two minutes after Jo talked to Bev, Tessa called to ask if Jo wanted to go to the mall. (20) Tessa lived across the street. (21) Her invatation, even if it was at the last minute, was immediately welcome news. (22) Jo immediately said yes.

(23) The mall had been built five years ago and was designed by a famous architect. (24) Later that afternoon, Jo and Tessa walked home together. (25) Jo found herself thinking that she might spend more time with Tessa.

(26) "Want come in and hang out?" Jo asked Tessa when they arrived at her house. (27) "OK."

(28) They went in the front door.

(29) "Surprise!" was shouted by twenty voices.

(30) In the living room stood Jo's family and friends. (31) Front and center was Bev who lost no time in throwing her arms around Jo and giving her a huge birthday hug.

(32) "Sorry I've been such a drag all week," Bev smiled. (33) "Plan all this was no easy job. (34) I had to make sure no one ruined the surprise. (35) I had to make sure Tessa called right after we spoke this morning, so she'd get you out of here today. (36) Your mom and I worked all afternoon to get the house ready. (37) I had no idea a surprise party would be such exhaust work. (38) But it was all worth it. (39) Happy birthday, best friend!"

51. Read this sentence from the passage.

"Surprise!" was shouted by twenty voices.

Which of the following correctly puts this sentence in the active voice?

A. "Surprise!" was shouted at Jo by twenty voices.

B. "Surprise!" twenty voices shouted.

C. "Surprise!" Jo was shouted at by twenty voices.

D. "Surprise!" was shouted out.

52. Which of the following is the correct way to write sentence 5?

A. They'd always been constant, steady inseparable companions.

B. They'd always been constant, steady, inseparable companions.

C. They'd, always been constant, steady, inseparable companions.

D. They'd always been, constant, steady, inseparable, companions.

53. Which of the following is the correct way to write sentence 33?

A. "To planning all this was no easy job."

B. "I planned all this and it was no easy job."

C. "Planned parties are no easy job."

D. "Planning all this was no easy job."

54. Read this sentence from the passage.

Her invatation, even if it was at the last minute, was immediately welcome news.

Which word is not spelled correctly?

A. minute

B. welcome

C. invatation

D. immediately

55. Which of the following is the correct way to write sentence 26?

   A. "Want to come in and hang out?" Jo asked Tessa when they came to her house.

   B. "Want come in and to hang out?" Jo asked Tessa when they came to her house.

   C. "Want to come in and to hang out?" Jo asked Tessa when they came to her house.

   D. "Want coming in and hanging out?" Jo asked Tessa when they came to her house.

56. Which of the following is the correct way to write sentence 37?

   A. "I had no idea a surprise party would be such exhaustible work."

   B. "I had no idea a surprise party would be such exhausting work."

   C. "I had no idea a surprise party would be such exhausted work."

   D. "I had no idea a surprise party would be such exhausts work."

57. Read this sentence from the passage.

> **Front and center was Bev who lost no time in throwing her arms around Jo and giving her a huge birthday hug.**

Which punctuation mark does this sentence need?

   A. a comma after *Bev*

   B. a semicolon after *time*

   C. a colon after *Jo*

   D. a dash after *lost*

58. Read this sentence from the passage.

> **This time she had to take her brother to the Dentist.**

How should this sentence be rewritten to have correct capitalization?

   A. This time She had to take her Brother to the Dentist.

   B. This time she had to take her Brother to the Dentist.

   C. This time she had to take her Brother to the dentist.

   D. This time she had to take her brother to the dentist.

59. Read this paragraph from the passage.

> **The mall had been built five years ago and was designed by a famous architect. Later that afternoon, Jo and Tessa walked home together. Jo found herself thinking that she might spend more time with Tessa.**

Which sentence should be deleted from this paragraph? Why should it be deleted?

_____

_____

_____

_____

60. Read this sentence from paragraph 3.

> **Jo and Bev had been friends since the first grade.**

The teacher of the student who wrote this passage told her to move this sentence to another part of the passage. Why should this sentence be moved? Where should it be moved to?

_____

_____

_____

_____

STOP

Session 2

Persuasive Prompt

Imagine that your city or town is considering a law that would require all bicyclists to have permits if they want to ride on its streets. Write a letter to the mayor arguing for or against this law. Be sure to support your position with details and examples that make your letter persuasive.

Use the checklist below to help you do your best writing.

Does your letter

❏ have a clear topic?

❏ show a point of view about that topic?

❏ have a logical structure?

❏ support reasons with details?

❏ connect reasons and details with the right words or phrases?

❏ use a style and vocabulary that is correct for the audience and purpose?

❏ have a solid conclusion?

❏ have good spelling, capitalization, and punctuation?

❏ follow the rules for good grammar?

Write your response in the space provided. You may use your own paper if you need more space.

SUMMATIVE ASSESSMENT

Glossary

act a larger division of a play; a collection of scenes (Lesson 1)

active voice the form of a verb in which the subject does the action in a sentence (Lesson 29)

affix one or more letters attached to the beginning or end of a word to change its meaning (Lesson 32)

allusion an indirect reference to a well-known person, place, event, or object in history or in a literary work (Lesson 6)

analogy figurative language that illustrates a relationship by comparing it to another relationship that is widely familiar (Lesson 6)

argument an attempt to convince someone on a topic open to debate (Lessons 11, 17)

audience the people for whom an author writes a text (Lesson 20)

author's purpose an author's reason for writing a text (Lesson 12)

bias a tendency to favor one point of view in an argument without fairly considering other sides (Lesson 17)

capitalization the use of capital, or uppercase, letters in writing (Lesson 30)

cause the reason something happens, such as an event or action (Lesson 13)

CD-ROM a compact disc containing electronic information (Lesson 24)

chapter a section of a longer work (Lesson 1)

character a person or animal in a story, play, or poem (Lessons 3, 19)

claim a statement of an author's point of view in an argument (Lessons 11, 17, 27)

climax the point in a plot where a character must grapple directly with a conflict (Lesson 2)

comma a punctuation mark used to separate ideas or elements in a sentence or to indicate a pause (Lesson 30)

compare to examine the similarities between two or more things (Lesson 12)

conclusion the last paragraph in a composition (Lessons 17, 18, 19)

conditional mood the use of a verb to express an action or idea dependent on a condition (Lesson 29)

conflict the problem that the characters in a story must solve (Lesson 2)

connotation the emotional weight a word carries, or the set of associations implied by the word (Lessons 6, 33)

context the words, phrases, and sentences that appear before and after a particular word in a text (Lesson 31)

contrast to examine the differences between two or more things (Lesson 12)

denotation a word's dictionary definition, or what it literally means (Lesson 33)

detail a piece of information that expands a reader's knowledge of a subject (Lesson 18).

diagram an illustration with labels that describes something or shows how it works (Lesson 14)

dialogue the words the characters in a drama or story say (Lessons 1, 3, 19)

dictionary an alphabetical listing of words that provides their meanings, pronunciations, and origins (Lesson 31)

discussion a type of conversation in which two or more people talk about a specific topic or issue (Lesson 25)

domain-specific vocabulary words used in specific areas of knowledge, such as social studies, science, or technology (Lesson 16)

dramatic irony a type of irony in which the reader or audience knows something that a character does not (Lessons 3, 6)

edit to correct errors in content, grammar, and style (Lesson 23)

effect what happens as a result of an event or action (Lesson 13)

ellipsis a set of three spaced dots used to indicate a pause in a sentence (Lesson 30)

em-dash a longer dash that separates two related parts of a sentence (Lesson 30)

example a piece of information used to develop a topic (Lesson 18)

fact a statement that can be verified, independently and objectively (Lessons 15, 18)

figurative language words used beyond their literal meaning for effect or to create an image in the reader's mind (Lesson 6)

flowchart a graphic that shows the sequence of steps in a process, typically with boxes and arrows (Lesson 14)

fragment a sentence missing a subject, a predicate, or both (Lesson 23)

generalization a broad statement made about a text (Lesson 7)

gerund a verbal ending in *–ing* that often functions as a noun (Lesson 28)

glossary an alphabetized list that defines important terms used in a book or other text, often appearing at the end of the book or text (Lesson 31)

graph a diagram that shows relationships between sets of data, such as a bar graph or line graph (Lesson 14)

graphics visual representations of information and ideas (Lesson 14)

illustration a picture that provides visual reinforcement for the words in a text (Lesson 14)

imperative mood the use of a verb to express a command or direct request (Lesson 29)

indicative mood the use of a verb to make a statement (Lesson 29)

inference an educated guess based on information and evidence in a text and the reader's prior knowledge (Lesson 7)

infinitive a verbal that consists of a verb and the word *to* before it (Lesson 28)

informative text or **informational text** text that informs the reader about a topic, using facts, examples, and specific details (Lessons 18, 22)

interrogative mood the use of a verb to ask a question (Lesson 29)

introduction the first paragraph in an argument or other composition (Lessons 17, 18)

irony a type of figurative language in which a statement means the opposite of what it says (Lesson 6)

leader someone who keeps a discussion moving forward, evenly balanced, and on topic (Lesson 25)

literary analysis a reader's examination of the characters, setting, events, and themes of a work of literature (Lesson 21)

literary reflection an analysis of a reader's emotional response to a work of literature (Lesson 21)

literary response an essay that demonstrates a reader's understanding of a work of literature (Lesson 21)

literature written work derived from a writer's imagination and creativity (Lesson 21)

loaded language exaggerated language in an argument that is intended to cause an emotional response in the reader (Lesson 11)

main idea the central statement made by a piece of writing (Lesson 9)

map a graphic representation of regions on Earth and their geographical features (Lesson 14)

meter the pattern of stressed and unstressed syllables in a line of poetry (Lesson 1)

misplaced modifier an error in usage in which a participle is not modifying a specific noun (Lesson 28)

moderator a person who makes sure rules of discussion are followed and who encourages participation within a discussion (Lesson 25)

mood the attitude a verb communicates in a sentence (Lesson 29)

motivation the reason a character acts a certain way (Lesson 3)

narrative a piece of writing that tells a story (Lesson 19)

opinion a personal belief or a point of view that cannot be proven true (Lesson 15)

participial phrase a phrase consisting of a participle and an object for the participle, often modifying a noun (Lesson 28)

participle a verbal often used as a noun or an adjective (Lesson 28)

passive voice the form of a verb in which the subject is acted upon in the sentence (Lesson 29)

periodical a text printed on a regular schedule, such as a newspaper, magazine, or journal (Lesson 24)

persuasive presentation a presentation or speech in which the speaker makes a claim and supports it with evidence (Lesson 26)

plagiarism the act of claiming the words of another writer or speaker as one's own (Lesson 24)

plot the sequence of events in fiction or drama (Lessons 2, 19)

point of view the perspective from which a story is told (Lessons 3, 19); also, a person's attitude toward a subject (Lessons 11, 12)

prefix an affix attached to the beginning of a root word to change the meaning of the word (Lesson 32)

primary source source material that is closest to a person, time period, or information you are researching (Lessons 12, 24)

publish to make something publicly available either by printing it, putting it on a Web site, or sharing it with classmates (Lesson 23)

pun a play on words in which a word that sounds like another word is used for humorous effect (Lesson 6)

punctuation the use of marks to make sentences flow more smoothly (Lesson 30)

purpose the reason for writing a text, for example, to persuade or inform (Lesson 20)

quotation a direct statement by a character or real person in a text, usually placed in quotation marks (Lesson 18)

reasoned judgment a statement based on an issue for which there is more than one standard of judgment (Lesson 15)

recorder a discussion participant who takes notes and creates an accurate summary of the discussion (Lesson 25)

reference source a source that contains factual information on a wide range of topics (Lesson 24)

resolution the ending of the story, when the conflict is resolved (Lesson 2)

resource something you can use to help you write a research paper (Lesson 24)

revise to write a final copy of a composition, based on changes to improve the content (Lesson 23)

rising action the bulk of the story, during which the character works to resolve the problem (Lesson 2)

root the main part of a word (Lesson 32)

run-on a sentence that is very lengthy and has no connectors or transitions; also a sentence that could easily be broken up into two smaller sentences (Lesson 23)

scene a shorter division of an act that takes place in one location in a drama (Lesson 1)

secondary source a source that discusses information originally presented elsewhere (Lessons 12, 24)

sentence structure the grammatical arrangement of words in a sentence (Lesson 23)

sequence the organization of information or events in the order in which they happen (Lesson 13)

setting the location and time in which a story takes place (Lessons 2, 19)

spelling the correct arrangement of letters in a word (Lesson 30)

stage directions the instructions in a drama that tell characters actions to perform or that describe the set (Lesson 1)

stanza a group of lines in a poem (Lesson 1)

structure the pattern of organization in a text (Lesson 13)

subjunctive mood the use of a verb to speculate or express a wish (Lesson 29)

suffix an affix attached to the end of a root word to change the meaning of the word (Lesson 32)

summary a short restatement of a longer text in the reader's own words (Lesson 10)

support descriptions, factual information, details, and examples that make an argument more credible (Lesson 27)

supporting details details in a passage that prove or explain the author's main idea (Lesson 9)

table an arrangement of information in columns and rows (Lesson 14)

table of contents a list of chapters in a book, with the pages on which those chapters begin (Lesson 1)

text evidence or **textual evidence** facts or information within a text that indicates why an inference or interpretation is reasonable or accurate (Lessons 7, 8)

theme the central message or lesson of a literary work (Lesson 4)

thesaurus an alphabetical listing that gives many synonyms of words (Lesson 31)

timeline a representation of events in chronological order (Lesson 14)

tone an author's attitude toward the subject about which he or she is writing (Lesson 6)

topic sentence the main idea of a supporting paragraph (Lessons 9, 17)

trait a quality that defines a character (Lesson 3)

verb a word that shows action or occurrence or describes a state of being (Lesson 29)

verbal a word formed from a verb that may function as a noun or an adjective (Lesson 28)

verbal irony the use of words to express something different from their literal meaning, sometimes for humorous effect (Lesson 6)

video an electronic visual recording, such as a film or documentary (Lessons 14, 24)

Web site an electronic page on the Internet with information (Lesson 24)

Mechanics Toolbox

 Pronouns

A **pronoun** is a word that takes the place of a noun. The form of a pronoun shows both person and number.

Person refers to the point of view expressed by the pronoun: first person (the person speaking, or *I*), second person (the person spoken to, or *you*), or third person (the person or thing spoken of, or *he, she,* or *it*).

Number refers to how many people or things the pronoun represents. A **singular** pronoun represents one person or thing. A **plural** pronoun represents more than one person or thing.

This chart features the personal pronouns.

	Singular	Plural
First Person	I, me	we, us
Second Person	you	you
Third Person	he, him; she, her; it	they, them

An **antecedent** is the word that a pronoun replaces. Pronouns and antecedents need to agree in person and number. Third-person singular pronouns and antecedents also need to agree in gender. The antecedent for a pronoun may appear in a previous sentence. It may also appear earlier within the same sentence as the pronoun.

> Examples:
> My class organized a fundraiser. We raised nearly $10,000! (correct)
> After Susan and Elfranko finished the laundry, they went swimming. (correct)
> When a person does well on this exam, they should be congratulated. (incorrect)

In the fourth example, the plural pronoun *they* does not agree with the singular antecedent, *person*. The correct sentence is:

> When people do well on this exam, they should be congratulated.

It also needs to be clear which noun is the antecedent of a pronoun. Consider this example:

> We piled tall stacks of books on the tables until they fell over.

The antecedent of *they* is not clear. Did the stacks of books fall over, or did the tables fall over? It is best not to use a pronoun in this sentence. The correct possibilities are:

> We piled tall stacks of books on the tables until the books fell over.
> We piled tall stacks of books on the tables until the tables fell over.

Sentence Pattern

A sentence is a group of words that tells a complete thought. It can stand alone. It can include various combinations of clauses and phrases, but it has at least one subject and predicate. The **subject** tells who or what the sentence is about. The **predicate** tells what the subject does.

> Example:
> They left.

They is the subject of this sentence. The predicate is *left.* It tells what they did.

 ## Phrases and Clauses

A **phrase** is a group of related words that does not include its own subject and verb. A comma should follow an introductory phrase.

> Examples:
> From the very first day, Tabitha liked her new school. (prepositional phrase)
> Walking on tiptoe, James creeped behind his little sister. (participial phrase)
> To tell you the truth, I did not like that movie at all. (infinitive phrase)
> A sleepy town next to nowhere, Riverdale was beautiful. (appositive phrase)

A **clause** is a group of words that includes a subject and verb. There are two types of clauses: independent clauses and dependent clauses.

An **independent clause** can stand alone as a sentence. It tells a complete thought. In the following examples, each subject is underlined once, and each verb is underlined twice.

> We argued.
> George agreed to walk his neighbor's retriever.
> They practiced hard that entire year.

Although it includes both a subject and verb, a **dependent clause** cannot stand alone. It is not complete. Some dependent clauses begin with a relative pronoun, such as *who, whom, which,* or *that.* The relative pronoun may serve as the subject of the dependent clause. Other dependent clauses begin with a subordinating conjunction, such as *after, although, because, however, if, until,* and *when.* In the following examples, each subject is underlined once, and each verb is underlined twice.

> Until we started to laugh.
> Although he dislikes dogs.
> Which ended with their first championship.

Duplicating any part of this book is prohibited by law.

On its own, none of these clauses expresses a complete thought. It needs to be joined to an independent clause.

Examples:
We argued until we started to laugh.
Although he dislikes dogs, George agreed to walk his neighbor's retriever.
They practiced hard that entire year, which ended with their first championship.

 Compound Subjects and Predicates

A sentence can include more than one subject. For example:

Yolanda enjoys reading. Ursula enjoys reading, too.

These sentences can be combined into one sentence with a compound subject.

Example:
Yolanda and Ursula enjoy reading.

Notice the change in the verb when the sentences are combined. The compound subject, *Yolanda and Ursula*, needs a plural verb, *enjoy*.

A sentence can also include more than one predicate. For example:

Yolanda enjoyed that book. She did not like the movie based on it.

These sentences can be combined into one sentence with a compound verb.

Example:
Yolanda enjoyed that book but did not like the movie based on it.

Yolanda is the subject of both predicates, *enjoyed that book* and *did not like the movie based on it*.

A sentence can have both a compound subject and a compound verb. For example:

Yolanda and Ursula enjoyed that book and are looking forward to reading the sequel.

Both subjects, *Yolanda* and *Ursula*, are the subject of both predicates, *enjoyed that book* and *are looking forward to reading the sequel*.

Duplicating any part of this book is prohibited by law.

Types of Sentences

Different combinations of independent and dependent clauses form different types of sentences. There are four basic sentence patterns.

1. A **simple sentence** includes one independent clause and no dependent clauses.

    Examples:
    The lilies bloomed.
    The violinist amazed the audience with her skill.
    When did you return home?

2. A **compound sentence** includes two or more independent clauses. In the following examples, each independent clause is underlined.

    <u>Michael lost his wallet</u>, but <u>a stranger soon returned it to him</u>.
    <u>We could get the books at the library</u>, or <u>my sister will lend us her copies</u>.
    <u>I wrote the lead article</u>, <u>Amy did the interviews</u>, and <u>Jimmy designed the layout</u>.

3. A **complex sentence** includes one independent clause and one or more dependent clauses. In the following examples, each independent clause is underlined once, and each dependent clause is underlined twice.

    <u>Our basement floods</u> <u>whenever it rains</u>.
    <u>The dress</u> <u>that my mother made</u> <u>is my favorite</u>.
    <u>Because Lisa usually visits him on Saturday</u>, <u>her grandfather worried</u> <u>when he did not see her that weekend</u>.

Notice that the dependent clause *that my mother made* appears between the subject and verb of the independent clause *The dress is my favorite*.

4. A **compound-complex sentence** includes two or more independent clauses and at least one dependent clause. In the following examples, each independent clause is underlined once, and each dependent clause is underlined twice.

    <u>Although they had never taken care of a garden before</u>, <u>their flowers were healthy</u> and <u>their vegetables were delicious</u>.
    <u>Whenever Allison practices the clarinet</u>, <u>her dog starts barking</u> and <u>the stray cats</u> <u>that live in the empty lot behind her house</u> <u>start yowling</u>.

Notice that the dependent clause *that live in the empty lot behind her house* appears between the subject and verb of the independent clause *the stray cats start yowling*.

Duplicating any part of this book is prohibited by law.

Concise Words and Phrases

Good writers choose their words carefully. They use vivid words that appeal to the senses. They also use words that convey precise meanings. Consider these examples:

> I was hot. (general word choice)
> Sweat poured into my eyes. (vivid word choice)

The second sentence is more vivid. It helps the reader feel the speaker's discomfort in the heat. Using the verb *poured,* it is more active. It is best to avoid overusing forms of the verb *be,* such as *was* in the first sentence.

Consider these other examples:

> Swimming in the <u>water</u> <u>made me feel better</u>. (vague word choice)
> Swimming in the <u>lake</u> <u>cooled me off</u>. (precise word choice)

In fewer words, the second sentence conveys much more detail than the first. It tells precisely where the speaker went swimming: in a lake. It also tells precisely how the speaker felt better: he or she cooled off.

It is usually better to use a vivid verb or precise noun than to add an adjective or adverb. Here are examples:

> Holly <u>walked quickly</u> across the parking lot. (verb and adverb)
> Holly <u>hurried</u> across the parking lot. (vivid verb)

Also avoid adjectives or adverbs that repeat ideas already conveyed through other words. For example:

> Neil Gaiman, my favorite writer, has written a wide variety of different books.

It is not necessary to use both *variety* and *different* in this sentence. The word *variety* on its own conveys the idea of difference. This sentence is better:

> Neil Gaiman, my favorite writer, has written a wide variety of books.

Duplicating any part of this book is prohibited by law.

Verb Voice and Mood

In a sentence that reflects the **active voice**, the actor is the subject. In a sentence that reflects the **passive voice**, the object of an action is the subject. Compare these examples:

My aunt donated the costumes for the performance. (active voice)
The costumes for the performance were donated by my aunt. (passive voice)

My aunt is the subject of the first sentence. She is doing the donating. *The costumes* is the subject of the second sentence. They are the object of the donating.

The active voice is generally preferred. However, there may be times when the passive voice is acceptable or even necessary. For example, you might use the passive voice in a letter of complaint if you do not want to write a direct accusation:

We have learned that some children were prevented from seeing the performance.

You might need to use the passive voice if the actor is unknown. For example:

The flowers for the performance were also donated. We have no idea who sent them.

Conditional sentences tell about events that are dependent on a condition that may or may not occur. The condition is given in a dependent clause beginning with *if*. The possible consequence of the condition is given in the independent clause.

The tense and mood of the verbs in a conditional sentence depend on the truth of the condition given in the sentence. The condition may be true, possibly true, or untrue.

If we <u>have</u> ice cream, we <u>are</u> happy. (true about the present)
If we <u>have</u> ice cream, we <u>will be</u> happy. (true about the future)
If we <u>have</u> ice cream, we <u>should be</u> happy. (possibly true about the future)
If we <u>had</u> ice cream, we <u>would be</u> happy. (untrue about the present)

Notice the verbs in the independent clauses of the sentences about possibly true or untrue conditions. They are in the **conditional mood** and include the helping verbs *should* and *would*. The conditional mood expresses possible but uncertain events. The helping verbs *could* or *might* can also be used in the conditional mood.

Also notice the past-tense verb (*had*) in the dependent clause that expresses an untrue condition. This verb is in the **subjunctive mood**. The subjunctive mood expresses untrue or hypothetical events. It is often used in clauses beginning with *if* or to express wishes. For example:

If I <u>were</u> you, I would give up now.
I wish I <u>were</u> in charge.

Duplicating any part of this book is prohibited by law.

Notes

Notes

Notes

Notes

Notes

Notes

Notes

Notes

Notes

Notes

Notes